A PIECE OF TRUTH

AMALIA FLEMING

A PIECE OF
TRUTH

Illustrated with photographs

HOUGHTON MIFFLIN COMPANY BOSTON

1973

First Printing   c

First American Edition 1973
Copyright © 1972 by Amalia Fleming

ISBN: 0–395–15474–x
Library of Congress Catalog Card Number: 72–6810
Printed in the United States of America

To those who fight for their ideals

AUTHOR'S NOTE

I would like to express thanks to many friends who have helped me with this book but who do not wish to be named in it, particularly to those in Greece who first came to me with the story of their experiences, and also to all those outside Greece who have been so generous with time and energy. My very special thanks go to a friend who with endless patience translated my English into English; to the lawyers who helped me understand the laws and traps of the illiberal constitution of 1968; to the friend who collected the data of the main events from 1944 to 1967; to Mr P. Lambrias for his precious help in finding for me newspapers of the time of each event, photographs and documents; to all other friends who also provided me with data, newspapers, photographs, Georgakis's letters, photographs and data, and who don't wish to be named; to Athena Panagoulis, mother of the young convict, who ignoring all danger managed to give me all the latest data I needed about her son's condition. My thanks go also to my two young friends, a lawyer and a poet, for their help while I was writing the book and who typed the manuscript.

I wish to thank the foreign press for attracting attention to the suffering of our small country, to all our friends in every country on my own behalf and that of all the Greek political prisoners and their families for the help they have given. I also wish to thank Philippe Grand d'Hauteville, the representative of the International Red Cross, who devoted himself to his work with a great sense of his duties and obligations but also with deep humanity, and made the existence of the International Red Cross worthwhile for us. Last, but not least, I would like warmly to thank those English people who made me so welcome in England—a girl in Cooper's, a waiter in the Ritz, and many others in shops and in the street.

AMALIA FLEMING

London, May 1972

CONTENTS

ILLUSTRATIONS

A PIECE OF TRUTH

PROLOGUE

During the occupation of Greece in the Second World War I took part in the resistance out of a natural feeling that people have the right to be independent, to rule their own country in the way they choose, and to refuse to accept that foreign forces should tread their soil or become their masters. Also I had and still have a strong feeling for the respect due to all beings, respect for their dignity and for their right to live in the way they like, provided this does not interfere with the same rights and freedom of other people. Everything I felt so strongly about was being crushed by the foreign occupation, and so there was not a minute's doubt in my mind that it was my duty to help all those who were in danger because they opposed the fascist enemy: Greek or Allied officers and soldiers, resistance fighters, and all those the enemy was after—the Jews, and later, after the collapse of Italy as an Axis ally, the remnants of the Italian Army. The Italians had entered our territory as masters, had beaten and imprisoned us, but did not want any longer to go on fighting beside the Germans, so that they were in danger of reprisals from their former allies.

When one starts getting mixed up in things like that, one goes on further; for instance, one tries to find ways of escape for the people in danger, and one does more and more that the enemy dislikes. Also, as the enemy one fights is usually stronger than oneself, has good informers, trained police, and cruel methods of getting information, the odds are that after some such activity one is found out, arrested, interrogated and imprisoned—if one is lucky enough not to perish in one way or another during the process. This was a general pattern in Greece during the occupation years, and I was not an exception. I was even one of the lucky ones: I was not tortured, as so many of my friends were. Although repeatedly threatened with execution during interrogation, I was not executed, nor did I suffer any particular anguish on the subject, because I have a very strong sense of the ridiculous, and being executed sounded too ridiculous even for people who took themselves so seriously. Nor did I die from starvation, as thousands of Greeks did, and, what is more, I was in prison during the great peak of the famine so I did not see small children, old people and even once-strong young men suddenly fall dead from starvation in the streets. I did not see the carts which collected corpses in the street and carried the starved dead in dozens every morning to a common grave.

This was the time when our allies were weighing which would be more valuable to them: to lift the blockade and allow food to reach their loyal and starving little ally, necessarily letting the occupying enemy share the food, or to keep up the blockade and let the Greeks starve to death. Would the survival of seven and a half million friendly people (the whole population of Greece) be of value and advantage to them after the war? Were they worth the stopping of the blockade or not? Fortunately for us the majority voted for our survival.*

At the time, most of us believed that the Allied nations confronting the Axis represented the ideals of freedom, democracy, and respect for human dignity. The Greek people paid a high price that these ideals should survive. About fourteen thousand villages were destroyed, and one-tenth of the Greek population perished. Today, although Greece still remains on the Western side, the Greeks have been forcibly de-prived of all the ideals for which they fought. This may explain the deep bitterness the Greek people feel today. Still, during the occupa-tion, believing that we were fighting for freedom in the world, we cheerfully risked our lives.

* Excerpt from the Warner Report, R 7038/96/19/G, July 16th, 1941, 'Summary of Outstanding Greek Questions', Paragraph 7, File Foreign Office 371/29840: 'This is likely to be the most difficult question of all. Greece produces little food and is almost entirely dependent on imported cereals. Her situation is probably one degree worse than that of Belgium. In private conversation members of the Greek Legation express the view that if we starve the people in Greece and the children suffer, the Greeks will turn against us. They will not, of course, turn pro–Axis, but will become violently xenophobe. The question is what is Greek goodwill worth to us? Is their shipping, the effectiveness of their passive resistance, and the armed resistance of their free forces worth more to us than the amount we might help the enemy by facilitating the supply of cereals to Greece? Is it important to have a healthy population of 7·5 million Anglophile Greeks to reinforce our position in the Eastern Mediterranean after the war? Or can we view with equinamity the reduction of the Greek population by famine, its health, particularly in the case of chil-dren, ruined and its outlook violently anti–British? The pros and cons must be very carefully weighed before we commit ourselves to starving Greece, and it must be borne in mind that the Greeks will not starve silently. The effects on opinion in the United States of America will also have to be considered ...

' ... Cyprus is our strongest trump card, and we may have to play it in an attempt to keep overseas Greek goodwill and shipping, particularly if we decide that we must starve Greece.'

From 1946 to 1962 I lived in England for most of the time, with the exception of the year 1952, which I spent in Greece helping reorganize the bacteriological and haematological laboratories of a Greek hospital. However, all these years I spent in Athens whatever holidays I had. In Greece my friends were telling me that things were getting better and better every day, and I believed them because I wished so much that it might be true. My visits to Greece were too short to allow me to have a clear picture of what was really happening in my country. In reality horrible events were taking place, and I am ashamed to think that being away, and so involved in my personal life, I was hardly aware of them.

The reasons for these horrible events are complex, and only un-biased historians will one day explain them. It seems to me they were roughly due to the following causes. During the hard years of the Nazi occupation, there was in Greece an overwhelming majority of people who, for the freedom of Greece and the victory of our ideals, sacrificed their well-being and even their lives. There was also a small minority belonging to one or the other political ideology who took advantage of the general upheaval to take personal revenge on people they had any sort of quarrel with. Another group of people of the extreme right collaborated with the fascists as they were fascists themselves, and handed over the resistance fighters, mostly the left-wing ones, to the occupying forces. Others, very few, collaborated with the enemy for simple mercenary reasons.

Their opponents of every group replied in kind. As usual in periods of great misery and great political differences, there was intense resent-ment between opposed groups. Grave errors, which in politics are worse than crimes, were committed on both sides, and on both sides killings took place which should have been but could not at that time have been avoided. At a later stage legal killings followed which not only should but could have been avoided: it is unfortunate that they were not.

This book is mainly my personal knowledge and recollections of life, especially from April 1967 and onwards, my description and judgment of events in which I was either personally involved or about which I have first-hand information. It is flashes from a history I have lived, flashes seen through my own eyes. I do not claim to be writing a general history of the time, and I ask the reader to take it for what it is: an honest description of what I know, and the way I personally judge it. Necessarily, events which happened before but have a bearing on what happened on April 21st, 1967, are briefly mentioned.

What I know about what happened between 1946 and 1962 comes from the scars and misery this terrible period left. I came in contact with this misery later, when I started spending more time in Greece, and I learned of it and tried to relieve it in whatever small way I could. I suddenly found out that there were a number of political prisoners, some of them already held for eighteen years. Naturally, I was horrified. I tried to help their families, and to use legal means to have certain cases retried or to help to obtain an amnesty for political prisoners.

On April 9th, 1953, I had married Alexander Fleming. He died suddenly on March 11th, 1955. These two years were the only ones when I had no longing whatsoever for Greece. My country was where my husband was. But a few years after his death, Greece, and above all Athens, started haunting me again.

From 1962 I started spending more time in Greece than in England. I lived for six months in Athens in 1962 and seven in 1963. From then on I considered myself a resident of Athens. I spent nine months or so every year in Greece, and then started moving house in order to settle in Athens for good. On March 15th, 1967, my last belongings arrived from London. Five weeks later, on April 21st, 1967, a group of what to most people were unknown Greek officers took over the country, abolishing all freedom and all our rights.

There had been rumours of something like this since 1964, when the Greek people had managed after many difficulties to obtain the liberal government they wanted. There were fears then because the forces and powers that seemed to rule our small state had never allowed a liberal government to be elected, or, if one gained power, allowed it to last more than a few months. We were afraid that the 1964 government of the Centre Union party would follow the usual pattern once again. We were afraid that George Papandreou, the leader of a party which came to power with an unprecedented majority — 53 per cent of the vote, a majority that no other party had ever had in the whole history of modern Greece — was not going to be allowed to govern for long. The 53 per cent was given to him by the Greek people, but the administration, and especially the army, repeatedly purged of democratic elements over nearly twenty years, were in the hands of the Right, and the key posts were in the hands of the extreme Right — of those who, whether they were fully conscious of it or not, were the instruments of a foreign influence.

In 1964 King Paul died and was succeeded by his son, Constantine. In July 1965 this young, inexperienced and ill-advised King managed by an assortment of tricks to overthrow the prime minister. In this he was helped by the Right, and also by a few members of the Centre Union party. These members of the Centre Union are called in Greek *Apostatai*, that is, renegades, and we believe that they have betrayed the people's vote which had brought them to Parliament. Their reason was one of personal interest. The prime minister was seventy-nine years old, he might die, and they were afraid of the great and daily increasing popularity of his son, Andreas Papandreou, who was a minister. It seemed to be a desperate fight for the succession to the leadership of the party; if George Papandreou was allowed to go on governing, and brought in the social and economic reforms Andreas suggested, when he died Andreas would sweep the elections. The leaders of the *Apostatai*, who had an eye on the succession, knew this and tried to alter the course of events. At least, this is how we, the 53 per cent of the people who were for the Centre Union party and its leader, George Papandreou, saw things. We gathered to give a tremendous ovation to the overthrown Old Man when he gave a public speech. We shouted that we wanted our prime minister back, the man we had voted for.

It was no use. The extreme Right exploited the people's protest against the violation of their expressed will by declaring that there was chaos.* It seemed to me like a funny story where burglars break into a house in the night, and the police arrest the owner who shouts for help on the charge that he is upsetting the neighbours' sleep and causing a public disturbance; in the meantime the burglars are allowed to get away with all the goods. Everything was being well taken care of; what was to come was slowly and safely prepared by obscure, foreign forces, with the collaboration of the King, the *Apostatai*, and the Right, who, without understanding what they were doing, were helping bring about the doom not only of Greece and the Greek people but also of themselves.

---

* With little respect for the truth which could so easily be proved, some right-wing newspapers let it be vaguely assumed that these huge demonstrations had taken place during George Papandreou's tenure and not after his overthrow, trying to give the impression that there was a lack of order when he was in power.

From July 1965 to April 21st, 1967, this murky combination of forces under the auspices of the deluded young King and the Right attempted to muffle the popular outcry and to find some device which would have the appearance of legality, but which they could use for their own purposes, not for what the Greek people demanded. They would much rather have a parody of democracy than come out in the open with a coup. But all these efforts failed in the end. The people refused to submit, and the King was obliged to allow elections on May 28th, 1967.

Information from all over the country spoke of a tremendous landslide for George Papandreou, the ousted prime minister. Everybody expected that this time he was not going to get 53 per cent of the vote but well over 60 per cent. How could we believe that the King and the Right would ever allow such elections to take place? Yet how could we believe, on the other hand, that in 1967 fascist dictatorship would be allowed to raise its abject head once again in Greece?

Dictatorship did not arrive on April 21st, 1967, because of any Greek need. It came because every other trick to smother Greek freedom had been defeated, and because certain organizations, presumably up to the level of the Pentagon, and some officers of a few NATO countries, were short-sighted enough to make one of the greatest mistakes they could make: they permitted or assisted (I do not know which) some specially trained Greek officers to use a NATO plan and American-provided tanks to enslave a free nation. This nation had fought beside the West precisely in order not to be subject to totalitarianism, and had later joined NATO only because NATO was supposed to be founded to protect the freedom and ideals in which the Greeks believed and for which they made so many sacrifices.

The Greeks now not unjustifiably believe that their NATO and American allies made an instrument of ruthless, retrogressive military men so that they could turn Greece into a colony that would support military bases. Greece was going to be an aircraft carrier attached to the Sixth Fleet. Yet the NATO countries ought to understand that this is not in their interest. If they need Greece as an ally because of its strategic position, they should make the Greeks believe it is in their own interest to be partners in NATO: as it is, the Greeks suppose they are being used only to safeguard doubtful foreign interests while their own freedom, progress, and interests are not only ignored but stifled.

It must be remembered, although it is well suppressed so that we can all forget it, that our small country, which has now been put in chains, once before refused to surrender to a powerful demand—from the Axis—for its use as a base. In order to preserve its right to free decisions, Greece fought in some cases to the last man. It was the small and ill-equipped Greek Army that gave the first victories to the Allies.

Most people of all countries learn at school that there exists a small country called Greece which has a brilliant ancient history, some remnants of ancient monuments, blue skies and blue seas. 'Fair Greece! sad relic ...' I wish to tell those who may not know it that this small country in contemporary times is inhabited by people who love democracy and freedom; that the Greek Army is a Greek Army, and will soon realize that this dictatorship now in power is a foreign dictatorship which is selling out the country. It is a foreign occupation, with one or more Quislings kept in power by foreign officials with obsolete ideas, and the sooner the foreigners understand that they cannot base an alliance on the goodwill of a few servile military men, while the whole nation's resentment against NATO and the Americans is growing day by day, the better it will be for all of us. Only their support keeps the Colonels in power.

It may be of interest to recall here that the resentment against the Americans is built up by the Junta itself, which barks like a small dog behind a Great Dane. 'Who do you think you are fighting?' I was asked by someone when in the hands of the military police, 'Us? You are fighting America. America is behind us, America is supporting us. All this—' he indicated everything around him with outstretched arms, 'comes from America.'

In November 1941 I was arrested by the military police of the fascists because I refused to accept their rule and helped their victims. On August 31st, 1971, I was arrested by the military police of the new occupying army. It seems to me that in some ways there is not much difference: the voice of the people is silenced again, its will is violated, the country is being pushed back into obscurantism. One personal difference is that then I was young, thirty years younger, but the reasons for my arrest seem very much the same.

My own experience of the beginning of the coup, of what happened immediately after it, of life in Greece, of the oppression, the brutal intimidation, the savage tortures and sentences, is perhaps worth briefly recording, although these matters are known to some people.

My experience after my arrest may also have some interest because

I have lived through some bad moments in the history of Greece, and have had the opportunity to observe a class of actors in our history which has often remained muffled: both the nature of the victims and what has been even more obscure, that of the victimizers.

Many reasons impelled me to write. I am writing for those who have no such opportunity, because I believe that it is useful, and imperative, that the truth should be known both inside and outside Greece, and because I have personal knowledge of a piece of this truth. Very much, I have been forced to omit; the nature of the Greek state in 1972 means that there are stories and details that cannot yet be told. All I state is accurately reported. The only exceptions are a few details and names that had to be altered to protect people inside Greece.

The principal interest of what I have to offer lies not so much in my own passionate indignation as in the reasons for it. All of us have lived through this period, but few of us are now in a position to describe, even partially, what it has meant. Fewer still have been presented, as I have, with the evidence of the destruction which has been inflicted. It may help if I try to convey for those who do not know it, who did not have the opportunity to feel it, the atmosphere which prevailed from April 21st, 1967: the sudden and confused events, the unexplained arrests and disappearances, the problems of tracing friends who at one moment were free and the next in unnamed prisons, and the system of torture and terror of which we became more and more conscious. When I come to it, the detailed account of my personal experience may also throw some light on both this nightmare and its actors. I have tried to describe the strange relationship of the interrogator and the interrogated, when the first uses all the means available to him, and the latter, while fighting not to betray, tries to understand the psychology of the torturer.

I have written in full consciousness of those many Greeks who, since April 21st, 1967, in prison, under torture, during difficult and frightening escapes, by their constant refusal to submit, have in this generation saved the honour of Greece. It was one of the glories of my life to be thrust for a few moments into their company, and one of the motives of this book is to express my deep admiration for them and the gratitude that I feel to them as a Greek.

1. The Colonels' Coup: Our Reaction

> For we alone regard the man who takes no part in public affairs,
> not as one who minds his own business, but as good for nothing;
> and we Athenians decide public questions for ourselves or at least
> endeavour to arrive at a sound understanding of them, in the belief
> that it is not debate that is a hindrance to action, but rather not to
> be instructed by debate before the time comes for action.

> THUCYDIDES 2, 40, 2, *translation by Charles Foster Smith*

Elections had been announced for May 28th, 1967. On April the 19th I
had some friends home for dinner. After dinner we played a sort of
referendum game: were we going to get these much demanded and
much hoped-for elections? As the oldest I was asked to speak first. I
said no, I could not believe it. There was not the slightest doubt that
George Papandreou would get in with a terrific majority, and I could
not see the obstinate and unimaginative young King offering him the
premiership on a silver platter. The King was known as the King of the
Right, not of all the people. His party was not going to allow him to
hold the elections. What new tricks they would devise to prevent
them I could not imagine, but they would find something. We were
not going to be allowed free, honest elections. Some were of my
opinion, others were optimistic and dead certain: we were going to
have elections and, of course, win them. Two days later, the Night of
the Colonels dissolved the elections into a lost dream.

Only once in my life have I voted, and that was in England. I voted
not to give my own vote, but that of my dead husband; he was
Conservative and I was Labour. An election occurred a short time after
his death, and it made me think I was bringing him back to life for a
few seconds when I gave his vote to the Conservatives. In Greece I
never even bothered to get my voting book. It is somehow a
complicated business, and I am by nature unbelievably lazy—or, to
tell the truth, an unbelievably lazy person who has always had to work
very hard throughout her life; and this is perfectly appalling. But

21

I was for George Papandreou when the elections of 1963 and 1964 took place. I did not know him personally, though I knew Constantine Karamanlis, whom I thought very handsome, and I very much liked his wife, Amalia, a gentle and perfect lady. All my friends were right-wing, very pro-Karamanlis, and I had neither the knowledge nor any wish to oppose them when they told me while I was living in England that everything was going well in Greece under his leadership. When I spent six months in Greece in 1962 and seven months in 1963, I was struck by a feeling of lack of freedom, a police state atmosphere, which had escaped the attention of my friends. I remember one little incident. In *Avgi*, the left-wing newspaper, there was a theatre criticism which I had been told was very good, and being a great theatre-lover I wanted to read it. I stopped at a kiosk almost outside my house, with one of my right-wing friends, and asked for *Avgi*. She went pale when I got it. She whispered, 'Hide it, put it in your handbag.' I asked why, what was happening, was it forbidden to buy *Avgi*? And if so why was it freely sold? She did not explain. Later I heard that people had got dossiers at the security police as communists merely because they had once been seen reading *Avgi*. It was not only *Avgi*; even the liberal papers were not to be found in provincial cities, let alone the villages, because the police were forbidding them. The police had complete power over the people. They could simply create a file saying that some remote relative was a communist, and on these grounds refuse to issue the legal clearance certificate needed for certain work permits. The human dignity of second-class citizens, that is, the liberals, let alone the third-class citizens, the left wing, could be trodden on at the whim of policemen.

Two days after Papandreou was elected I was on a boat going to Aegina. A newspaper boy walked about on the deck before the boat left, calling out the names of his papers: '*Vima, Kathimerini, Avgi ...*' When I heard *Avgi* being freely sold, I felt that people now believed there was such a thing as civil rights, and that the police could not now persecute them for selling or reading a non-prohibited newspaper. I thought that, rightly or wrongly, people believed that with Papandreou in charge of the government a change had come, and the police state had been abolished. I felt that just for the sake of this moment, just for this feeling of freedom that Papandreou's government had given to the people, it was worth supporting.

I was not going to Aegina just for a holiday to a beautiful island. My own personal circumstances, and the experience of very much suffering among those I had known, had dragged me deeper and deeper into a preoccupation with freedom and with the rights of those wrongfully imprisoned. I was going to see a man I believed to be innocent, Kostas Filinis, who was in prison. He was a political prisoner, and for some time past, through my friends the Ministers of Justice, I had been trying to help him towards freedom through a revision of his case or a pardon. I did not know him when I first heard of his case. He came from a very good family; he was a communist because he believed that communism would in the end bring freedom and equal rights to everyone. As a boy of seventeen he joined EPON, the young people's branch of EAM, the anti-Nazi resistance organization.* Like so many brave young men, he joined in order to fight the Nazi occupation of Greece. It was during this period and the events that followed that he became a communist. The day did come when he was freed, and I came to know him better. I don't think there is anyone in the world for whom I have greater esteem. He is a pure idealist, a man of immense intelligence, courage, and humanity. He has spent most of his life either living clandestinely, for fear first of the German and later of the Greek police, or in prisons. In some ways he has remained an idealistic boy of seventeen. He managed to escape the mass arrest of the night of April 21st, 1967, but only to be arrested in August of the same year, in connection with the communist resistance organization against the dictatorship, PAM, which Mikis Theodorakis, the composer, founded. For being a member of PAM, Kostas Filinis got a life sentence and is still in prison.

My concern for Filinis was a human rather than a humanitarian matter; it had been a revelation of modern history for me to discover his case and his plight. If that needs explaining, I must explain it in terms of my own experience of life.

Thirty years earlier, my part in the resistance had started with helping the needy families of those engaged in the war. I then progressed to hiding people: Greek and British officers who had escaped from concentration camps, resistance fighters the enemy was after, or those who had already been arrested and had escaped from prisons; I remember that one of those I sheltered had been sentenced

---

* EAM are the Greek initials for National Liberation Front. Its secret leaders were communists, but their original aim was resistance to the fascist occupation. The majority of its members were not communists.

to death twice for sabotage. We had to find a way for them to get out of our enslaved country. In the same way we had to help the Jews to avoid the cattle trucks to Belsen; the police would forge identity cards for them and give them Christian names, and we would find them houses to hide in. Radio operators could not transmit messages more than twice from the same place before being found out. This danger created the need to help them, too, harbouring them while they transmitted and between transmissions. The operators were too precious to be allowed to run unnecessary dangers, so we young girls would carry the radio equipment on our shoulders from place to place. We made it look like sacks of potatoes. And if they seemed very heavy for our shoulders, what wouldn't one have done during the famine of that time for one sack of potatoes!

Eventually I was arrested and imprisoned in the Averof Prison in Athens. I was held for six months, and threatened with torture and death to make me give my friends away. I was then judged by a military tribunal and provisionally released. And thus I was able to continue what I had been doing before. When I entered Korydallos Prison after my recent trial, I could not help remarking aloud that I seemed to go to prison whenever the country was under occupation, and for similar charges.

After the end of the Second World War I applied for a one-year British Council scholarship to work at the Wright-Fleming Institute, under Alexander Fleming. Besides university study records, character and behaviour during the war years were among the factors considered for the granting of the scholarship, and I topped the list of forty-five applicants.

I went to London in 1946. Fleming had accepted me to work with him for six months. After this, he said, I should spend the remaining six months of my scholarship at another laboratory. Things turned out differently. Apart from one year in Athens, I remained at his side for the rest of his life.

In London, both before and after my marriage, a great number of sick people from Greece trusted that being a Greek I would do all I could to help them. Complete strangers would ring me up from Athens or the villages to ask me to choose a doctor and a hospital, to go to the airport to fetch them, to interpret for them and to look after their relatives.

If they were to be operated on, they begged that I should be present in the operating theatre. They said they felt more confident if they knew I would be there. The surgeons gave me a stool to stand on so that I could see better, thinking that they were doing me a favour. How many skulls did I see being opened? And how could I have told them, without sounding ridiculous, that I could not stand it? Doctors must not get personally involved, but I was not made to be a doctor. Many patients came when they were already beyond medical help. Each time, when they died, I felt as if I was losing someone dearly loved. The sorrow of their families inevitably became my sorrow, too.

This intensified after my husband died in 1955, perhaps because he was no longer there to help me and give me strength with his protecting presence, perhaps because I was too distressed personally, or because I had more cases to deal with as people found that I had more time to give them. The families rarely spoke English, and often I had to help them deal with undertakers about returning their dead to Greece. Instead of hardening, I felt that I was getting more and more morbidly sensitive. I think that the final breakdown came when I realized that all the undertakers in London knew me. I tried to sever all connection with hospitals and sick people, but it was not easy. Years later, when I was on holiday in Greece, perfect strangers used to come to me for information about British doctors or, if they were poor, to ask me to secure for them in Athens free medical care, or a free bed in a hospital, or whatever else they needed. This went on even at a time when I could not hear of an illness without feeling the need to be sick—I always feel that way when I am upset. But how could I tell these unfortunate people what I felt? How could I make them understand? Was I not meant to be the strong one?

For three years after my husband's sudden death, I did very little, almost no, laboratory work. Instead I devoted all my time to collecting the material for his biography and helping André Maurois write it. During these years I did not go to Greece, but once the biography was published I started going back, and gradually I stayed longer and longer. In 1962 and 1963 I stayed for up to six or seven months every year.

My longing for Greece had become an obsession. My stay always seemed too short, and leaving was always a heartbreak. I decided to experiment, to stay without giving myself a limit and to leave only when I had had enough and really wanted to get away. I stayed on and on, and that day never came. Then I knew for certain that Athens was the only place I wanted to live, that I belonged there, that in spite of all my years in England, in spite of how much I loved my British friends, I had remained thoroughly and incurably a Greek. I knew then that these people that I loved so much, extrovert, bad-mannered, vivacious, interested in everything and everyone, with their warm and generous hearts, were my people, and I belonged with them. As much as I loved London, the strong link which had attached me to it for such a long time had gone with my husband's death. Deep inside myself when I was in England, something seemed disturbed and upset; my feelings seemed to be in conflict. It was not so in Athens. There I felt at one with the people, with nature, the sun, the sky, the sea. I felt as if the granules in my cells were moving with the same rhythm as the dust in the air. Balance and calm were slowly coming back to me.

So I decided to return to Athens for good and to settle there. I would still travel, go back to London, see my many friends and rediscover treasured memories—those memories travelled with me, anyway, they were part of me. But I would live in Athens and never, never be uprooted again. I would at last have rest, peace. I would lead the uneventful life I wanted after so much upheaval, such a disturbing sequence of happiness and unhappiness. On March 15th, 1967, almost the last of my possessions arrived from London. I was settled for a quiet life.

Five weeks later, on April 21st, 1967, a terrible calamity, in the form of the military coup, fell upon us.

On that April 21st, at about 1.30 a.m., I was sitting with a friend in Kolonaki Square, a few yards from my home, eating an ice-cream. The night was calm and beautiful. We had no fear of any sort, seeing no sign of or reason for the calamity that was already on its way. We did not know that the coup had started, and that the tanks, under Colonel Pattakos, were converging on the quiet capital. We went to bed after two o'clock; everything was still peaceful as far as we knew, except for some road-drilling in Scoufa Street, almost next to my house.

I had to make an urgent call at seven o'clock in the morning. I tried, but my telephone was not working. I tried again and again. Then I heard some noise at the bottom of the marble steps which lead up to my dovecote, and I thought it was the concierge; I called out to him to ask to make a call on his telephone. It was not the concierge but the tenant of the flat below mine. He said he was trying to get the concierge on the internal telephone because his telephone was not working. Then I remembered the drilling in Scoufa Street, and I told him it was that, they were repairing the telephone lines, soon they would be working again. He thanked me and walked back into his flat.

At eight o'clock I heard banging at his door, loud voices, and then he called me to tell me that a military coup had taken place. I said, 'They have done it.' I never imagined that I knew so many bad words, but I used them all. We were not going to get our elections. Our last chance of liberalism, of social and economic reform, of equal rights and progressive education had withered away at one blast. Who had blown that blast? Wild rumours circulated in the first moments. The King and some of his generals? This is what we were expecting, this is what had been whispered for some time now, but it was supposed to happen later, on the eve of the elections or the day after. Whoever they were, the people who had taken power had started out with a lie: the communiqué they broadcast to the bewildered population at about eight o'clock in the morning of April 21st, 1967, was stated to have been issued and signed by the King and the government (a conservative one at the time). However, the King as we learned later had not signed, though he did some five hours later. The whole government and all Members of Parliament and thousands of other people had been arrested in the night, in their sleep. Convoys of buses of prisoners drove from the villages on that day. The communiqués announced that all articles of the constitution guaranteeing the protection of the people from abuse and arrest, their right to free speech and even to private opinion, and in fact all their rights, were now suspended. We did not know yet who 'they' were, so we called them the Junta.

For foreign consumption, and for those of the Greek people the Junta thought they might deceive, the reason given for the coup was that before April 21st, 1967, there had been chaos and danger of communism.* It was said that Greece had been standing on the edge of a precipice. Some Greeks commented that with the coup it had evidently taken a step forward. In the early afternoon we knew some

* This was the original justification given for the coup. Truckloads of evidence were promised, but never produced. Later the regime claimed that it was not the Left but the whole parliamentary system which was the target. A further claim was that the danger was of anarchy, not communism.

of the names of our new masters. There were some colonels, George Papadopoulos of the KYP, the Greek equivalent of the CIA, Brigadier Pattakos, who was chosen because he was commander of the tank corps, and Makarezos. There were also two generals, Spandidakis and Zoitakis.

They had taken over power by deceit, by abusing the confidence of the people and the government who had trusted them with arms, with tanks, and with the NATO plan which was supposed to protect Greece from enemy attack. They used the arms, the tanks, and the NATO plan to enslave Greece and to deprive its people of their rights, safeguards and liberties.

Orders over the radio came one after the other, interspersed with military music. We had to stay in our homes, keep quiet, everything would be all right, it would all revert to normal soon. We were not to use our private cars. We were not to be out after 8 p.m. on any excuse. The soldiers had orders to shoot on sight anyone who was out after 8 p.m. A young friend arrived and asked me if I could take her in my car, which had the Aesculapius sign showing that I was a doctor, to people she wanted to contact because her father had been arrested.

We set off, but it was terribly difficult because police stopped us everywhere and made us go round and round, most streets being closed to traffic. One thing I noticed with pleasure: the police we met seemed as fed up and angry with what had happened as we were.

People were trying to get supplies of food. I got some evaporated milk and tinned fish for the cats. There was a terrible feeling of doom in everyone. What was happening? The voice on the radio went on telling us throughout the day that no one was to be out after 8 p.m. No one. Whoever disobeyed this order would be shot. I could not believe that this voice would succeed in enslaving us. I imagined that no one would accept it. I walked out after eight, got into my car and went for a drive around. It was dark — there were only tanks and soldiers in the streets. I did not go very far; I was ordered to go home and I did. I was shivering with cold terror. The doctor's sign on the car had protected me. But others had died. Down in Patissia Street one woman and one young girl were shot down. A friend of mine witnessed this from his window, in his unlighted room. An officer in a tank had given the order. He saw the soldier's hand tremble when he fired.

Very early I started learning about atrocities, unheard-of brutalities.

The nightmare of learning about hardship, misery and illness had been my lot almost since my early youth, as I have said. Somehow people had felt or heard that if I could help I would try to do so, and they came to me. One evening, when I was in my twenties, we were sitting in an open air café, and my first husband said, 'Stop calling all the beggars around you.' To my bewildered 'How am I calling them?' he answered, 'You look nicely at them.'

I was never interested in party politics or the intricate details of party machinery. But I have a strong feeling about such things as human dignity, and rights, and freedom of speech and thought. In the course of one night, of that terrible night of April 21st, all that world was crushed and gone. Thousands and thousands of people were taken to concentration camps for transfer to a barren, waterless, foodless, uninhabited rock, the island of Yaros. Others were taken to prison. Their crime was that there were files with the security police some thirty years old, saying that at a time when most of them were fifteen, eighteen, or twenty years old they had had leftward ideas; or that they were now Members of Parliament, or leaders, or potential leaders.

Relatives of people who had been arrested while ill, and the neighbours of small children who had been abandoned when their parents were suddenly taken away by force, flooded my apartment. They came to ask me to tell the head of the Greek Red Cross what had happened and secure his help. For about seven months I visited this man, Constantine Georgakopoulos, almost every day. He is a very old man, he must be nearly eighty, and because of his great age he must be forgiven.

I was always well received. He had some affection for me, having known me since I was a young girl. Each time I described to him the misery of a case, I had to listen to a long, political, heartless speech against the communists—everyone who had been arrested was labelled as a communist. Why was I interested in the families and children of such criminals? Each time I replied that if he wanted to, he could give me his views on the punishment that the small children of supposed communists should suffer; or on the hardship that sick or old people should be suddenly subjected to all over again, because some thirty-year-old police files stated that they were communists, although when they were arrested they were peacefully sleeping in their beds; he could give me his views—but in another place, not in the office of the

Red Cross. He could come and see me in my house on a social call, or ask me to his, and give me, if he liked, hours of tuition on how to make sure that small hungry children had no communist parents before I gave them something to eat. But I had to remind him that there, in the offices of the Red Cross, he, as its head, and I, as a doctor, had only one duty and should have only one aim: the relief of suffering. I even copied out for him something my husband had written in his diary in 1935. It was an extract from a speech by Lister, the great British surgeon who had saved so many lives in Britain by applying antiseptics for the first time. In 1898, on being given the freedom of the city of Edinburgh, he said, ' ... I regard all worldly distinctions as nothing in comparison with the hope that I may have been the means of reducing in however small a degree the sum total of human misery.' I gave this to Georgakopoulos and asked him to keep it on his desk and to try to remember the message. But however much I pleaded and begged, whatever promises I managed to obtain, nothing, but absolutely nothing, was done. I should have known better than to waste his time.

Georgakopoulos belonged politically to the extreme Right, to the party the Colonels had come from. He had been a minister in the Cabinet of another dictator, Metaxas. He was the only man I heard say 'we' when speaking of the Colonels; everybody else in Greece said 'they'. I should not have been surprised at his position. I knew that on the morning of April 21st, after the deposed prime minister, George Papandreou, aged seventy-nine and running a fever, had been arrested and taken away to an unknown place, one of his doctors had rung Georgakopoulos at his Red Cross office to ask his help for the sick old man. Georgakopoulos's answer was a stream of abuse against the prime minister. The doctor, before putting the receiver down in disgust, had said, 'I do apologize, I must have got the wrong number. I thought I was speaking to the head of the Red Cross.' I should have known that there were no longer any legal means of helping people. But I went on, and it required two major incidents to stop me from asking the help of the Greek Red Cross.

The first occurred after I had been told in Geneva that there were forty thousand parcels for the political detainees waiting to be taken into Greece and distributed. I was asked whether I would be able to persuade the Greek Red Cross to deal with them. I said I would try, and once again visited my friend Georgakopoulos to be told the same old story. Why should I, and these international bodies, be interested in the families of criminals?' 'We', he said, 'will accept these parcels if it is left to us to distribute them through the police to the poor that we shall choose. Why are you not interested in helping the poor in general?'

I explained that I was, very much so, and he had known me long enough to understand that, but that firstly, there was the express wish of the senders to consider, and secondly, the poor in our country had somehow managed to survive, while this present case was a sudden emergency: between one moment and the next the breadwinner had been taken away; children had been left with nothing to eat. Georgakopoulos refused, and I left in anger, saying that *I* was going to take these parcels through the customs and *I* would personally go to distribute them. But how could I? The Red Cross would have got them into the country duty-free, but I would have to pay customs duties far beyond my possible resources; and even if I did get the parcels in, how could I go and distribute them when it was illegal to help families of detainees: people had been arrested for giving them only the equivalent of a pound or two in Greek money.

The incident that put a final stop to my visits to the Greek Red Cross and to my efforts to help people through legal means was still more upsetting. The child of a deportee was dying. If my memory is correct, she was a little girl aged ten. She was crying for her father, and he asked to be allowed to be brought back, under guard, to see and kiss his child for the last time. He was told that he could only do so if he signed a document renouncing his beliefs and ideals. He refused. Because of his refusal, he did not get permission to be brought to Athens, and the child died without seeing her father.

Georgakopoulos's reactions and mine were so different that I felt I could never see this man again in my life. He believed that the father should have signed the humiliating renunciation of the ideals of his whole life, and his conclusion was to call the man a criminal, a fanatic, a monster. But who were the criminals, the fanatics, the monsters?

Despite my efforts to explain that I had no means of helping, people kept coming to me to ask for help. The word had gone round that I was prepared to do *anything* possible, and, hope being inextinguishable, they kept coming. With them they brought descriptions of the atrocities that were going on.

The Colonels needed to use torture to put fear into the hearts of the people, to prevent the people from rising and throwing them out of power. Reducing the people to silence was necessary if the entire enterprise of the Junta was not to be doomed from the beginning. Also they had to use torture, and horrible torture at that, to obtain the names of the newly emerging resistance groups. About a week after the Colonels had gained power I learned about the methods the Junta was using to stifle the people's reaction. I learned of them by a mere coincidence.

A woman I had known for years, who lived in one of the working-class suburbs and whom I had not seen for a considerable time, came suddenly to see me. She sat down and just looked at me, without speaking, tears running down her face; I asked her to tell me what was wrong, but she would not. It was about a week after the Colonels had seized power. For a few days the woman kept coming almost every day; she would just sit and cry. All I could get out of her was that she wanted to tell me why she was crying and what had happened to her, but she could not; and then she would add, what was the use, what could I do? At last she spoke: early one morning, some men from the police station had come and taken her husband away. He was an elderly, hard-working man who had never before been in any trouble. He returned late at night, haggard, bloodstained, unrecognizable. His face was swollen and covered with blue-red bruises. He could hardly walk. He collapsed, and when she tried to help him on to his bed, he screamed with pain. He was passing blood instead of water. When she saw his body, it was all blood and bruises. She tried to run for a doctor, but he stopped her. He was terrified. They had told him to speak to no one and not to dare call a doctor or they would work him over again. He could not speak or cough without great pain in his chest. Twelve days after this treatment he still could not cough without the pain. His wife finally persuaded him to come and see me. He told me that through a whole day he had been kicked and punched and beaten with truncheons all over his body and his head. He had tried to save his face by covering it with his arms. This lasted until he fell unconscious. Then he would be revived, abused obscenely and beaten again. When the first policemen had had enough, others would take over. Then they would stop for a while. They would look at their watches and say they would be back in an hour. And they were. The same process started all over again. They never asked him any questions. From time to time they would make him say, 'Long live the King', or 'Long live the revolution', and when he did, they would laugh and go on beating and abusing him, saying that they knew he had gone to election speeches for EDA, the legal left-wing party, and that they would beat it out of his system. This lasted for seventeen hours. 'It was only that long for me,' he said, 'because I am old and frail. For the young it was hell. There was a young boy there who had been going through it for five days. They gave you as much as they thought you could take, short of dying.'

I took the man immediately to a friend of mine, a very good doctor, an honest, nice man with very right-wing political views. From the medical point he could do more for the old man than I could, and I wanted my friend to see him and to believe. It was twelve days after the beating. His chest, his back and his arms and legs were black and blue. His face was swollen and red, his genitals swollen, bruised, and aching. Two ribs were broken near the region of the heart. They had been punching him there with particular brutality, telling him they would break his heart.

He said that men from sixteen to seventy were taken in every day, about ten or fifteen a day, and put through this treatment. I heard that this happened in almost all the working-class districts. It was obvious that it was being done on orders from above. The pattern was always the same, even if the brutalities varied. For instance, in the case of one boy, the police had formed two groups. One group beat him up and then threw him like a football to the other for the same treatment. His spine was dislocated. It seemed to be a well organized, widespread programme of terror. There was no doubt that the police station was obeying orders, detailed orders, to terrorize people into silence, to annihilate any idea of revolution. At some police stations the local chief of police refused to obey these inhuman orders, but only a few districts were lucky.

This time I did not go to the Greek Red Cross. I went to Mr Collendon, the representative of the International Red Cross. I told him of the first case, the man I had seen myself, in detail. I gave him the name of the police station, despite the promise I had made to the poor old man that I would not say anything, but I did not give his name. Collendon took notes. He seemed very annoyed, and said he would go straight to Pattakos, the Minister of the Interior, and tell him. He said, 'This thing must stop.' He asked me how I had come to know, and this also seemed to me to annoy him. He gave me the impression that he cared more about the image of the Colonels than about the poor tortured devils. But I may be wrong; I was just too upset to have a clear judgment.

Perhaps Collendon's intervention did something, or perhaps by the time I saw him the operation was almost over. It had certainly brought beautiful results; people were struck dumb. More miseries came to my knowledge every day. I did not know where to turn for help. I had used all the legal means I could use. These children, these people, had to be helped. But how?

The Great Terror spread. There were rumours of terrible bestiality in the police posts of Piraeus and Salonika. There were rumours of many deaths, especially of officers and soldiers who had resisted the coup. There were rumours of informers, of soldiers and police in civilian clothes mixing with the people, encouraging them to talk and arresting them at the slightest adverse comment. So nobody spoke.

Yet, in spite of all this, the boys and girls of student age started writing slogans on walls and distributing leaflets with information from foreign radio stations. These were all we could rely on. In the early weeks of the coup, foreign newspapers were not allowed, and no one believed the local radio, which was in the hands of the Junta. The newspapers had been taken over as well. Some of them were closed down. Others closed of their own will, and those that remained were all identical: the same size print, the same headlines, the same text, the same news in the same column—all exactly according to the same detailed orders. In every editor's office sat a military censor.

Some of the active young, most of whom were students, were arrested and subjected to terrible tortures. The torturing stopped only when they fell into a coma or broke down and spoke and gave away the name of a friend. Then this friend would be arrested and treated in the same way until he also spoke. The department of security police headquarters that specializes in beating up students is called the 'Intellectual Department'.

The most common torture is falanga* — beating the soles of the feet. This is done with a metal bar, a wooden club, or a heavy twisted wire — whatever is at hand; usually they use one after the other. When

* The word falanga is derived from 'phalanx', a formation of soldiers lined up in rows. The punishment the word describes is extremely ancient; the word came to describe the beating of the feet, or bastinado, as the blows on the feet would be aimed to cover the soles with systematic rows of welts.

the feet are swollen and cracked, the victims are made to stand and even run so that circulation returns to their feet and with it the full agony. Then the beating starts again. Usually there are four or five torturers taking turns: one beats the feet of the victim, another will crush or twist the genitals, or tie them tightly with a string, or beat them, a third will bang the head of the victim on the bench to which he is attached, or pull out his hair, or gag him with a dirty cloth (drenched with urine which runs down his throat) so that he cannot scream, or beat the bones of his legs, hips and chest with a metal rod. When he faints, filthy water is showered on him, and the torturers start again.

Starvation, deprivation of water, standing for days and nights, electric shocks, the torturing of the victim's girlfriend, cigarette burns —all these were used. The details have been written a hundred times. Why repeat them? Because they still continue. Because I have met some victims and listened to their stories and seen their scars.

One of the first boys I saw who had been treated like this was only eighteen. The beating had been done in the room on the terrace of the security police headquarters at Bouboulinas Street, in Athens. This place, at the beginning, was more infamous than any other for its terrible tortures. Today the Special Interrogation Centre of the military police has the honour of holding this disreputable championship. The police building in Bouboulinas Street has just been demolished. The security police have moved to another building where, I suppose, special measures for stifling the sound of the victims' screams must have been devised. Something like a television studio, no doubt.

The boy was a student; he stood the tortures for about twenty hours, then he spoke; he gave away his best friend. He was carried down to the basement, a place called the Well, and was left in a cell without a bed or blankets until the swelling in his feet and other wounds no longer showed. Then he was transferred to Averof Prison, and later court-martialled for distributing leaflets. He was sentenced to eighteen years' imprisonment. When he came back to Averof, a common-law convict who saw him dressed in a suit and tie asked him if he had been up for trial. He said 'Yes.' 'How much did you get?' 'Eighteen years.' 'Did you kill a man?' 'No,' said the boy. 'Two?' asked the convict with admiration.

Some time later an amnesty freed all these youngsters. This is when I saw him, and he told me his story. I shall never forget what he said, his eyes darkened and filled with an implacable hatred: 'We who were forced to betray will never forgive.' Shortly afterwards he was re-arrested. He had become involved in resistance activity again. And again he was tortured and again imprisoned.

So much for my dreams of a quiet, uneventful life. How many tortured people I saw; young boys, young girls. Sometimes for the girls it was worse. Often they would be stripped of all their clothes and tortured naked by a group of men and threatened with rape. Young boys, also, were threatened with sexual assault. I met one boy who had had two of his toenails wrenched out. He told me how he had seen a friend carried down to the Well in a blanket dripping with blood; this is how they carried them when they had totally collapsed.

Besides the central security police station at Bouboulinas Street, a new place of torture was becoming known: Dionysos, the commando training-camp just outside Athens. Terrible tortures were reported to be taking place there, and, what was worse, some were carried out by the young conscripts, boys of twenty called up to do their military service. These boys were ordered to torture, instructed in it, and trained to become sadists.

But it must be stressed that not all the police or all the army had suddenly changed into monsters. Far, very far from it. The information about the fate of people who had suddenly disappeared, and whose existence the police would pretend to ignore, came from *inside* — inside the police stations, inside the military camps. And so did the details of their torture. Anonymous phone calls, typewritten notes in capital letters, giving precise and almost invariably accurate information, reached the relatives, and through them it often reached me.

I heard of young soldiers who were forced to torture and could not stand it, and who suffered breakdowns. A young girl told me of a small incident which occurred when she was back in her cell after terrible tortures and humiliating abuse. She showed me the traces of cigarette burns on her breasts. She knew she was right in opposing this un-acceptable dictatorship which was ruining her country, but she felt shattered; the world seemed to have changed into something horrible, evil, unjust, and dirty. She was lost and alone, and what could she do? What could anyone do? She felt short of breath and crawled to the door. She managed to stand and reach the spyhole for some fresh air. Outside stood her guard, a young soldier with a gun, a conscript of about her own age. He was shaking, and tears were running down his cheeks. The girl felt that she was not alone, and that the world had not changed; all evil was the work of a few. Bitterness left her; she felt at peace and strong again.

How much did I see and hear of horror and atrocities? How and where did I see it? What did I do to try to stop it, to stop the tortures, and to stop this sadism from spreading, in fact to save both the tortured and the torturers? I cannot say. I cannot speak at this time. It is too early yet. But these things, and much more, were proven. The European Commission of Human Rights investigated and found the Colonels guilty of horrible atrocities. The investigating committee was helped by a number of men and women who had suffered horrible tortures, and many had scars to show. On their release from jail some had the immense courage and self-sacrifice, knowing well what they were risking, to escape the prison that was Greece, go to Strasbourg, and testify. It was helped by men and women still in prison, and therefore at the mercy of their torturers, who had the courage to smuggle out signed statements describing their ordeals and asking to testify to the European Commission of Human Rights. Some of them, very few, managed to do so, despite great resistance from the Colonels' regime.

A lawyer, Angelos Tsoukalas, defended the Colonels at the Council of Europe. He denied the tortures, and yet he had good knowledge of them, since his own daughter-in-law, the wife of his only son, had been arrested with a group of young people who had been badly tortured. She saw the tortured, and she heard their screams. She told him, and so he certainly knew only too well. For all his efforts he lost his case, and the Colonels were forced to withdraw from the Council of Europe. However, they were grateful for his defence, and Angelos Tsoukalas was rewarded for having tried so hard to serve them against the Greek people; he is now the Minister of Justice.

The Colonels themselves, on their 'word of honour as officers', had denied all charges of torture. They still do so today. Pattakos promised to hang any proven torturer in Constitution Square. He has not yet hanged himself. The ambassadors and press attachés, almost all newly appointed, issue denials which, when challenged, they do not usually dare to repeat. They are instructed to deny the truth of bestialities which are eventually all proved to be true.

Oppression in other forms, milder but equally effective, was also applied and still is. Thousands were fired from their jobs: professors and university teachers, educationalists, officers, and public servants. The secure tenure of judges, which was the traditional safeguard for their freedom of judgment, was suspended for three days, and twenty-one judges were dismissed, among others Christos Sartzetakis, the original of the impartial judge of the film, Z. No one was secure any longer. Everything that was best in the judicial and educational worlds was got rid of, dismissed without any other explanation than the vague phrase 'anti-national activities'. Dismissal from jobs is a very serious thing. People know that once they lose their job they might be prevented from obtaining another. A mere telephone call from the security police would deter most potential employers. Most people depend on their salary. What happens when it is stopped?

Among all these miseries we also heard of dismissals which had their funny side. For example, there was the case of a high civil servant who was offered the post of minister of the ministry in which he had been working for many years. He refused it. They insisted, he refused again, and then was dismissed as 'inefficient'.

The schoolbooks were destroyed. New ones appeared with unbelievably regressive contents. Children were taught a falsified history. Vernacular Greek, our own native language, the one we write and speak, our true living language, was forbidden to be used in the schools—the order actually said that from their third year of schooling, children should 'no longer use their mother tongue' but 'Katharevusa', a language that was introduced at the time of the liberation of Greece from the Turks to classicize the Greek language. It has however never been spoken and has never been a living language.

Teachers were forced to deliver speeches praising the new regime. Banners all over the country proclaimed the same message. On national anniversaries, and of course the anniversary of their seizure of power came first, people were obliged, by order of the police, to hoist flags. All apartments had to do so, and the blocks of flats came to look like cakes decorated in very bad taste.

What had happened to my country? How could I help the families of the detainees, the families of the dismissed, all this misery? Who were these men who were systematically ruining the people, brain-washing them, training informers and sadists? They were moulding a new generation into either fanatical idiots or revolutionaries.

Where did these unbelievable people spring from? Who trained them, and where, to be liars, dishonest, cruel, unprincipled? What for? Who gave the wrong twist to their mind? Who harmed them, when they were youngsters, as they are harming our young people today? They too were children once, one presumes, perhaps with the same dreams that we had. Who ruined them?

I remembered the talks I had in 1966 with Christos Sartzetakis when I first met him in Paris. I had liked him immediately. He was integrity itself, with a childish candour. He was proud of being a judge. It was obvious that he could not have chosen any career that he would have liked better. As a young judge of thirty-three, Sartzetakis had been charged with the investigation of the death in Salonika of the left-wing Member of Parliament, Grigoris Lambrakis. In spite of great pressure from Kollias,* the Supreme Court judge (who was to be the first prime minister of the Junta), Sartzetakis had proved that the death of Lambrakis was actually a murder. He had disentangled an almost unbelievable saga, and in the end arrested more than one general officer of the police, indicting them for having instigated the murder and for trying to cover it up. Sartzetakis was proud to be *the* judge, impartial and unbiased. For this reason he refused to belong to any one political party or to express personal opinions. We had however the same liberal ideals; we both dreamed of a progressive Greece, and we both wanted the Greek people to be allowed the culture and education that they deserve, and to be what their natural intelligence leads them to be: free-thinkers, tolerant, real democrats, kind and helpful, objecting to any illegal interference by the government machine. *But*, I used to say, if we are to have all that, some other element has to stop: the brain-washing in the army and in the schools. This seems to be exercised and imposed by an invisible force, and it leads to the elimination, by prevention of promotion, dismissal from work, exile or even imprisonment, of anyone expressing liberal ideas. It especially affects everyone dealing with education, from teachers at primary schools to university professors.

---

* In the spring of 1943 Kollias was appointed by the 'authorities of occupation' to the security committee of Attica, under Kivotas, the provincial governor. Kollias was the man who, by putting pressure on others, deported to the prison of Acronafplia the young K. Arkendis, Yannis Destounis, Anastasios Papoustanis and Dionysios Papaconstantinou, who were arrested by the well-known butcher of special security, Lambrou. When Acronafplia stopped being used as a prison, the five young men were transferred to the special security of Athens, where Arkendis was executed (Spyros Yannatos, *George Papandreou* [Toronto, 1971], p. 211).

Since I first started to think about things I have believed that everything depends on an atmosphere of intellectual freedom and enlightenment. And here I use the word 'intellectual' to mean not only the world of the scholar but also that of anyone who is conscious of what is happening to his country and the people, and who cares. Sartzetakis would not speak of anything touching on politics. But we agreed on the two main subjects, the governmental machine and intellectual atmosphere: something that was wrong in both seemed to crush every free and liberal thinker. But we thought everything was going to be put right. We never imagined that everything was to become so much worse! What a beautiful Greece we were going to build! There I was, feeling very young again, dreaming the old dream of my youth during the enemy occupation in the Second World War, the dream of a free, progressive, independent, proud Greece where human rights and human dignity would be respected. That dream had given the fragile young woman I was then the courage to face interrogations and imprisonment with a fierce spirit.

And now? Now? Now I had no hope any more. Only despair.

2. *The Junta in Control*

The arrests, the horrifying tortures, and the savage sentences went on until they were a routine. Ten, fifteen, twenty years of prison for circulating pamphlets or translations of articles from foreign newspapers.

There was a universal upheaval. Protests came from every kind of humanitarian organization and even at government level. The Junta answered by denying all atrocities and all illegal measures. They were just purifying the universities, the ministries, the army and the schools from 'corrupt elements'. Soon a beautiful and pure democracy would come into effect.

On May 21st, in an address to the people, King Constantine announced the birth of the heir to the throne and on the same occasion promised a new constitution.

This happy event [he added] coincides with the assurance I was given by the government concerning the progress of the revision of the constitution. A committee will be named before the end of the month, and within six months will lay the draft of the new constitution before the government, which after a final work of revision will put it to the approval of the people through a referendum.*

A number of lawyers probably chosen by Kollias were asked to prepare the draft of the new constitution. Among the lawyers whose names appeared in the newspapers as members of this constitution committee were some who had refused to take part in this new parody, but who had no means of saying so publicly; so most of the population believed they had accepted to serve on the committee. It was also announced that the people would have the freedom to criticize the draft of the constitution, and that their suggestions would be taken into consideration.

In fact nobody cared about these announcements and no one believed a thing. We had already heard enough lies. Only the

* *Ethnos*, May 22nd, 1967.

American Embassy, the State Department and some high American officials expressed their approval of these measures of future liberalization. They pretended to believe that they were real and that we were heading towards normality, legality and freedom.

The young King had accepted the Junta after a few hours of resistance, hoping, along with many of his right-wing friends, that it might eventually work in their favour, and realizing, anyway, that it saved them from the immediate humiliation of a crushing electoral defeat. He began to discover that things were not going his way, and that the Colonels were tougher and more shrewd than George Papandreou; they were not going to give him the chance of re-using his old tricks in a situation that they commanded.

Once again ill-advised, the King mounted an abortive military counter-coup on December 13th, 1967. The way he did it made many people believe that it was a piece of play-acting conceived to disengage him from the Junta, and that he never believed he had the slightest hope of success. He seems not even to have tried to win. When he left his palace to lead his loyal officers to war against the Junta, he took with him his mother, his young wife, his babies, cases of his most precious belongings, his maid, his poodle, and his prime minister, Kollias. Kollias had become the first prime minister of the Junta at the King's demand, in exchange for his recognition of the Colonels. That was yet another mistake of this inexperienced monarch, who had never behaved according to the constitution, and who was not the King of the Greeks, which is his title, but the King of one party, the right-wing party. If he had had better advice, and had troubled to know how the people reacted, he would have known that Kollias was far from being popular after his scandalous interference in the Lambrakis murder investigation. He had attempted from the powerful position of a High Court judge to influence and almost force the young investigating judge, Christos Sartzetakis, to cover up the guilt of the police and not to indict them.

As soon as he reached Kavala, a town in north-east Greece, the King gave a speech which was both arrogant and ill-timed. All the same, such was our desire to get rid of the dictatorship that our hearts filled with hope. We thought that to attempt a counter-coup the King must have been assured of significant support, and that we were to see the end of the catastrophic Junta. Apparently this was not the case. The whole story is an absolute mystery to some of us. Before even being defeated, the King, his family and his prime minister left the country, leaving his loyal officers at the mercy of the revengeful Junta. A large number of officers, some of very high rank, were arrested, humiliated, imprisoned for months in absolute isolation, and then exiled to remote villages or islands. Some were tortured, others simply ill treated. Naval officers and sailors were arrested and taken for torture as ships returned to port.

After Kollias's departure, Papadopoulos became prime minister. His humourless speeches would have been greeted as masterpieces of parody, an incomprehensible sequence of pompous words, if we had not been so unhappy. A day will come when we shall be able to laugh, reading them again, without feeling a cold shiver going down our spines or an icy hand twisting our hearts. Besides the funny parts, I don't think that any man has ever insulted a people in such a way. In the beginning, one of Papadopoulos's favoured themes was that the Greek nation was a sick man under treatment. He, Papadopoulos, was the great surgeon. He would cut off the sick and rotten parts, and put us in plaster. He would wait some time for the result of the treatment, and from time to time he would break the plaster to see if we had recovered—that is, if we had given up wanting freedom and civil rights, and were willing to accept the rule of the Junta. If we had not, he would clap us back in plaster. The Greek people seem to be really sick and incurable. After five years we are still in plaster.

In response to pressure, Papadopoulos from time to time promised a return to normal life and a new and real democracy. The drafts of the constitution were going on being prepared, subjected to the people's criticism, changed and rechanged. Every newspaper appeared with a headline above the name of the paper saying 'The Constitution of the People, by the People, for the People'.

In the meantime Papadopoulos was completing his own programme, purging the army and the administration of any element he considered insufficiently secure, placing some officers of whom he was absolutely confident in high administrative posts, and dismissing fully qualified civil servants. What mattered was not efficiency but absolute devotion to the new masters. Most of the officers put in key positions were first made to retire from the army, as did Papadopoulos, Pattakos and Makarezos, our triumvirate. But the people continued to call them Colonels. Later, such officers were placed at the head of all intellectual institutions, such as universities, the archaeological service, the elementary and secondary schools, etc. The Greek people called them 'commissars'. Hundreds of policemen, in civilian clothes, of course, were registered at the universities as students. At the smallest demonstration by the students, some of them would drop the mask and arrest the culprits. Young boys of eighteen or twenty would also be bought as informers, and followed closely all the other students might say. Secret police would often act as a nucleus, start a resistance organization, and then have the whole group arrested. A law was prepared, though I think that it was not officially applied, that 10 per cent of the university places would be given to candidates who, even if they had failed their entrance examinations, had shown at school behaviour 'of high loyalty'. The children of the military or police officers who supported the Junta seemed all to have given proof of 'high loyalty' at school, so they were all able to register as students.

All the students who had been taken away in the mass action of the first days of the coup were expelled permanently from university life. Later, the 'commissar' of each university chose a committee of professors to judge young students who had been sentenced to prison terms for anti-Junta activities. To their shame, they expelled the students for ever from their university, even if they had been sentenced to one year's imprisonment, and were by then free to continue their studies, or even, as happened in some cases, if they had only to pass one more subject in order to graduate. As these students were not allowed passports, this meant they were effectively debarred from higher education. Most of them were among the more brilliant students at the universities. Their long-standing request to have tuition by correspondence, and in this way to become accepted students of foreign faculties, has not yet had any result.

It was not only the students who could no longer go on with their studies. The professors of the universities, the archaeologists, and the teachers who were dismissed, and among them were the best we had, not only could no longer go on with their teaching but they were also refused passports to leave the country when they were invited to teach in foreign universities. Since nothing at all in Greek life is general, some of these professors, after great pressure from foreign countries, and because the Colonels were afraid they might lose financial or military aid, finally did get permission to leave. A number of students, fearing arrest with all it involved, left the country. So, for various reasons, did thousands of workers. The great exodus had started again.

Special measures were taken to deceive the tourists. As most of the taxi drivers were anti-Junta, like most of the population, three thousand new drivers' permits were issued to people bought by the Junta. These drivers knew a few foreign words, and would start a conversation with foreign passengers, telling them their honest and unbiased opinion as men in the street. A foreign friend told me of one of these new taxi drivers on a long journey who, after an hour and a half of absurd propaganda, admitted he was talking nonsense in which he did not believe, but explained disarmingly that in his provincial town they were all instructed what to say by the police, twice a year.

All the tourist agencies were also made to see that tourists were told the 'right' information, or at least that they should be well protected from the truth. I experienced an example of this personally. An American friend who used to visit Greece every year, and who was actually one of us in her feelings against the Junta, wished to go to Lefkas, a lovely island which is inhabited almost exclusively by real democrats. As I had some very good friends in Lefkas, and loved both the island and the drive (although an island, it is so near to the mainland that you just have to get into a ferryboat at one end and get out a few yards further on at the other), I told her I would like to join her. She said she would do the hotel booking through the tourist agency she always used. But after trying through her agency, which had some new staff, she told me that unfortunately all the hotels were fully booked and we had to go to a private house which was letting rooms. When we arrived I was amused to see that the owner was expecting V.I.P. American ladies. I asked him please to telephone to a number of my friends, as there was not even a telephone in the house to tell them that I was there, and that I wanted to see them as soon as possible. After some time only one arrived, the one who knew me best and trusted me, and one of his first questions was, 'Can you please tell me why you are in *this* house?' I answered naturally that it was because there was not one room available in any hotel. He seemed astonished, and asked me to wait for him a few minutes. He went out and came back to tell me that every single one of the hotels had numbers of rooms free. 'Do you know', he added, 'that you are in the only pro-Junta house in the island?'

Greece is always Greece, our beautiful Greece. The Colonels have not managed to ruin everything; the sky is blue, the sea is blue and clear. There are no tortures in the streets, and people will be afraid to talk or to tell you what they really think. The cafés and the tavernas are full. We are used to living out of doors, because it is usually nice and warm. But don't misunderstand us. For one thing we must go on living, we must survive, we must have the strength to fight and therefore we need to laugh. Laughter is a national characteristic, in spite of the fact that our folksongs are usually sad, and we enjoy them that way.

One evening something happened—I shall describe it later—to upset me terribly. I was expecting a friend to come for dinner at home. When she arrived I told her that I was so distraught that I felt myself suffocating in the house, and asked her if she would not mind if we went out to a taverna for dinner. We did so; the place was full, the musicians played, the people ate heartily, and laughed heartily. I was shocked and disgusted. On such a day, after what had happened, when we should all be ashamed and in some kind of mourning, all these people were out enjoying themselves in a taverna! And suddenly it occurred to me that there I was as well, with what distress in my heart.

Tourists, remember: we would rather that you did not come to Greece now, that you did not help the Colonels. We, the Greeks who consciously oppose their regime, would like to see every sort of boycott imposed on our country. Foreigners say, but would this not bring hardship to the Greek people? And we say yes, it will. But one has to choose between two evils and choose the lesser one. If financial boycott could shorten the life of the dictatorship, and therefore lessen the catastrophe we believe it has brought to the country, is not that better?

Take a hotel owner, for instance, who has two boys to bring up. He certainly wants to have guests, to earn the money to bring up his sons. But will he want this if it means that the dictatorship will be strengthened, so that the results fall upon his boys? By their retrogressive teaching the schools will change his sons either into fanatical idiots or, by reaction, into open opponents of the government; he may see his sons arrested, tortured, imprisoned—will he want that? And if, to take the most pessimistic view, the Junta stays in power so long that eventually the nice soft Greek people get fed up and start a real, open fight, and his boys are killed, would he prefer that to a short period of financial hardship?

3. *Alexandros Panagoulis: The Assassination Attempt*

Early in the morning of August 13th, 1968, a rumour started that there had been an attempt to kill Papadopoulos as he was driving on the coastal road which leads from Sounion to Athens, at twenty to eight in the morning.

Papadopoulos spends his summer in a villa by the sea, halfway to Sounion, near Lagonisi. It must be the best protected place in the world. Coming from Athens, a few yards before one reaches the villa one passes a military police camp that has been set up on the opposite side of the road. There are continual police patrols in the neighbourhood of the house, and boats patrol the sea offshore. At the gates one has to undergo a full identity check and search, and inside the area itself one has to cross a number of fully manned trenches before reaching the house.

On August 14th, 1968, Papadopoulos himself spoke to the press:

My life will be safe as long as God, who is a philhellene, connects me with the interests of Greece ... With the democratic regime that we have, anyone can move freely, can have a revolver in his pocket freely and can shoot it freely, or he can have a piece of dynamite in a bag and put it somewhere to blow up. But God has always been a philhellene and he continues to be a philhellene to the great annoyance of our enemies ... Do not feel distressed or worried ... the blue sky, the beautiful beaches and the islands are waiting for the foreigners to come to a country where hospitable Zeus will always be eager to serve them. This is the best country for holidays ... the best place for people to spend their holidays in joy and happiness ... Do not be in anguish. The referendum [on the new constitution] will take place whether the enemies of democracy who present themselves with the mask of democracy wish it or not. Greece will get a constitution, democratic and free. And all should be certain that liberty which flourished in

47

this country will continue to flourish in this country. This annoys [the enemies] because they will no longer be able to speak of a dictatorial regime where there is no freedom ... With these few words and with my appearance before you in good health, I thank you for your anxiety and also for the help you will give in calming the anxiety of those at home and abroad ... *

The newspapers carried a photograph of the man they had arrested, who had given his name as George Panagoulis. The photograph had the caption: 'The instrument of fascism who, imitating the OAS, attempted to murder the founder of the new democracy.' But the photograph was of Alexandros Panagoulis.

Stamatopoulos, the official spokesman of the government, also spoke to the press:

> ... you may have in mind one of the latest declarations of the State Department that the government has firm control of power in the country ... The Greek people gives its full support to the government. Our country goes steadily towards the referendum, that is, the democratic procedure moves towards normality, exactly as the prime minister had foretold. No power will be able to hold back this evolution towards new, contemporary democracy ...

He then announced that 'something had happened' — an attempt to kill the prime minister, at the thirty-first milestone on the Sounion road.

> The murderer-to-be, who was supposed to escape in a Chriscraft, was arrested easily by the police as the Chriscraft was unable to approach because of the large number of bathers who assembled. He was in bathing trunks and was jumping from rock to rock and had in this way torn his feet. I shall now describe to you the would-be murderer. He is George Panagoulis, son of Basil. He was a regular captain in the army. In August 1967 he deserted ... I am sorry to say that the man who wanted to murder the prime minister is not a communist. George Panagoulis was and is the instrument of fascist and of reactionary forces who wanted to

---

* *Bima*, August 14th, 1968. Since the censorship was in full control, whatever was published was given out by the government. These were Papadopoulos's actual words.

murder the leader of the revolution, the President of the government, that is, the man who is leading the new forces which are
founding democracy. The National, the Political, the Social and
Economic Revolution whose future is guaranteed by the new
constitution ... There is no doubt that the Greek people, and the
public democratic opinion of the world, when it learns that the
so-called democratic forces entrusted their design to a fascist, will
draw their own conclusions ... The God of Greece has once
again put under his blessed protection our people, peace and
democracy.

On the next day, August 15th, 1968, Stamatopoulos said again:
'the country is moving steadily towards the referendum, and the
revolution is founding the new democracy with wisdom, with
progressive ideas, and with determination.'
He said also that Andreas Papandreou had said that Panagoulis was
a hero—and that this proved that he was the instigator of the murder.
He attacked Sweden and the Swedes, and President Erlander, who
supported Andreas. On August 17th, Stamatopoulos issued a new
communiqué. It was not George Panagoulis who had made the
attempt, but Alexandros, his younger brother. He said that Panagoulis,
like all murderers, 'was a coward, had volunteered to speak and was
speaking freely—so much so that the person who telephoned abroad
from Athens to say that Panagoulis was suffering "pressure" to speak
made a great mistake'. (Unfortunately we already knew of the
appalling tortures to which Panagoulis was being subjected.) Asked by
the press if he was accusing Andreas Papandreou of instigating the
attempt, Stamatopoulos answered that the fact that Andreas was the
only one to have defended Panagoulis, to have said that he was not a
murderer but a hero, was a revealing factor. He added that 'even
the communists do not take up the defence of Panagoulis, but
Andreas Papandreou has, as reported in the British press, asked for
the intervention of a number of organizations for Panagoulis.' On
Sunday, August 18th, it was announced by the Archbishop of Athens
that in all churches a *Te Deum* was to be sung to thank God for the
miraculous rescue ...
About the technical details of the attempt, Stamatopoulos said that
Panagoulis had tried to blow up the road, but the explosion
occurred a few seconds after Papadopoulos's car had crossed over the

danger spot. Moreover, most of the explosives had failed to go off, for some reason unknown to us but well known to the spokesman: 'God Himself who loves Greece has saved our prime minister,' he said. The only damage was two small holes on the side of the road, in a recess of the rocky hill not covered with asphalt.

Much later, when I was a prisoner in EAT ESA,* the commanding officer, Theodoros Theophyloyannakos, explained to me that the explosives had been placed in an enclosed place, inside a road drain under the asphalt with a hill rising above one side of the road. Because of this, the detonator ought to have been put two or three yards closer to the road itself if it was to create the very big explosion that was necessary. He also told me some other technical information about it that I did not understand at that time and cannot now remember. He gave me all these explanations because I had said that I had no proof that Panagoulis meant to kill Papadopoulos; perhaps he simply wanted to frighten him. Theophyloyannakos was definite: an enormous amount of explosive had been placed at two spots, and if the placing of the detonator had been more accurate, the road would have been blown up, and Papadopoulos would in fact have been killed. Theophyloyannakos may have spoken the truth; I must suppose he sometimes does.

If Stamatopoulos could suggest no other explanation for the failure of the attempt than the special desire of God to keep Papadopoulos alive, he did speak at great length about the 'murderer', who he thought at first to be a royalist officer, George Panagoulis, who had deserted the army soon after the Colonels had taken over.

We had heard of George Panagoulis. He was one of the best parachutists and frogmen of his unit, admired and adored by his soldiers for his achievements and courage. After the officers' coup and the betrayal of Greece by a group in the army, he had deserted from that army and escaped to Turkey by crossing the Evros river where it runs along the frontier. From there he eventually reached Israel. The Israeli authorities handed him over to the Junta officials, who sent him back to Greece in the boat *Anna Maria*. When the *Anna Maria* arrived in Piraeus, George Panagoulis was no longer in his locked cabin. The glass of the port-hole had been broken, and a cord made of the bedsheets was hanging from the opening. It was assumed that he had tried to escape by jumping into the sea. A careful search was carried out

* Special Interrogation Centre of the military police.

over the sea near Athens and the nearby island of Aegina, but George Panagoulis was not found alive or dead.

Until late in the night of August 13th, Stamatopoulos went on issuing communiqués. He reported that in Paris a resistance organization EA (Hellenic Resistance) had announced that bombs were exploding all over Athens, and the city was in flames. He claimed that explosives had in fact been planted in various parts of Athens, but that Panagoulis, without being in any way pressured, had shown where the bombs were, had volunteered complete information, and had betrayed all his collaborators. Actually two or three small explosions did occur on the day of the attempt without causing any damage.

When Stamatopoulos gave his second version, that it was Alexandros, and not George, Panagoulis who had made the attempt, he gave some further information about Alexandros. He was an ex-student of the polytechnic, who was doing his military service when the coup took place. Like his brother George, he had deserted from the army after April 21st, 1967. Alexandros Panagoulis, continued the communiqué, had already been tried for 'anti-national activities' in 1967, had been sentenced to prison and then amnestied.

The next day there was a new communiqué. It was not Alexandros who was tried by a military court in 1967, but the youngest of the three Panagoulis brothers, Stathis, and he had not been sentenced but acquitted.

A full-length photograph of the handsome young man in bathing trunks who had been arrested had appeared in the newspapers. Identified first as George, and then as Alexandros, Panagoulis, he had the healthy face of a young man, in spite of his sad expression. We were never to see this healthy face again – the next photographs, taken three months later at his trial, showed a drawn, very pale face, with protruding cheekbones and sunken eyes, eyes brilliant with will and courage.

In spite of the thousands of congratulations sent to Papadopoulos on his miraculous escape, among them those of King Constantine, the great majority of Greeks shared Andreas Papandreou's opinion. Panagoulis was a hero. I remember being told that a friend who had heard the first communiqué rang his brother to tell him about the attempt. He started by telling him in an outraged voice that a 'frightful creature, some vermin,' had tried to kill 'our prime minister'. 'What happened?' asked his impatient brother. The man's voice dropped to a moan. 'He failed,' he said.

We heard of mass arrests, including some of royalist officers, but more particularly of members of the Centre Union party and friends of Andreas Papandreou. Alexandros Panagoulis, who was born on July 2nd, 1939, belonged to the youth branch of the Centre Union party, the party of Andreas's father, prime minister George Papandreou.

The official communiqués were the sole source of information, since only information supplied by the authorities was published; the story they told seemed so strange that many people doubted whether there was any truth in it at all, wondering whether the whole affair might not be a put-up job to justify the arrests. However, I knew that there had been a real event of some kind. I had heard from a friend, who had driven down the coastal road half an hour after the time of the alleged attempt, that helicopters and planes were flying very low, searching the sea, and that a very large number of police were on the road, especially near the thirty-first milestone from Athens, checking all cars and drivers.

Stamatopoulos had first said that a Chriscraft had been waiting to take Panagoulis away after the explosion. Three days later this story too was changed: a car was to have waited for him a little further down the road, but the police had not permitted it to stop. Its driver, Nikolaos Lekanides, had been arrested. He, like Panagoulis, had 'volunteered to confess'.

Panagoulis's father, a retired colonel, Basil Panagoulis, and his mother, Athena, were also arrested. A thorough search of their house in Ano Glyfada, some hundred yards from the very fashionable beach of Glyfada, produced some money amounting to about one thousand dollars and a few thousand drachmas, and nothing else at all. Athena Panagoulis was thrown in a basement cell of the police station of Glyfada. Her husband was taken to Petroupolis police station, where after a few days he suffered a brain haemorrhage. Both parents were then transferred to the Nosileftikon Hospital, where families of military people go. There they were kept in complete isolation, and did not see each other until November 24th, when they were allowed to go home.

A large number of Alexandros Panagoulis's fellow students at the polytechnic were also arrested and interrogated, some under torture, others only under threat of torture. Some were kept for weeks or months, others were released after a few hours. It is common in Greece today for people to be arrested, interrogated, and made to sign statements condemning and renouncing their beliefs and ideals, whatever these may be. At this time, the main theme was Andreas Papandreou. 'Are you for Andreas? Do you support his ideas? What do you think of the attempt against the prime minister? Write down your answers in detail.'

Very soon news reached me of the appalling tortures suffered by the newly arrested. It came from very reliable sources from inside the place of torture, as usual, and it was cross-checked. Again and again I wish to repeat that the tortures are the actions of a few, very few, army or police officers who are a stain on the honour of the Greek Army. The others are sufficiently appalled to inform on them; nor is the horror with which they do so unmixed with a justifiable fear.

Already, on the day after his arrest, the government spokesman Stamatopoulos had mentioned the 'wounds Panagoulis had received on his feet and legs while he was jumping barefoot on the sharp rocks', and the wounds on his head he had got by plunging into the sea. According to another communiqué he had injured his head by trying to hide in a cave. But the full-length photograph taken after he was arrested, published the following day, had shown clearly that head and legs and feet were in a perfectly healthy condition. We knew how he had got the injuries on the soles of his feet — we had already heard enough about falanga — and what we knew was confirmed by the letter that Panagoulis smuggled out of prison in November 1970, which summarized some of the tortures to which he had been subjected. It spoke of 'whipping with wires and with twisted wires all over my body, beating with clubs on the soles of my feet so that my right heel was fractured ... beating my head against the wall and against the floor'. News of terrible tortures to his genitals also came to me. His letter added details of appalling subtlety: 'Burns with cigarettes on my genitals. Insertion of a long metal wire into my urethra and heating of the exposed part of the wire with a cigarette lighter.'*

Three days after the abortive assassination attempt there was another explosion in the centre of Athens in Syntagma Square; once again there were no casualties.

At the 'spontaneous' request of many organizations it was decided that the gratitude of the people to the Heavenly Powers for the escape of Papadopoulos should take a more concrete form. A church should be built in the place where the miracle had taken place. Eventually a mosaic representing the Virgin was placed on a rock that stands up

* Letter of Alexandros Panagoulis, November 1970, see page 92.

beside the road. Strangely enough, and unlike other advertisements of the Junta, it is discreet and in good taste.

The 'miracle' had certainly been assisted by the police who always cover Papadopoulos's route. This patrolling of the road when the prime minister drives has never occurred in Greece before. About an hour before he starts, policemen in cars, on motorcycles and on foot are to be seen every eight or ten yards, and a great number of plain-clothesmen are around. In the city itself, secret police with guns stand on the terraces. Papadopoulos's car is said to be bulletproof. He has often been seen to sit uncomfortably, ready to dodge, and once even to duck under the seat when the tyre of another car burst. He certainly does not seem to have great confidence in the 'love of his people', and according to those who know him he is a physical coward.

We continued to hear of more and more arrests. The names of the arrested were not revealed, and it became more difficult than ever to trace them, partly because of the renewed wave of fear. There were wild rumours about the number of these arrests. Semi-official statements implied that the arrests of royalist officers had nothing to do with the assassination attempt but were simply a preventive measure against a possible counter-coup. Former Members of Parliament who were known to favour Andreas Papandreou, and who had been arrested at the very beginning of the coup but released after a few months, were re-arrested now along with other Centre Union sympathizers, because, according to the Junta, by declaring that Panagoulis was a hero Andreas Papandreou had confessed to instigating the murder.

Fourteen young men alleged to make up the whole of Panagoulis's group were arrested. They were all tortured, but infinitely worse tortures were suffered by Panagoulis himself. We learned that he had twice been transferred to the military hospital in a coma, and that even in his coma the handcuffs he had been wearing since his arrest had not been removed. Nikolaos Lekanides's and Yannis Klonizakis's tortures ranked second in intensity.*

The government spokesman kept repeating that all the men had confessed. Yet in spite of the facility with which the people controlling our country are able to lie, Stamatopoulos said that Panagoulis had only partially confessed. We had heard of at least one other young man who had confessed nothing, and most probably knew nothing: Elef-therios Beryvakis, a young lawyer of great courage and character. He

* See p. 238 for Klonizakis's statement.

had previously been arrested, tortured, and imprisoned for resistance activities. There was no evidence whatsoever that Beryvakis was involved in the attempt.

The official versions continued to be many and varied. The only story that remained tragically the same was the one that we continued to get hold of ourselves. It told of the most bestial tortures. Panagoulis was being tortured to admit a number of things, but in particular to say that Andreas Papandreou was behind the assassination attempt, and he was refusing to do so.

4. *The 1968 Constitution*

In the meantime, and to distract people's attention from the complete abolition of every kind of freedom, much fuss was made over the notorious new constitution which was to bring Greece a real free democracy. Its articles, after many changes and corrections, had been published for the people to study and 'freely' comment on; according to the government spokesman, over five thousand enthusiastic letters were received. The referendum was fixed for September 29th, 1968. It was compulsory to vote. After having voted, a certificate would be issued to each person stating that he had voted.

It is worth remembering that on August 14th, 1968, Papadopoulos had said that Greece was to get a constitution both democratic and free, and that everyone should be certain that 'the liberty which flourished in this country will continue to flourish in this country'. After this constitution the enemies of the regime would no longer be able to speak of the 'dictatorial regime where there is no freedom'. And on the same day the government spokesman had said that Greece 'goes steadfastly towards the referendum, that is, the democratic procedure moves towards normality ... No power will be able to hold back this evolution towards new, contemporary democracy.'

What in fact is this new constitution, which is known as the 1968 constitution? Personally it reminds me of one of the funniest and most tragic books I have read: Joseph Heller's *Catch 22*.

The constitution which was to guarantee the return to democratic normality and real freedom had in fact one aim: the legalization and consolidation of the rule of the Colonels. The essence of the constitution is disguised control by the dictatorial regime itself of every individual or civil right. It creates a constitutional dictatorship which stifles any individual, collective, private, or public expression. It is the suffocation of freedom.

The drafters of the constitution faced one basic problem: how, in the context of twentieth-century Europe, to construct a system that furthers the interests of the few while seeming to protect the rights of the whole people, and thus avoid arousing distrust in the free world, Greek or foreign. The new constitution is full of noble expressions of principles and values for which generations have fought and are still fighting.

All power originates from the people, exists for the people, and for the nation ...

All Greeks are equal before the law.

Personal freedom is inviolable.

No one can be arrested or imprisoned without a warrant.

No one may be deprived of their right to vote or to stand for election to public office.

The establishment of extraordinary tribunals, under whatever name, is prohibited.

Every person's home is inviolable.

Every person is entitled to freedom of expression both in speech and in writing, in the press, and in whatever other way he wishes.

The press is free ...

Secrecy of correspondence or of any other sort of communication is inviolable ...

The right to peaceful and unarmed assembly is guaranteed.

The Parliament shall consist of members elected according to the law by direct general and secret ballot by all citizens who are twenty-one years old and have the right to vote.

Greek citizens who have the right to vote can freely establish political parties, participate in the activities of these political parties and be elected in these parties.

But all these praiseworthy provisions of the Colonels' constitution are very badly abused. Careful reading of the 138 articles almost invariably reveals *Catch 22* sort of traps which abolish all these rights, principles and values and change them into an elegantly written parody.

The new constitution has weapons to hurl against anyone daring to challenge the enduring rule of its creators.

The individual rights so generously provided and secured are always subject to the trap of Article 24, paragraph 2: 'whoever uses the inviolability of his home, freedom of expression, especially in the press, secrecy of correspondence, freedom of assembly, freedom to establish associations or unions, the right to private ownership, to oppose the established regime ... is considered to abuse these rights and is deprived of them as well as of all other rights that the constitution guarantees.' How does one *abuse* one's rights? What is the border between right and wrong use of the citizens' rights, so that they know where they stand and may protect themselves? Who decides that an individual right has been abused? The answer is simple: everything is decided and judged by the dictatorship, which this constitution changes into a 'constitutional' dictatorship, and which is helped to decide and judge by its police and its secret agents.

Besides, to achieve this, and cover it up, the constitution establishes a wonderful mechanism: the Constitutional Tribunal. This mechanism is omnipotent; it decides the fate of Greek citizens, and has absolute power to deprive them not only of their individual rights but also of all their civil rights. And the Greek has no means of defending himself against it because the decisions of the Constitutional Tribunal are irrevocable, even in cases of evident ill judgment. But what in fact is the Constitutional Tribunal? It is the fortress of the dictatorship, established by the Colonels; it is the dictatorship itself. Although it is called a tribunal, it is a purely political instrument and need have no relation to any judicial branch. Its structure and powers, carefully described in fourteen articles, make it the single most important device for the Junta's exercise of absolute power. Its members are appointed by the Council of Ministers, which is the dictatorship itself. They can be professors of the faculty of law, distinguished lawyers, public men who have distinguished themselves in political, economic or scientific life, or high public functionaries. All this, of course, sounds good, and would be a guarantee of fair judgment if these people were not chosen and appointed in the first place by the regime of the Colonels; in this way they are able to appoint only those who will serve their aims, and exclude any undesirable or unbiased judge. The Constitutional Tribunal is thus one of the many disguises of the regime. Everything of any importance is in the sphere of its unchallengable powers:

i. the right to approve the charters of political parties, to control their activities and decide on their dissolution;

ii. the power to deprive citizens of individual and all civil rights when it decides that these rights are 'abused';

iii. the right to depose Members of Parliament (previously this responsibility was vested in Parliament);

iv. the competence to rule on objections concerning the conduct of parliamentary elections and to rule on the validity of elections;

v. the competence to rule on the constitutionality of the regulations governing Parliament;

vi. the competence to rule on the scope and extent of the powers the constitution gives to the King and the Parliament and the government.

One theme echoes throughout the new constitution: Greeks are entitled to their freedom only if they do not intend to oppose the form of the state or the established regime. This vague terminology, which has already made possible many prosecutions and heavy sentences against citizens who only wished to restore democracy, is the dictatorship's protection against its opponents. It is revealing to note the articles in which the Junta provides these dangerously vague exceptions. They form a trap which totally negates the ostensible intention of the beautiful and liberal articles of the provision: all the articles are valid *unless* they are used against the form of the state and the established social regime. So the articles of the new constitution start all over again with a series of 'unlesses'.

Individual rights are provided and protected unless ...

All Greeks above the age of twenty-one have the right to vote unless ...

The parties can function unless ... in which case they become illegal.

Any Greek can be elected Member of Parliament unless ...

Any Greek can be elected mayor, president of a community, town or communal counsellor unless ...

Any person with an ideology aiming at ... cannot be a public employee.

Any person with an ideology aiming at ... cannot belong to the army.

But the meaning of 'opposing or overthrowing the form of the state or of the existing social regime' is of course interpreted and judged by the military dictatorship and its agents.

Article 129 makes the army virtually omnipotent. 'The military forces ... have as their aim the protection of national independence, the territorial integrity of the country, *the established form of the state and the established social regime* against any attempt made against them' (my italics). And with this article the army has the right to intervene and abolish every freedom and every democratic function of people any moment it considers that the 'taboo' forms of the state and established regime are in danger. This the army can do, according to Articles 129 and 131, independently of the wishes of or opposition from the Parliament and the government. To defend these 'established forms' the army can interfere even in cases of peaceful and democratic expressions of the people's will, i.e. in elections, referenda, etc., if the army thinks that the results might reverse or in any way oppose the establishment.

One would imagine there would be some parliamentary provision for checking the army's power to intervene; that some other elements in the administration of law, and especially in the government, should be able to decide if the country was in the sort of danger which would justify such an intervention. But the constitution assures exactly the opposite: the complete independence of the army from the government. According to the legislative decree 58/1968 the government assumes the command of all the armed forces, through the head of the armed forces. This high and all-powerful officer is elected for a life-long term by the Supreme National Defence Council which consists of (1) the prime minister (2) the deputy prime minister (3) the Minister of National Defence (4) the Minister of Co-ordination (5) the Minister or the Deputy Minister of Foreign Affairs (6) the Minister of the Interior, and (7) when he is first elected, the head of the armed forces. The above members of the Supreme National Defence Council are of course at the moment the Junta itself which, according to the constitution of 1968, will elect the head of the armed forces, who will remain the head until his death, according to the same constitution. Whatever government may, in the meantime, replace the Junta, this offspring of the Junta will evidently continue the tradition of the Junta, and act independently of any contrary wish of any other government. It is also he who, in fact, elects the heads of the army, the air force and the navy: because these are theoretically elected by the Supreme National Defence Council but *compulsorily* from a list submitted to them by the head of the armed forces who is not only a life member of the council but also one of the most important ones; no quorum is formed if he is absent.

Article 131 completes the absolute independence of the army because:

i. the promotion and retirement of regular officers from the army takes place through a royal decree, issued at the proposal of the Minister of National Defence according to the decision of councils consisting of high-ranking officers;

ii. postings and transfers of the high and highest-ranking officers are decided by councils consisting of highest-ranking officers;

iii. all these decisions of these councils are *compulsory* for the Minister of National Defence, and there is no possibility of appeal to the Council of State against any such decision.

Is there any doubt, after all this, that the military become the true rulers of the country according to the constitution?

Most of the provisions of the constitution which deal with individual and civil rights, with regional self-government, and with the competence of various courts to hear political cases have not yet come into force. They will be applied when the Junta wishes to apply them, and as things have evolved now, in 1972, it is in the hands of one man, Papadopoulos, to decide if and when they will be applied. As yet it is in vain that the Greeks wait for the application of even the Junta's own laws.

Some more details of this 'liberal' constitution establish that 'revision of the constitution will not be permitted until ten years after the referendum has approved the constitution;' that 'the first elections will take place under the supervision of the National Revolutionary Government;' and that 'the official language of the state and of education is the language in which the constitution and the laws are written.' This, as I have said, is the dead, artificial language Katharevusa, which no one speaks or writes, which children do not understand, and which hinders their powers of expression.

And so, in the Greece of the end of the twentieth century, the Colonels have with their constitution done their best to smother every freedom, annihilate all opposition, and destroy the minds of future generations. The referendum took place on September 29th—92·6 per cent of the Greeks were declared to have voted for it. It was a splendid success for the Junta: in six thousand years of known Greek history, no one had ever before succeeded in making 92·6 per cent of the Greeks agree on one subject.

5. The Indictment of the Fifteen

On October 19th, 1968, Major Theophyloyannakos, the chief interrogator and, according to Panagoulis, one of his main torturers, issued a long report on the findings and conclusions of his investigations. As Stamatopoulos had done before him, Theophyloyannakos said that fifteen men were indicted and all had confessed to all sorts of things, without of course saying how they were persuaded to do so. On page 238ff one of them, Yannis Klonizakis, in a signed statement smuggled out of prison gives a hair-raising account of the methods used. However, about Panagoulis's own confession Theophyloyannakos seemed reticent and confused. He clearly seemed not to have found out the truth, which perhaps only Panagoulis knew. Panagoulis himself both openly at the trial and in the letter smuggled out in 1970 (see p. 92) accused Theophyloyannakos of having inserted in the prosecution's brief a false document said to be his confession, and which actually did not bear his signature.

From the different communiqués, we knew in advance more or less what Theophyloyannakos was going to say about the fifteen accused. But his report created an enormous stir. It named Polykarpos Georkatzis, Cypriot Minister of the Interior and of Defence,* as one more instigator of the attempt, crediting him with being the 'military advisor'. Georkatzis was alleged to have given a false passport to Alexandros Panagoulis while he was in Cyprus, to have helped him return to Greece, and to have sent him explosives through the Cypriot Embassy.

The fact that the name of Georkatzis was brought into this affair in the way it was puzzled me considerably at the time. My information was that he was a friend of Papadopoulos, and that our 'prime minister' was to be the best man at his wedding. People had seen Georkatzis twice in Papadopoulos's office having very private and apparently friendly talks. Even when I heard that Panagoulis had defended Georkatzis with vehemence during his trial, and that he denied that Georkatzis had helped him, I kept wondering whether Georkatzis had not been

* He was forced to resign after pressure from Archbishop Makarios.

playing a double game, whether he had not both assisted Panagoulis and betrayed him. The attempt, later, on Makarios's life, in which he was said to have been involved in collusion with certain Greek officers, naturally did not disperse my doubts. But I do not know anything about this personally, and Georkatzis is now dead, murdered. He can no longer speak, or defend himself, or tell the truth; some people saw to it that he should never do so.

The inconsistent communiqués, as well as the unfounded accusations in the interrogator's full report, confirmed our conviction that Panagoulis was the only one to know the truth, and Panagoulis had not spoken.

The soldiers, the officers, and the policemen who told us about Panagoulis's prolonged martyrdom spoke of his courage, his spirit, his dignity. The lawyers present at the trial were to tell us the same things, and to add one more element, that of his great intelligence.

The trial of the fifteen was fixed for November 4th, 1968. As the day approached, the defendants, or at least those who had not yet been allowed to do so, must have been looking forward to seeing their parents and relatives, if only from a distance, in the military court-room—all of them, that is, except for Alexandros Panagoulis.

Alexandros's elder brother was never heard of again after his disappearance from the *Anna Maria*. He must be dead. His younger brother, Stathis, had got safely abroad. His father and mother were, it was said, ill in a military hospital, but no information was available on the nature or cause of their condition. On the first day of the coup an old man I knew was beaten to tell the hiding place of his son-in-law, which of course he did not even know. He remained bedridden for some months before he died. Alexandros's father never recovered to tell what had happened to him when he was arrested and taken to the police station of Petroupolis, where he suffered a brain haemorrhage. Maybe it was because of anguish for his son, maybe for other reasons. He was never, till his death in 1970, in a condition to tell.

6. George Papandreou

While we were waiting for Panagoulis's trial, there was a tragedy in Greece which was also a resurrection. George Papandreou died. George Papandreou, the legal prime minister who was ousted on July 15th, 1965, had been arrested in the early hours of the first day of the Colonels' coup. Although he was seventy-nine years old and running a high temperature, he was made to leave his bed and follow his captors. His only reaction when he saw them was to ask, 'Are you the Junta?'

He was taken first to a military centre in Goudi,* as all other politicians were, including his son Andreas. The following night they were all transferred to an hotel at Pikermi.† Soon afterwards George Papandreou was transferred to a hospital, and after a couple of months back to his home. From the first day of his arrest to October 7th, 1967, he was kept in isolation. He could see only his maid, his devoted bodyguard, and sometimes his doctor. Guards were posted by the Junta in a wide circle around the house, and they kept it well isolated from any possible access. It was a great relief to all of us who knew and loved the Old Man to learn on October 7th that the house arrest was lifted. We knew what a hardship and misery it must have been for a man like him, who delighted in intellectual discussion, to have any such possibility cut off. However, he never submitted, never complained, and never stopped his open criticisms to the Junta officers. As soon as I heard that he was allowed to communicate with people, I rushed to Kastri, his house. It was noon; he had already spoken with many people and both the emotion and the fact that he had got out of the habit of speaking had tired him enormously. Also he was still in his dressing-gown, and out of *coquetterie* he did not want me to see him. He asked whether I could call to see him the day after, which of course I did. This time he was smartly dressed and sparkling; we spoke about many things, and about his son Andreas, who since May 10th had been in

---

* A suburb of Athens where there are some military camps.
† Pikermi is about halfway from Athens to Sounion on the inland road.

isolation in Averof Prison.* Referring to the differences he had had
with Andreas, who was against the compromises the Old Man had
accepted in a conciliatory effort to prevent illegal developments like
the dictatorship, which however he was unable to prevent, George
Papandreou told me, 'Andreas was right.' When I asked him why he
had let the right-wing people keep almost all the key posts they had
secured for themselves over the years of their own government, he
answered, 'Because I have not the makings of a dictator.'

The Junta did more than stop the house arrest: they said they would
allow him, if he so wished, to leave the country and go abroad to look
after his badly shaken health. George Papandreou refused. When, on
December 13th, 1967, the King made his abortive counter-coup,
Papandreou was arrested again, and freed again a few months later;
but not for long. On April 21st, 1968, the first anniversary of the coup,
which that year coincided with Greek Easter, George Papandreou
smuggled out of the country a recorded address which was read by the
announcers of all foreign broadcasts to the Greeks and was heard by the
whole country. As a reprisal, the Junta inflicted house arrest once again
on their indomitable old opponent. This time the conditions were
harder. His bodyguard was taken away, George Papandreou could now
see only his maid, and, when there was need, his doctors, but both only
in the presence of the Junta guards, even when his doctors were examin-
ing him. No humiliation was spared. This time the Junta had sentenced
George Papandreou to death, by natural causes.

At 2.30 a.m. on October 25th, 1968, George Papandreou, who for
some time had suffered from a gastric ulcer, was urgently transferred
to the Evangelismos Hospital with a haemorrhage. As soon as I heard
of this, I got into a taxi to go to the hospital to find out about his
condition. My sorrow and my anger at people who could behave so
heartlessly to a man of his distinction and age were such that I forgot
all restraint, and kept telling the driver, 'They are killing him, they are
murdering Papandreou. How could he stand such isolation?' To my
amazement I discovered that the driver had no idea that the legal prime
minister of the country had been kept for so long under house arrest.
The censorship had indeed been successful. 'How do you know all
that?' he asked. 'Are you a relative?' And, like a coward, I said, 'Yes.'

* American economists, all of whom knew Andreas from his studies in America, united
to put such pressure on President Johnson that he asked and secured the liberation of
Andreas on December 24th, 1967, and his departure from Greece on January 16th, 1968.

On November 1st, 1968, Papandreou died, and was first laid in the little church of the hospital while the Junta was offering his family a state funeral. But his sons, George, whom he adored, and Andreas, of whom he was very proud, and the rest of the family remembered that he had said, 'Do not let them even touch me,' and they refused. Again I got into a taxi to go to the church. Again I spilled out all my indignation: 'They managed to murder him.'

'Is he in the little church?' asked the driver. 'Do you think that I might dare go in the church?'

I said, 'It is up to you.'

'I would so much like to go, but it may be dangerous. What do you think?'

I was disgusted. Oh Lord, why are people so frightened. I repeated, 'It is up to you.'

He said, '*They* may take my permit of work, I have a family to feed, but I would so much like to go in.' His voice sounded as if he was crying.

I softened, I understood. 'Don't go,' I said. 'I shall go twice, one time will be for you.'

There were only a few friends. Few people had learned that the Old Man had died, fewer where he was. With sorrow I thought that there would be only very few people at his funeral; many people would not know where to go, most would not dare.

The Junta, not imagining what was to happen—who ever did!—had allowed the funeral service to take place in the cathedral; probably they had imagined that the few people who would dare attend would look even fewer in the large cathedral. It was Friday; they allowed the funeral to be on the following Sunday.

Towards the evening, I went again to the church of the hospital. I was told that he was to be moved to Haghios Lefteris, the little old church next to the cathedral, and I decided to wait to see him taken away. There were some people in the church and at the church door, and only three or four passers-by in the street. The houses all round were unlighted; their inhabitants must be out?

The coffin was brought out in absolute silence, and suddenly terrific applause broke out. We looked at each other for a moment, and shuddered, because not one of the followers was applauding; it seemed as if we were in a world of invisible ghosts. The thundering applause was coming from the lightless houses.

The day after, in the morning, I went to Haghios Lefteris. I thought that again there were to be a few people, but there was a long queue. I went four times during the day trying to get into the church, but the queue was only getting longer and longer in spite of the hostile presence of a large number of police. By the end of the day I knew that the feelings of the people were this time stronger than their fear. I had sent a wreath for the funeral; I asked that on the ribbon be written in big letters, 'With admiration and love', with my full name underneath. It was Sunday, November 3rd. Five years before, on November 3rd, 1963, George Papandreou had won the election.

The funeral was to start at 11.30 a.m. I left home at 10 a.m., but when I reached Constitution Square, a cordon of police let no one through. Already, though, a very large number of people were crowding the cordoned area; they had started much earlier than I had done. I had to go round and round to reach the vicinity of the Cathedral Square. It was almost empty, kept empty by the police, who did not allow anyone to approach the church. Why did they do that? Did they hope that by keeping the Cathedral Square empty and by obliging people to scatter round, they could make the press photographers show a poor crowd? No one, neither the police nor we, the people, dreamed what a farewell was to be given to the Old Man.

By 11 a.m. the number of people was estimated by some reporters to be over 300,000 and by others to be 500,000. The police, it seemed like the whole police force, were everywhere. I went to an officer, who seemed to be the chief of the police, who was refusing access to the square and the cathedral. I said I was a personal friend, would he allow me to go to the church? He said no. I asked why they were keeping the square empty, and he did not answer. So I went to a little side street where masses of people were already waiting. We could see the entrance of the cathedral and the whole square. We could see the wreaths being brought by the dozen and left to lean on the walls of the cathedral. I cannot remember how many there were, but they covered the enormous circuit of the walls. We were made by the police to stand on the pavements; the street was for them, and they were going up and down our little street watching the people press one on another in a compact mass. Across the square as far as we could see, behind us, everywhere, there was a compact mass of people.

The coffin was taken from Haghios Lefteris to the cathedral. Two George Papandreous were carrying the coffin, the son and the grandson of the Old Man. Thunderous applause, and a huge cry of 'Pa-pan-dre-ou', marking every syllable, burst out. It was the first time since the coup that anyone had dared to shout his name. For a moment we were startled, then the applause and the cry 'Pa-pan-dre-ou' started again, and then other forbidden words: 'Democracy', 'Liberty'. The crowds started singing part of one verse from our national anthem: 'All was silent because threats filled us with fear, and slavery was crushing us,' and the last words, 'slavery was crushing us', were repeated again and again. Our little street was full of people whose eyes shone with tears of happiness and pride. But no one in our street as yet dared to speak. There were too many police round us. At one point, in answer to the shouts of 'Democracy', 'Freedom' from across the square, one young man in our street shouted, 'Democracy', and some more people repeated the cry. Police officers got hold of them immediately, took a couple of people away and the identity cards of others. There was absolute silence again in our frightened street, but from the other streets the shouts, 'Democracy', 'Freedom', 'Today we bury the Junta!' In a frenzy, I started applauding. People looked at me, smiled, and the fear was broken and our whole street started again applauding and shouting, 'Democracy', 'Freedom'. The police did not dare to stop us this time. A high-ranking officer spoke to the eager policemen. I think that he gave orders to let us shout, at least for a moment. The officer who took the identity card of the young man behind me came and stood beside me, looking at me threateningly, but he could not approach too close because I applauded with outstretched arms.

While we went on applauding, and the people looked round and drew strength from one another, seeing how many, how strong we were, there were shouts, 'We are the 7·4 per cent' (referring to the referendum which brought in 92·6 per cent for the Junta's constitution). 'Papandreou, you are our prime minister!' 'Papandreou, you are not dead!' 'Papandreou, you are immortal!' And then one man shouted the most moving cry, 'Old Man, rise up to see us!'

A father has on his shoulders his little son, about five years old, and he tells him, 'Look, listen, my boy, so that you will always remember.'

The coffin comes out, and young men rush to the wreaths and each one gets hold of one and starts on foot towards the cemetery while the coffin follows. All the roads are black with people, the police make way for the coffin. All the balconies and all the buildings are full. Now, from time to time, the police make raids, start hitting people with clubs, arresting some of them. A large crowd has gone early in the morning straight to the cemetery. Police again club the kneeling people, and make more arrests. The coffin is taken in. But the police stop us at the gate; we are not to enter. Some police officers clearly show their own emotion; one politely, in an apologetic way, tells me, 'Please, now go away, we cannot let you in.' I go further and find a little gate which is open. I enter. But when I try to approach the grave I am stopped again by a large number of police who cordon a large area around it. I am told roughly to go away. I tell the commanding officer of the group which stops me, 'I want to see the wreath I have sent. I want to see if it was made as I ordered it.'

The policemen look at me aghast. 'You have sent a wreath?' they ask. But I have no time to answer. A woman whom I don't think I have ever seen before says, 'There it is,' and yes, there in front of me, among the many hundreds of wreaths, is my wreath with my name. I stand and look, and I am as amazed as the policemen who stand startled around me. Then the officer recovers. 'Well, you saw it,' he says. 'Now, please go.' I go.

At about five in the afternoon we go again with a small group of friends, five or six of us. We carry flowers. The gates are guarded; we cannot enter, says the officer. But one friend says that she wants to go to her husband's grave; she shows him where the grave is, gives her name, and we get in. We go to that grave and lay down the flowers. Police are lurking behind each grave but we manage to get out passing in front of George Papandreou's grave which is nearby. It is guarded by some fifteen policemen. We stop. 'Is this Papandreou's grave?' I ask a young policeman. He says yes. I say, 'Why do you guard him? Are you afraid he may rise up?'

'Anything is possible,' answers the young policeman.

Why did we not know our strength? Why were we not organized? That day we could have taken Athens. That day we could have thrown the dictatorship we hated out of power. Why don't we know that we can still do it? Do we need the Old Man to rise and lead us?

7. Panagoulis's Trial

On November 4th, the day after the funeral of George Papandreou, the trial of Panagoulis and of fourteen other young men who were accused with him started at the special military court.

At that time the military court was just down my street, a hundred yards from my house. Jeeps and police were all around. The police had hardly recovered from the shock of the day before, when, incredibly, the people had in a moment of great emotion broken their chains and the plaster which had paralysed their movements. They had taken out the gag which had silenced their voice since April 21st, 1967. 'We are voting today,' they had been screaming. They had proclaimed their opposition to the Junta, and their longing for freedom, democracy and elections. If anyone needed the slightest proof that the referendum was the result of coercion and falsification, the reaction of these 500,000 people had given the answer. I do not believe the number in the streets was any less.

The Colonels, who imagined that only some hundreds of people might dare to demonstrate, had given orders to the police to let them be. In this way they would have a chance to let off steam and the regime would show its tolerance. But when things took the turn they did, and the funeral, even though it was performed with emotion and respect, became a universal condemnation of the Junta and a cry for freedom, when the American Ambassador was openly and loudly booed, the police took the initiative. Had people got over the intimidation, the terror? It had to be brought down on them. They had to be encased again in fresher and stronger medical plaster. Clubs came savagely down on the demonstrators in many parts of the massive crowd, and over two hundred people were arrested. Of these, forty-one were given sentences of between eighteen months and four and a half years on the following evening.

The censored papers on the next morning spoke ridiculously of some hundreds of hot-heads who had desecrated the funeral, but the press all over the world reported the insurrection of a whole population against their brutal masters. Only the relatives of the prisoners were distressed. The rest of us were still living the unbelievable thing we had witnessed, and with gratitude and emotion thought that the Old Man, dead, had inflicted upon his torturers and his murderers their greatest defeat.

One other thing was in our minds: Alexandros Panagoulis had suffered the most inhuman tortures with extraordinary heroism. He had not spoken, except to say the absolutely obvious things. When arrested for his attempt against the life of Papadopoulos he had said, 'I did it, and I did it alone. There is no one else.' He kept to this even after he knew without doubt that Yannis Klonizakis and Nikolaos Lekanides, two of the young men accused with him, had admitted having known of the plot, having helped Panagoulis, and many other things such as the involvement of Georkatzis and the Cypriot Embassy in Athens which were probably not true. As to how voluntarily they had done so, Klonizakis's handwritten and signed statement* gives us some idea.

We had no hope for Panagoulis. We knew he would be sentenced to death. We had only great admiration for his courage and deep concern for what he had suffered. 'I did not want to kill, I did not care about the success of my action,' he had said. 'It was a warning.' And we believed him. Anyway, we could not easily forget what we learned at school with some pride of ancestry about the laws of ancient Athenian democracy: 'It is enacted by the Lawgivers', says a marble tablet found in the Agora of Athens and dated 337–336 B.C., 'that if any person shall make an insurrection against the people, or shall contribute to establish tyranny, or shall put down the people of Athens or the democracy of Athens, let whoever shall kill anyone that has done this be considered innocent and holy.' Measured against this ancient law, Papadopoulos, who abolished democracy and enslaved Athens, deserves condemnation, and Panagoulis, who disinterestedly and for the freedom of his country knowingly risked execution and, what is worse, torture, deserves praise. Statues were erected to Harmodios and Aristogeiton, the two youths who killed the dictator Hipparchos to make Athens free and because he had abolished democracy; and a song was sung at dinner parties and taught to children to remind Athenians for ever of the fate of those who interfere with freedom, of the duty to kill them and of the glory which should come to those who do so.

As for those who collaborate with the dictators, and who enact or

* See p. 238.

even debate laws without the approval of the people, the same law preserved in the same inscription says:

> It shall not be permitted to the Councillors of the Council of the Areopagos while the people and parliament of Athens are put down to assemble in their assembly or to consult about any matter whatsoever. But if while the people and parliament of Athens are put down any councillor of the Areopagos shall go to the Areopagos or assemble in the assembly or consult about any matter, let him be dishonoured and deprived of all his civil rights, he and his seed after him, and let his property be public property and let one tenth belong to the goddess.

Those were the laws of ancient Athens.

The newspapers published whatever was given to them, under the censorship law, and so we read what we were meant to read – the confessions and repentance of the fourteen men accused with Panagoulis, which were of course extracted through torture. Actually thirteen declared their repentance; one refused to do so, and only narrowly escaped the death sentence.

The accused men were: Eleftherios Beryvakis, 33, a lawyer; Yannis Klonizakis, 30, a civil engineer; his brother, Artemios Klonizakis, a physician; Nikolaos Lekanides, 29, private employee (driver of the alleged getaway car); Nikolaos Zambelis, 22, a taxi driver and first cousin of Panagoulis (he escaped from Aegina Prison in June 1971); George Eleftheriades, 39, a taxi driver; George Abramis, 30, private employee; Efstathios Yotas, 28, a lawyer; John Valasselis, 32, an airline employee who had been active in his trade union before unions were banned after the coup; Anthony Printezis, 29, private employee; Michael Papoulas, 36, motor engineer; Alexander Sigalas, 37, a taxi driver; Demetrios Timoyannakis, 61, private employee; Basil Anastasopoulos, 27, private employee.

We read their confessions and declarations, filtered through the censorship.

What I write here is taken from what I can remember the lawyers at the trial told me, from what I could get out of the Greek and foreign papers of the time, connecting the news in the papers with what I already knew, and from the detailed account the French lawyer Denis Langlois, who followed the whole trial, gives us in his book.*

* Denis Langlois, *Panagoulis le Sang de la Grèce*, Cahiers Libres 161 (Paris, 1969).

From the beginning of the trial, when he was asked to give his name, Panagoulis accused the people who had held him at their mercy for eighty-two days of having used medieval methods of torture against him. He told the court that they represented his torturers and had no right to judge him. A sentence of two years was immediately passed on him for contempt of court.

Panagoulis's defence counsel said that he had not yet been given an opportunity to speak with his client, and that neither he nor Panagoulis had had a chance to read the indictment which had just been handed to them; for the eighty-two days since his arrest Panagoulis had been kept handcuffed with his hands behind his back; long periods of hunger strikes had weakened him to such an extent that he would be unable to follow the proceedings, and he asked for a postponement of the trial. Panagoulis was examined by a doctor who found the tortured and emaciated young man absolutely fit. But Panagoulis got something out of this. The handcuffs were removed for the first time, and he could rub his wounded wrists. He would be allowed, as long as the trial lasted, to be without handcuffs for a few hours each day.

The witnesses for the prosecution were all police, who as usual had no need to justify their accusations, or give their sources of information. One miracle phrase was enough: 'National Security Secret.'

When Police Lieutenant Evangelos Mallios, the most horrible of all the torturers of the Security Police Headquarters, came to testify, Panagoulis could not restrain himself. 'You are the specialist in sexual tortures,'* he shouted. 'You cannot testify. You crushed my hand and cut a tendon by treading on it.' Mallios, of course, denied everything. Then it was the turn of Petros Babalis, of the same security police. Panagoulis accused him of being the expert on falanga, and of using it on him for hours and days on end, breaking his heel. Among the many who tortured him, Panagoulis named three as the main and worst torturers: Theophyloyannakos of the military police, Mallios and Babalis. It was in their hands that I was to find myself three years later.

Most accused took advice from their defence counsels, who saw no other way to save them from the danger of the death penalty than to say that they repented or else that they denied any connection with Panagoulis. Panagoulis himself said that he did not know most of them. Panagoulis denied that he had been helped by Andreas Papandreou or

---

* See Panagoulis's letter, p. 92. ' ... burning of my genitals with cigarettes, insertion in my urethra of a long metal wire whose extended part was heated.'

Polykarpos Georkatzis the Cypriot Minister. Nikolaos Lekanides and Yannis Klonizakos said he was. They claimed to have gone to the Cypriot Embassy to get explosives sent in the diplomatic bag. Panagoulis said these confessions had been made under orders by the torturers and obtained by torture. He denied any connection with that embassy. He placed all moral responsibility on the coup which abolished our freedom, and stated that he on his own had taken all the measures necessary for his attempt. He said he did it by himself, on his own initiative, with no one else's help or knowledge, and that he knew he would be executed. He finished his short and proud speech with the words: 'There is no better swan-song for a patriot and a lover of freedom than the death rattle in front of the firing squad of a tyranny. Violence begets violence. After me, others will come who will succeed where I have failed.'

One other man refused to say that he repented what he had done. He was the lawyer Eleftherios Beryvakis. There was no evidence against him other than that he gave seven thousand drachmas (less than a hundred pounds) to Panagoulis which he had received from another defendant, John Valasselis, as coming from Andreas Papandreou. But both he and Valasselis stressed that the money had nothing to do with the attempt. Beryvakis refuted every accusation. But he had two things against him: firstly, that he had been sentenced at the very beginning of the coup for subversive actions against the Junta, when he was tortured, imprisoned, and then amnestied; and secondly, that he was intelligent. The public prosecutor, Liapis, took the line that Beryvakis was dangerous: there was no evidence against him because he was intelligent and destroyed such evidence, and took precautions by not seeing anyone but his friend Panagoulis. 'Men like him must not survive.' He demanded the death sentence for Beryvakis!

But before the sentences were given, the indomitable Panagoulis accused Major Theophyloyannakos, one of his main torturers, of having threatened him the night before with much worse tortures after the sentence if he went on giving details of his tortures.* The President answered that as this had taken place outside the tribunal it did not concern the court!

On November 19th, 1968, the verdict was published. Panagoulis was sentenced to death twice: once for being a deserter, and once for

---

* The day before my trial Theophyloyannakos threatened me that if I spoke against them I should pay dearly for it (see p. 183).

attempting to overthrow the 'established regime'. He also got 15 years in prison for the attempt, and another 3 years for using explosives and for contempt of court. He heard his sentence with indifference. Beryvakis got a life sentence. Yannis Klonizakis 24 years, Lekanides 23 years, Zambelis 18 years, Abramis 16 years, Eleftheriades 18 years, Yotas 10 years and Valasselis 2½ years. There were some more sentences and some acquittals.

8. *Panagoulis's Escape and Recapture*

I must win
Since I cannot be defeated
from 'I Want', by Alexandros Panagoulis

The intervention of the world, including the Pope, saved Panagoulis's life. We were for him, not because of the laws of ancient Athens but because we did not consider him a 'deserter in wartime'; he had simply left one group of the army which had taken both the army and the country over; that much for the one death sentence. As for the second, for the intent to overthrow the 'established social regime' which, after all, we did not consider perfect or holy, he did not intend to overthrow it, only the dictatorship of the Colonels. Personally I am against any violence, because I believe that violence only breeds violence and brings no good whatsoever. I am against any war, I am against the death penalty. However, if violence or wars come, I try to judge who started them and put the blame on them. Most people were delighted that Panagoulis's life was being spared — for the moment, at least; the death sentence had not been commuted and they could execute him at any moment. I was not sure I was happy. I kept learning about his still being tortured, kept handcuffed, suffering mock executions, suffering hell. For myself I would rather have the short anguish of a quick execution, but of course this does not apply to a man of Panagoulis's age and spirit. Many people were sorry that he did not succeed in killing the dictator, but I was not among them. I consider Papadopoulos and all these people the victims of what they defend with such apparent fury: the established order of things, which brought it about that from the age of fifteen these people went through a proper brainwashing themselves. Unlike many others, I don't believe that I should enjoy seeing them hang, so much so that my friends tell me to be careful because they will know where to search for them when the time comes!

I must say here, however, that I am afraid that people who see me as a sort of forgiving angel are greatly misled. The proof? Last year I saw a play in Paris where all that is to me bad and contemptible was represented: exploiters of the poor, society ladies with their lovers, drunkards who kill in a frenzy, and an old decrepit lady who one thought would turn to dust at the slightest touch and who was called '*democratie totale, totale*', something, I suppose, like the totalitarian regime that the Colonels call democracy. When the curtain rose on the last scene, we saw all these people hanging by a cord around their necks, and my heart filled with such relief and joy that since then I am not so sure that I should not after all enjoy seeing certain people hang!

Independently of all that, I consider that Panagoulis is the greatest hero this unfortunate period of our life has produced, and also the greatest victim. Other, many other people have been tortured, but for all of them sooner or later, after a few weeks, or at the most in some cases a few months, the end of the torturing period came. Not so for Panagoulis. His fate, details of which I kept learning, obsessed me,★ so it was with immense relief that we heard that on the night of June 5th to 6th, 1969, Panagoulis had escaped from his military prison with the help of a guard called Corporal George Morakis.

Four days had gone, and by now we were sure that Panagoulis and his guard were safely out of the country. We supposed he could not have arranged his escape all by himself, but that some group had organized everything, with boats, yachts, etc. Just when we were allowing ourselves to forget our anguish about his possible re-arrest, and to celebrate his freedom and the end of his miseries, we heard the terrible news: Panagoulis had been re-arrested on June 9th at 2.40 p.m.; we heard about it that evening (it was the evening I described on page 46 when I felt that I was suffocating in the house and had to go out). The same night Corporal Morakis, the guard who had helped him, was also arrested. In the letter Panagoulis smuggled out in November 1970 (see p. 94), he gives the names of the people who he says had betrayed him. According to what I learned, the cousin with whom he was staying in hiding, until help came from outside Greece to take him away, gave the police the address and the keys of the flat, just for the sake of the money that had been promised to whoever gave Alexandros away. When the key turned in the lock, Panagoulis did not worry; only his cousin had the key. I can imagine how he felt when a number of policemen fell upon him.

He had been arrested by the rural police, which had control of the

★ Because of this, I hope I shall be forgiven for sometimes repeating some of the horrible tortures this man went through.

area where the house he was hiding in was. He was taken to Nea Ionia police station, and I know what his life was for the first five days. He was on the cement floor, hands and feet tied, and five men were round him, bending over him. The eyewitness who told me was not able to see what these five policemen were doing to him. It is probable that they were not caressing him.

Apparently no one else was involved in the escape. Alexandros Panagoulis persuaded his guard Morakis, who must have been appalled to witness the suffering of the young man, to help him. They had between them just the money to take a bus to Athens, which they did. Panagoulis went first to an aunt of his who lived with her daughter, but it was decided that he and the guard would be safer in a flat belonging to a male cousin of Panagoulis's mother. This was apparently the person who for 500,000 drachmas (about £6,000) gave him away.

How much more and for how much longer Panagoulis was ill treated, I don't know. Corporal Morakis got a sixteen-year prison sentence. The aunt and the cousin of Panagoulis who had helped him the first day by giving him a little money were also arrested. I believe that the aunt was freed after a while, but the cousin was ill treated and sentenced to some years of prison, and if my memory is right she suffered a breakdown from the beating and was in an asylum for a while.

On October 18th, 1969, Panagoulis tried to escape again, but was arrested before succeeding in doing so. He was again chained, beaten, deprived of food, left chained on the bare cement floor.

9. Resistance: Karageorgas, Georgakis and all the Others

Meanwhile, resistance was going on in more ways than one.

On July 14th, 1969, Dionysios Karageorgas, a brilliant young professor of economics who had studied at the London School of Economics, was arrested in the hospital where he had been hurriedly transferred with wounds suffered while he was handling explosives. He and a number of lawyers, chemists, economists, students and other professors,* General George Ioannides, and four young women were arrested within a few days of each other for being involved in subversive actions and, more especially, in explosions.

Dionysios Karageorgas had made his basement office into a small laboratory, and there, with poor means and great courage and determination, he had been making up little bombs, and with the help of his friends had planted them at hours and in places which would assure that there would be no victims. He was holding one of these bombs in his right hand when it went off, severing three fingers and part of the palm. His right eardrum was damaged by the explosion and his right eye wounded. Unfortunately, a police car patrolling nearby heard the explosion and arrived immediately; they soon found another thirteen bombs in the basement workshop. They rushed to the hospital as Karageorgas was coming out of the operating theatre. He had not recovered from the anaesthetic when they started torturing him, pulling out his hair and twisting the flesh of his chest until he relapsed into unconsciousness.† The police were abusing him because he, a professor of economics, was using explosives. Still semi-conscious and under torture, he answered that it was more appropriate that *he* should take this risk to protest in this resounding way against what he believed to be the catastrophe of the nation than that illiterate peasants or working people should get into danger by doing it.

* Among them George Mangakis, lately famous for his departure from Greece in a German military plane which took off from the American airbase in Athens.
† See page 240 for Karageorgas's statement.

All those arrested were tortured by different torturers and in different ways. Hallucinogenic drugs were also used; it was the first time that I had heard of their use in interrogation. Some of the torturers were rural police officers, for instance Moroyannis and Favatas; others belonged to the central interrogation centre of the military police, like Major Theodoros Theophyloyannakos, who with his own hands beat a young chemist called Spyros Loukas till he was a mass of blood, and unconscious. He remarked afterwards that the process gave him great pleasure.

What was important in this case were the names and characters of the accused. They were mostly intellectuals, scientists with brilliant careers. It is important and significant that people like them chose to use explosives to attract the attention of the world to what was happening to our small country. Under normal conditions it would be absolutely impossible to imagine that people of such character would be ever involved in, associated with, or accused of such things.

Conscious of the possible repercussions of the step I was taking, but weighing the pros and cons, I decided to appear as a character witness for the defence of Karageorgas and Christos Rokophyllos at their trial in April 1970. For about an hour, Liapis, who was the public prosecutor of Panagoulis's trial, the president of the court, and the four military judges tried to make me condemn violence and explosives. I did not. I will say what I condemn when I can speak freely of all the things I do condemn. It is from that day that Theophyloyannakos's hatred for me started. He seems to have sworn that he would corner me and arrest me.

The trial of the thirty-four intellectuals, as it came to be known, was important to the Junta because of the status of the people who had done or tried to do these actions. Small explosives, always positioned with extreme care so that no one would be hurt, had been exploding since the beginning of the coup. Usually, rightly or wrongly, they were attributed to young students.* This time mature men of brilliant intellect, career and character were the accused. It made a great stir in the world, and the greater the stir the greater was the fury of the Junta and their torturers. The names of the witnesses for the defence were also impressive. Among them was the former prime minister,

---

* A large number of brave youngsters, mostly for belonging to the Left students' resistance organization Rigas Feraios, had been arrested, terribly tortured and given savage sentences: eighteen, twenty years' prison.

Panayiotis Kanellopoulos. In the American Congressional Record, where the names of the witnesses were given, it was added that they all seemed to come out of the *Who's Who* of Athens.

Heavy sentences were given again. A student against whom there was no evidence whatsoever got five years because he refused to condemn the actions of Karageorgas, who was his professor, saying that he had been taught to respect his professors and not to judge them. A young man called Konstantopoulos* got eight years because he was supposed to have attended two discussions on what could be done so that Greece might be free again. When after the trial a lawyer asked the military judge, 'Why eight years for Konstantopoulos?', the answer was, 'Because he is a potential leader.'

Still, we were happy. We had been afraid that the Junta would sentence Karageorgas to death as an example. Yet again it was pressure from foreign countries that saved his life. The Junta struck immediately at the witnesses for the defence. Professor Emmanuel Papathomopoulos, a historian at Ioanina University, was suspended for six months, and the suspension was renewed for another six months. Those witnesses who had not already been refused the right to travel outside the country had their passports withdrawn. I was one of them. But soon afterwards a letter in *The Times*,† followed by a public outcry about the loss of this simple human right, made them lift the ban on my travelling and I did get out of Greece, with some apprehension, fortunately at the time unfounded, that I might not be allowed back. All seemed forgotten and forgiven as far as I was concerned. But Theophyloyannakos never forgets.

The struggle of the Greek people against the Junta has had not only its heroes but also its martyrs. Such a one was a Greek student, Kostas Georgakis, a young man of twenty-two, who on September 29th, 1970, burned himself to death in Genoa as a protest against the abolition of freedom in Greece.

On the evening of his self-sacrifice he took his fiancée to her home without telling her anything to make her guess that she was seeing him for the last time alive. Then he got back into his small car and drove to the Piazza Matteotti, whose name ought to remind us of one of the victims of Italian fascism. He arrived there about midnight, and when

* See p. 243 for Konstantopoulos's statement.
† May 1970.

he made sure that no one was there to see him, he poured petrol over his clothes and set himself alight. From far away some dustmen saw him and ran to his aid, but Kostas started running like mad round his car trying to avoid them, screaming in Italian, 'I did it for Greece, I did it for Greece!' At last he fell down in flames, and when the dustmen managed to put out the fire with their coats, Kostas was dying.

His decision to kill himself in this dreadful way was not an act done in a moment when the balance of his mind was disturbed, but something well and long thought through. This is proved by the letter he sent to his father and family in their island of Corfu.

My dear father,
Forgive me for what I am going to do, and do not cry. Your son is not a hero, he is a man like any other man, perhaps with more fear than others. Kiss for me the soil of our country. After three years of violence I cannot stand it any longer. I do not wish that this action of mine put you in any trouble. But I cannot live and think in any other way than that of a free human being. I am writing in Italian so that people may straight away get interested in Greece's problem.
Long Live Democracy.
Down with Tyranny.
Our land where Liberty was born will annihilate the tyrants.
If you can, do forgive me.
YOUR KOSTAS

In another letter left for a friend, he wrote:

My dear friend Michali,
Today I am in a position to give the great acceptance or the great refusal that Kavafis writes about. I do not want this action of mine to be considered heroic. I know that it will be considered by some people in Greece the act of an anti-Hellene. On the other hand, it may wake up others and make them realize how we live. Under whom we live ... I am sure that sooner or later the European people will understand that a fascist regime, like the one we have in Greece, which relies on tanks, is not only a shame to their own dignity but also a continual threat for Europe itself ...

The tragic suicide of Georgakis influenced those people in Greece whom he most cared about, those who suffered for the same ideals for which he had given his life: on the first anniversary of his death, the political prisoners of Korydallos Prison went on a hunger strike and smuggled out of prison a message in which among other things they wrote:

> The student Kostas Georgakis protested in the most tragic way for a European, by burning himself to death, against the existence in Greece of an unacceptable dictatorship. He is not our only dead. In our minds are the names of the victims of the dictatorship, the names of Tsarouchas, Tsikouris, Angeloni, Chalkidi, Fragopoulou, Zarkada, Parianou, Mavrogeni, Sotiropoulou, the victims of April 21st and of December 13th, and all the others whose names we shall know one day. Some of them died trying to help the overthrow of this accursed dictatorship, others were murdered by the dictator's agents, others perished because of the conditions they were made to live in.

10. *Resistance: Koronaios and all the Others*

On December 3rd, 1970, I left for London again, and I returned to Athens in the early hours of the 24th to spend Christmas at home with my friends and my cats. Not with all my friends, since by then a number had been in prison for a long time, while others like the lawyer Takis Touloupas were in exile in remote villages, some thousand or so metres up in the mountains. Hair-raising reprisals had not stopped the resistance. Three months before that Christmas, a lawyer, Nikolas Koronaios, had been arrested and accused of placing a home-made bomb, which made more noise than it did harm, in the National Gardens, just outside the Parliament office where our self-elected prime minister, Mr Papadopoulos, sat talking with the American Secretary of Defence, Mr Melvin Laird. Many people were arrested later in connection with the placing of this and of other bombs. At that time, I knew two of them, Peloponniseus and Andreas Frangias,* the latter a civil engineer of high standing, and a hero of the resistance against the Germans in the Second World War. The others, like Koronaios, were lawyers.

Stories of the terrible tortures to which some men had been and were still being subjected had reached us. The sources were such that we had no doubt they were true in every detail, and, of course, by then we had become used to seeing people who had been tortured and also to hearing the Colonels deny any use of brutality.

Tortures and lies for nearly five years now. Hundreds of cases have been described to me, and during my recent experience I had to listen to the screams of a tortured man. And, like many of us, I have my collection of the regime's lies, every one of them guaranteed by 'our word of honour as officers'.

All the same, on that Christmas Eve of 1970, in spite of all that I knew about the sudden arrests, the oppression and the tortures, the

---

* I believe that some 200 people were arrested. Many were tortured, some absolutely inhumanly. After months and in some cases over a year of ill treatment and imprisonment, many were released. The Junta did not want the people to know how strong the pro–Andreas people were.

fear in my own heart was mixed with joy at being back in Athens. In spite of Them, in spite of the horrible shadow over our lives, Greece, our own Greece, was as beautiful as ever, and home was home.

It was four o'clock in the morning when I arrived, but friends had come to meet me at the airport to take me to my small apartment. Day came, and we sat talking well into the morning of Christmas Eve. I inspected the cats. They had been well looked after, and they crowded around me purring. The plants and flowers on the two terraces seemed less happy. No one but me would give them two hours of attention a day.

I asked about every friend and all kinds of home news. There had been some new arrests, but this in our Greece of today is an almost everyday event. Who were they? Lawyers, scientists, all from the Centre Union party, which means liberalism, the same ideology as mine. I knew a few of them. Most had been arrested by the military police; the few arrested by the security police were later handed over to the military police too. They were being held at EAT ESA. The initials stand for the Special Interrogation Centre of the Greek Military Police, and this is a place more dreaded than the Security Headquarters. I did not know then that I was to have personal experience of it not too long after. Ironically enough, it is situated behind the statue of Venizelos, the great liberal leader, next to the American Embassy. Returning to Athens now, one always asks which of one's friends have been in trouble or arrested. That day most of my friends were all right. One of them, Christos Sartzetakis, had left the day before for Salonika to spend Christmas, which is also his name day, with his family.

I was always worried whenever Christos went to Salonika. It was there that the left-wing Member of Parliament, Grigoris Lambrakis, was assassinated in 1963. Sartzetakis, as a young investigating judge aged thirty-three, had charged some generals with instigating the murder, among them General Mitsou. General Mitsou's son was now himself high up in the gendarmerie in Salonika. So, apart from being sad that I had missed Sartzetakis by only a few hours, I also felt uneasy for him. I had left for England without seeing him or other friends and without telling them. In the Greece of today, if you are known to be an opponent of the government, you try *not* to see your friends when you are leaving and for a time after your return, for fear of implicating them in having foreign contacts. The Colonels are anxious and insecure, and they are afraid of messages that may have been taken in or brought back by word of mouth.

As I mentioned before, I had met Sartzetakis in Paris in 1966. He was on educational leave. After April 1967, he was ordered back to Greece to Salonika. We met again in Athens in 1968 and resumed a friendship based on those surviving dreams and on mutual esteem, a friendship which became closer and closer every day. Greece was occupied again. To me, this time it seemed worse, because the occupying force, the people who had deprived us of our freedom and were throwing Greece back in obscurantism, the oppressors and the torturers, were Greek. I was distressed, and above all ashamed.

At about six o'clock in the evening of Christmas Eve 1970, Christos rang me from Salonika. How was I? How had I enjoyed London? What news? One does not say anything even slightly touching on politics on the telephone in Greece, still less on a long-distance call. So I went on and on about my health, the tests the doctors had made, and what they had suggested, etc. etc., until I got a bored sort of an 'All right' from Sartzetakis. When was he coming back? January 1st or 2nd. 'Well, Christos dear, happy Christmas to you, happy name day, happy New Year. I shall see you when you are back.'

Minutes later Sartzetakis was arrested. Of course, without a warrant, and after sunset, although both these things had by this time become illegal once again, even by the Junta's own laws, since Article 10 of their own constitution had come into force. It covered both circumstances: no arrests without warrant and not before dawn. Still, anyone who asked to see a warrant while being arrested was answered with ironical laughter.

For a whole week Christos's father, himself an ex-officer of the gendarmerie, his brother, a friend who was a lawyer, and all his other friends tried desperately to find out where he was being held. The Salonika gendarmerie had promised his father to let him know if Christos was to be moved. But in their usual way they were lying to him when they told him that Christos was still in Salonika. In fact he had been transferred to Athens in the night, within hours of arrest. The security forces were anxious to perform their functions with no possibility of public knowledge. Finally, on January 1st, 1971, we discovered, with a shiver of apprehension, that he was at the Special Interrogation Centre of the Greek military police, the EAT ESA of ill fame.

New Year's Day is a very special day in Greece. I rushed around with a basket of food plus the traditional New Year's cake. At the gates the military guards refused to admit that Sartzetakis was there. I assured them, and it was true, that the officer on duty that day had said he was, and had also said that food would be allowed. A soldier went in to ask, and came back and took in the basket. It was not given to him; at that very moment Sartzetakis was in the middle of six days and nights of torture.

News of more arrests continued to pour in. Also some of the exiles had been brought back to Athens and handed over to the military police; they too were at the EAT ESA, and among them was my friend, the lawyer Takis Touloupas. Like Frangias, he was also a hero of the resistance during the Second World War. He had been tortured during the occupation, and not only did he not speak, nor of course give anyone else away, but he did not even scream; not a sound came from him until he collapsed alone in his cell. Now, in this new occupation by the Colonels, this man was in exile in remote villages. He had been moved from one to another as soon as he thought he was settled in one place. Such was the 'method'. And all this time he was under strict gendarmerie supervision. What could he have done? What information could the Special Interrogation Centre possibly expect to extract from him?

Details of further torture reached me; among others, I learned that Sartzetakis, who refused to speak, to admit imaginary charges or give away friends, was made to walk all around his small cell for six days and nights without stopping. The cement floor was inundated with water, which made walking still harder. They had taken away his glasses and his coat, and as it was winter the cold was unbearable. He was allowed one glass of water a day, and sometimes a bite of some horrible food, but he was not allowed to stop walking even to drink the water or to eat. He was also forbidden to touch the wall. Soon, of course, he fell from exhaustion or fainted. Then the soldier who was in the cell to make sure that the torturing walk was strictly carried out, according to orders, would call the beating squad – five or six strong, bestial soldiers who by kicking him brutally, punching him, and even jumping on him, would force him to stand on his feet and start his walk again. In this way, his knee was badly injured, and this became a blessing because it brought the torture to an end, although not immediately. They went on beating and kicking him to make him stand.

As soon as the tortured people felt better, and could stand on their feet, the torture would start again till they either broke down in despair and spoke, or were injured again to such an extent that the doctors might say their life was in danger, and torture would stop—they apparently had strict orders not to kill.

The news that my friend Sartzetakis, the brave and impartial judge, was being tortured had, as usual, reached me from inside EAT ESA almost as soon as I had found out where he was. The soldier who told me had witnessed his martyrdom, had seen him carried by soldiers in a state of collapse. He had seen him for days afterwards being carried to the WC by three or four soldiers and had heard the abuse and humiliations he was subjected to. Since Sartzetakis was not freed until after my expulsion from Greece, I have had no opportunity to check this information with him, but I have never received news of that kind that was not true, whether or not it was admitted by the tortured man, and I checked with another officer. I was more than sure that Sartzetakis was not involved in any resistance organization at all and had nothing to admit; anyway, he didn't speak. Certainly and definitely he was against the dictatorship and the continual transgression of every rule of humanity and legality. But what honest man was not? There could be no evidence of any 'illegal' action by Sartzetakis. Was it to admit some nonexistent crime that he was being tortured? Or to pay for his insolence in daring to indict generals of the gendarmerie, and in refusing to cover up Lambrakis's murder? Or was it also *pour encourager les autres*, to serve as an example for all other investigating magistrates who might one day dream of searching for the truth instead of giving the judgments desired by the Colonels?

Tortures, tortures, horrible nightmarish tortures everywhere. One young man had been and was still being tortured more than anyone else, longer than anyone else, and his tortures seemed to have no end. Alexandros Panagoulis. The thought of his suffering did not let me sleep. How to stop this horror? What to do?

Since my teens I have believed, and I still believe, in something perhaps childish: that only a small minority is using the whole consciousness open to what we have in mind when we say 'human being', and that a true enlightenment, understanding, and tolerance, not just learning, or polite hypocrisy, or superficial goodness, could change this minority into a majority. Then would the lives and rights and happiness and dignity of the people be respected?

Is there any such hope? Or is it that in spite of my age I am really eighteen, as the sadistic commanding officer of the Special Interrogation Centre used to tell me with contempt in between his shouts and his threats? But then how, if he is able to torture people, and he undoubtedly is, and he undoubtedly did and does torture, how can a man who inflicts torture ever understand that I cannot sleep because of the mere thought of the suffering of a young man I have never met? Alexandros Panagoulis has been maltreated on and off for years now, after having been inhumanly tortured during interrogation, sentenced to death, subjected to three mock executions, and living with the death sentence still hanging over his head. There are no legal means to end his suffering as long as he remains in their hands. He is a slave with no rights, a human being treated as no wild beast should ever be treated. How could this commanding officer and the others like him understand that since it was impossible for me to bear the thought of so much suffering I would accept any risk to help him or others in his position?

11. *Panagoulis Plans a Third Escape*

In the beginning of 1971 I began to hear that some of the two hundred people arrested from November 1970 onwards had been 'persuaded' while prisoners at EAT ESA to admit resistance contacts with me. It seemed that Major Theophyloyannakos, who had been after me since I appeared as a witness for the defence for Professor Karageorgas and Christos Rokophyllos, was doing some very good work here. In the end he overdid it. He managed to make some of the poor wrecks attribute so much to me that they could hardly be brought to trial unless I were also arrested and judged with them as the main culprit. For some of these people this seemed a safeguard, since they hoped that the Junta would not like the publicity my name might give to a trial, and that there would therefore be no trial for them either.*

It may also be that they hoped that if they came to trial with me as a co-defendant, foreign legal observers and correspondents would be present. It would be reasonably expected that because of this the Junta, who are very sensitive to adverse publicity abroad, would not press the bench for terribly harsh sentences, those dozens of years of prison which are so generally demanded and imposed.

It must be remembered that at the military courts, four of the five judges are simple officers who have to obey the orders of their superiors. Only the president is a trained lawyer and a qualified judge. To the credit of the legal body, there have been numerous verdicts with four votes for and one against a massive sentence.

As mentioned already, among the arrested were my close friends Christos Sartzetakis and Takis Touloupas, the latter having been taken to EAT ESA from the village where he had been living in exile for

* When once the interrogation is over, and the arrested man has been transferred to a regular prison, life for someone awaiting trial is much better than that of a sentenced prisoner. The prison for those to be tried is Korydallos, near Athens, which is new and the only one where living conditions are human. The prisoner awaiting trial, if he is not incommunicado, can see close relatives three times a week. But the sentenced prisoner can be sent to any prison in the country, and most are terrible. According to his sentence, he may be permitted to see relatives anything between once a week and once a month. This explains why many of the prisoners preferred not to be tried by a military court which rarely acquits people.

almost two years. There were also a few others arrested whom I more or less knew.

A plea reached me from inside prison that I should please not go abroad as long as those people were held awaiting trial. This is why 1971 was the only year in which I did not leave Greece at all until the police forced me into a plane on November 14th.

This group of prisoners, who were former Members of Parliament, lawyers, scientists, and officers, were supposed to be supporters of Andreas Papandreou. The charge against them was that they belonged to PAK, the pro-Andreas resistance organization. I do not know what the individual political opinions of all these men are, but I suppose them to be liberals, and that most had voted for the Centre Union party of George Papandreou. Whether they would vote for Andreas if an election were held now, or whether any of them belonged to PAK, I really do not know. Even to be suspected of being pro-Andreas, even as a matter of private opinion, is a terrible crime. The Junta knows that Andreas is their most dangerous opponent, and that in free elections he would get the majority. That is why the Junta is trying to stifle not only the activity of PAK but also all mention of it. I was convinced that the government would not expose any of Andreas's supporters who had been arrested to the publicity of a trial as it had never done so before. The first trial in which PAK was implicated was in January 1972, of eight young men charged with having explosives.*

I am for Andreas. I believe that his social and economic programme would make Greece a progressive and developed country where liberty and human dignity and human rights would be respected. But I do not belong to PAK or to any other particular resistance organization because I am for all the resistance. I was certainly ready to help any victim of the Junta, and whatever I could do, I did.

In November 1970, Alexandros Panagoulis smuggled the following letter out of the prison cell especially built for him in Boyati military camp:†

I am writing with the hope that my letter will reach every human being who feels his duty to be indignant about crime and to fight

* *Bima*, January 1st, 1972.
† From the Congressional Record, Senate. February 17th, 1971.

for its abolition. With the hope that the support of world public opinion for the struggle for freedom, democracy and progress will become more substantial. I am writing with the confidence that the progressive powers of all the world will help the many prisoners of the junta and with their assistance prevent our physical destruction. I am writing lastly so that from the isolation of a prison of the junta the anathema of someone who suffers reaches all the world and hits all those who help the completion of the crime that is perpetrated against our people. At the same time I want our gratitude to reach all those who stand by us in this terrible moment.

For two years now I am in absolute isolation. I have been subjected to terrible tortures. In summary I report:

Whipping with wire and wire rope all over my body. Beating with clubs on the soles of my feet with the result that my right heel was fractured. Beating with iron bars on my chest and on the ribs with the result that two or three ribs were broken. Burns with cigarettes on my hand and genitals. They put a long metal needle (wire) inside my urethra and heated the extended part of the needle or wire with a cigarette lighter. With their hands they closed my mouth and nostrils (ways of breathing) almost until the point of asphyxiation. Kickings. Punching with the fists. Pulling the hair. Beating of my head against the wall and floor. Preventing me from sleeping. (The protagonists: Major Theophyloyannakos, Police Officers Mallios and Babalis.) Brutal and torturing ways to forcefeed me by Dr Panagopoulos. I was permanently handcuffed. I was refused every possibility of defending myself by their refusal to allow me to see the brief of the prosecution prior to my trial and their refusal to allow me to see my lawyer except once on the eve of the trial and this in the presence of officers of the junta. Threats and pressure by Theophyloyannakos during the trial. Withholding the charges I made and submitted to the Military Tribunal against Major Theophyloyannokos and Hadzisisis for forging (which is proved) my supposed defence plea produced in the brief of the prosecution. Document which is not valid and has not got my signature. These all before the trial.

After the 'trial' transfer from KESA (Centre of Training of Military Police) in gangsteristic way 20th of November 1968 to the arsenal (NAFSTATHMOS) and from there in a naval boat under the signal R.25 (P.25) to a cell at the back of the prisons of Aegina (island of Aegina). They notified me that I would be executed the next morning and asked me if I wanted to ask for pardon. I refused. At dawn a detachment came outside my cell and I could hear orders being given—after a while the detachment left. I was notified that they would execute me the following day because 'Today is the Annunciation of the Virgin Mary and executions cannot take place.' I refused again their suggestions that I should make confessions and ask for pardon. In the morning of 22nd of November I was told again that the execution would take place on the morning of the 23rd. In the afternoon I was transferred to NAFSTATHMOS with the naval boat P-21 and from there to the special interrogation centre of ESA.* A Sergeant (surely under orders) told me that the newspapers had announced that I had been executed adding that now 'they are going to question you as they like.' At dawn on Nov. 23rd they put me in a car telling me 'Now all this gimmickery is over and we are definitely going for the execution.' And we went to the prisons of Boyati. They threw me in a cell without a bed. The walls were damp and green with mould. Still permanently handcuffed I started a hunger-strike, or rather I continued it because from the day after the trial I was not taking any food. The hunger-strike lasted until the 21st of Dec. when they allowed my mother to visit me and promised amelioration of the conditions of my imprisonment. However, I remained handcuffed and on the floor until the end of March. My wrists had ulcerated and pus was running from them. My cell smelt so badly that the guards couldn't stand outside the door. Inside the cell there was a hole which I had to use for all bodily functions. From the 20th of March it was impossible for me to bear the handcuffs (because of the wounds) but all they did was to remove them for 2–3 hours in the morning daily. From the 8th of May after I had been on a hunger-strike since Easter they put a bed in my cell and a table and they accompanied me for 15–20 minutes in the prison yard after they had closed the other prisoners into their cells. On June 5th I escaped.

* The Greek Military Police.

I was betrayed by Patitsas and Perdikaris and I was arrested on the 9th of June. I stayed handcuffed in a cell in the Security of Neo Ioania. I refused to make any testimony. I went on hunger strike. I was transferred to KESA (Centre of Training of the Military Police) on the 13th of June, they removed the handcuffs. They locked me in a cell. On the 20th of July I went again on a hunger strike. On the 24th of July I was transferred to Boyati in strict isolation. I continued the hunger-strike until the 5th of September (47 days). Then they promised that they would allow me to get out in the yard, when I would be able to walk and that I would get food from home and newspapers. I started taking food. On the 10th of September I started again on a hunger strike because except for the newspapers, there was no amelioration. On the 24th of September they gave me food that my mother had sent and I started eating again. On the 18th of October I was arrested while trying to escape. Handcuffs, chains at my feet, removal of the bed, no newspapers, no cigarettes, no food from home—I started a hunger strike. I was absolutely exhausted; from the 13th of November they started subjecting me to different tortures, psychological pressures, etc. The sort of the tortures I reported to the Representatives of the International Red Cross who visited me on January 16th. I have no room and I need to write many things to give you a clear picture. My hunger-strike ended on December 21st (44 days) when in a coma they put me on a bed they brought into the cell. And they removed the handcuffs, and they gave me newspapers. It took many days for me to recover. On the 16th of January the International Red Cross visited me. On the 19th of January, transfer to KESA, strict isolation and tortures!! 9th of February transfer again to Boyati to a special cage-cell of cement 3 metres by 1½ in dimension, other conditions known to the International Red Cross. They went on tormenting me. I am writing in summary so it is difficult to give a full picture of the conditions I faced. Now I am coming to the most tragic, for me, and more telling event for the criminal mentality of the junta!

9th of April—attempt to murder me. After the failure the junta tried to present it as an attempted suicide. I told, in as clear a way as I could, all that had to do with the attempted murder to the Representatives of the International Red Cross on the 1st of

June. I asked to see the Public Prosecutor at the hospital where I was transferred, still ill. This was refused. They also refused to allow me to get in touch with my mother.

To protect myself from similar acts of the fascist junta who have not for a moment left their murdering intent, I make this accusation publicly. With the hope that this letter of mine will be a testimony with the power and the ability to protect also the life of other prisoners who are in strict isolation, I certify on my word of honour and on oath the truth of my denunciation. I would not have done this publicly if I didn't know that, as perfectly as the junta had prepared my murder, they did make one mistake. When there will be justice in our country again I will bring all the evidence and testimonies which prove this criminal act. From the personnel of the prisons only one or two people are involved in this. From the 22nd of April until the 21st of May (30 days) I did not take food. They brought in the Military Doctor Panagopoulos who repeated his tortures on the 20th of May. On the 21st I was told they would allow me to see my mother and I accepted food.

Let the world's morals and sense of justice protect us.

Signed: A. PANAGOULIS

This letter, written on pink toilet paper, had I believe been written in June. It reached a young friend of mine, the lawyer Kostas Androusopoulos. Kostas was a friend of Alexandros and loved and tremendously admired him. When he showed me the letter, it brought back all my distress and bitterness for what Alexandros had suffered, and for what a young human being was still suffering, and all the indignation and the shame I had felt because Greeks, for money, had handed him back to his torturers when he had managed to escape. Now we had the names of these vile traitors from Alexandros himself. I remembered my own feeling after his first escape: why had he not come to me; at least I would not have betrayed him.

I knew already most of what was in the letter. But we learned that what we had heard of as an attempted suicide had been an attempt to murder Panagoulis. We also learned some of the appalling details of what he had called at his trial 'sexual tortures'. It was a sad satisfaction to realize how accurate our information was; we had known every place he had been moved to, one after the other, with extraordinary measures of secrecy. We had known all that, and yet we could not help him; the fact was that no one could help him.

In July 1970, Panagoulis had already spoken of his cement tomb-like cell. I now know that it has a little window high up near the ceiling with iron bars and a heavy metal mesh; this is the only means of ventilation. In the iron door there is a small, heavily meshed spyhole which his mother describes as the size of an envelope. There is a toilet hole and a little basin, but no running water. The water is brought to him in little jugs and he has many times been deprived of water for days at a time so that the hole fills with waste and the foul smell is such that the guards cannot even stand near the spyhole.

When Alexandros heard of the prison cages in Vietnam he smuggled out a letter addressed to the American Senators asking as a favour that such a cage should be sent to him as it would be healthier than the one he lives in (see opposite). For four years Alexandros Panagoulis was allowed out of his cell on only a few occasions. The public outcry against his misery, and against the conditions in which he was held, caused the Greek authorities to remove his handcuffs, which he had worn for eight months, and let him out in the yard for some twenty minutes a day. After a few days, reporters were allowed to see him from a long distance, and photographers were allowed to take pictures of him happily kicking a football! In spite of the distance, some photographs showed the swelling on his wrists that the handcuffs had caused.

About two months later Androusopoulos came again. He was happily excited: one of Alexandros's guards had brought him a letter. Panagoulis was ready to escape again. He was asking Kostas whether he could have a car waiting near the camp at a place the guard would show him, in order to take them both to a safe hiding-place.

Androusopoulos could provide a good hiding-place but had no money, no car, and in fact did not know how to drive. I was happy that he asked me if I could help; there was nothing I wanted more. I knew one thing: that if Alexandros managed to escape, I was ready to do anything that lay in my power to prevent his being betrayed and tortured again. I said at once that I should be delighted to help, but that I was afraid that perhaps it was a trap that the military police

A LETTER FROM ALEXANDROS B. PANAGOULIS*

Σ. Φ Μ
Β. Σ Τ 902
Ἰούλιος 1970

Προσκαλῶ τὰς Ἀμερικανὰς Γερουσίαστες,
ποὺ σὲ πρόσφατη ἐπίσκεψή τους εἰς Νότο
Βιετνάμ, εἶδον καὶ εἶχαν τὴν ἐντιμότητα
νὰ καταγγείλουν τὶς φυλακές-κλουβιὰ τοῦ
καθεστῶτος τῆς Σαϊγκόν, νὰ μὲ ἐπισκεφθ...
εἰς Στρατιωτικὲς Φυλακὲς τοῦ Μπογιάτι.
Ἀκοίβει τους, μιὰ νέα ἐμπειρία γιὰ τὶς
μεθόδους τοῦ φασισμοῦ στὴν Ἑλλάδα.
Ἴσως τότε τὰ φιλανθρωπικὰ αἰσθήματα
τῆς Κυβερνήσης τους, τὴν παρακινήσουν
ὥστε μαζὶ μὲ τὰ ὅπλα πὰ στέλνει στὴ
φασιστικὴ χούντα νὰ στείλει κι ἕνα κλουβὶ γιὰ μένα. Ἕνα κλουβὶ... περισσότερο
ὑγιεινὸ ἀπὸ αὐτὸ ποὺ μοῦ προσφέρει
ἡ Χούντα. Τοὺς περιμένω . . . .

[Ἀλὲξ Β. Παναγούλης]

* Boyati Military Prison, B.S.T. 902, *July 1970*. To the American Senators, who in a recent visit in South Vietnam witnessed and honestly exposed the existence of the prison-cages of the Saigon regime, I extend an invitation to come and visit me in the Military Prison of Boyati. They will be rewarded with a new experience about the methods of fascism in Greece. This might stimulate the philanthropic sentiments of their government, who might decide, along with the armaments they are shipping to the fascist Junta, to ship also a cage for myself. A cage ... healthier than the one provided for me by the Junta. I'll be awaiting them ... ALEX. B. PANAGOULIS

were laying for us. Androusopoulos assured me that if Alexandros had chosen this guard, then the young man was all right, and we should trust him. He added, and it sounded plausible enough, that for a trap they would have chosen someone more experienced. The guard who had brought the letter was a boy of twenty-one doing his military service; he seemed to be a democrat who violently resented the barbarity he was obliged to witness; Kostas had spoken with him for two hours, and he appeared to be genuine. Could I please on this same night at about nine o'clock drive them both to Boyati so that they could fix the place of the meeting? I agreed to do so, but in the evening it was pouring with rain. I dislike driving in the dark at the best of times because the lights of the on-coming cars blind me, and like it even less in the pouring rain. So I rang Yannis, a taxi driver I knew, and asked him to drive me somewhere out of Athens. I did not tell him where we were going, but simply directed him to go straight on, right or left. I do not believe he can have realized where we were when we reached the place in that rainstorm, or that he can have understood what we were speaking about.

The guard, Takis Bekakos, was dressed in civilian clothes and looked quite innocent and determined. But I was still worried; I asked him whether it was really possible for Alexandros to escape from such a well guarded place. He said yes, that it was, that Alexandros had worked it out and planned everything with him.

We really had no choice. Panagoulis had said he was coming out of the camp, and this part of the escape was inevitably his own responsibility, we could not assist him in it. But if he did come out, how could we possibly refuse to help him to reach safety? I asked about the other guards. Surely Bekakos was not the only one? What about the sentry at the watchtower? And both Androusopoulos and I insisted on one condition, that absolutely no one was to be hurt. I remember saying, 'I don't want to help one young man out of his suffering if it means that another innocent young man will be wounded or killed.' The guard said that there was no question of any such thing happening, that everything had been worked out. He himself was to choose an evening when the sentry was a new conscript who would be impressed by him and obey his orders, since Bekakos had already been a soldier for a year. Bekakos would go to the watchtower and hold the sentry in conversation, keep him inside and distract him, so that he could not see Panagoulis jump out of his window and run to the barbed-wire compound fence. He had already been practising for some time with the young sentry. There were some heavy bars in the watchtower which they were lifting to see who was stronger, and the sentry was innocently playing the game. As soon as Panagoulis had reached the fence, Bekakos would follow him and cut the barbed-wire with a cutter he had smuggled in. Before the day of the escape he would have given a file to Panagoulis to cut the bars of the cell window. It was as easy as that: they were sure of their success. All Bekakos wanted and demanded was to leave Greece immediately after the escape.

I said, 'That is not possible,' but Androusopoulos shook his head furiously at me and said, 'Of course it is possible, it will be arranged.'

The place of meeting having been arranged, Bekakos told us that he would ring Androusopoulos a couple of days later to fix the date of the escape. It depended on when he was to be on guard outside Panagoulis's cell from 7 to 9 p.m., which was the best time because it would be dark, and on whether the sentry at the watchtower was the right one.

On Androusopoulos's initiative I gave Bekakos one thousand drachmas (about thirteen pounds) just in case he needed to buy a few things before departing. I did not like Bekakos's accepting the money. Kostas was adamant: Panagoulis had written in his letter that Bekakos was all right. It did occur to me to ask myself whether Panagoulis never made mistakes.

For over twenty days we did not hear from Bekakos. Then he rang Kostas again, and they met. He told him that he had been punished for being caught on the watchtower speaking to the sentry. I was somewhat wary about this, but Kostas's confidence would not be shaken. He had counted the days, he said, and they fitted Bekakos's story; the only reason I worried and doubted was that being a woman I had naturally not done my military service and did not know how easily one 'gets twenty days' in the army. Kostas was jubilant. Bekakos had told him that all was ready, and that he had given a file to Panagoulis who had cut the bars of his window already. He had covered the cut with Nescafé, and it could not be seen.

But, said Kostas, Bekakos was worried because I had said that he would not be able to get out of Greece the very day of the escape. Panagoulis had assured him that he would have a foreign passport and could get away at once. Kostas insisted it was essential that Bekakos's trust in both Panagoulis and us should not be shaken; Bekakos was afraid we might look after Panagoulis's safety exclusively and abandon him. I had to agree that this was natural, and that it was even a proof that Bekakos was genuine. We had to do something to reassure Bekakos, even if it meant deceiving him. The deceit did not matter as it would not affect the substance of things; naturally we would not under any circumstances abandon him, indeed we would do as much to prevent Bekakos's arrest as we would do for Panagoulis himself. We knew this, but equally naturally Bekakos could not be sure. It was then that I remembered something Stathis Panagoulis had told me. The only member of the Panagoulis family I have ever met is Stathis, whom I met in London in December 1970 for a few minutes. His only concern was Alexandros; he was distressed by the fact that Alexandros had managed to escape the first time only to be betrayed and re-arrested. 'If I had known what the guard he escaped with looked like,' he had told me, 'I would have found two young men looking more or less like him and Alexandros, and I would have gone to Greece immediately with them to take Alexandros and the guard out on their passports.' We were counting on Stathis now to take Alexandros and Bekakos out of Greece. Stathis I thought should have a photograph of Bekakos; I should ask Bekakos for a photograph, saying that it was to be used for a passport, and in this way I would reassure both him and Kostas.

We were to meet again in the evening to settle every detail of the escape. I asked Bekakos for a photograph for the passport he so much wanted to have. He said he did not have one. I suggested that he could have one taken at an automatic photographic machine. It was only then that I noticed that, in the meantime, Bekakos's hair had been cropped to half an inch. He looked exactly what he was, a young Greek doing his military service. Where on earth was Stathis going to find a foreign passport with a photograph looking like that?

I remembered that I had a wig with long hair. I left Kostas and Bekakos waiting for me, went home, cut the hair to a hippy length and returned with it. It was a terrific success. Bekakos looked like any other hippy of any nationality. Stathis would have no difficulty as far as this was concerned. The photos were taken, and Bekakos arranged again that the escape was to take place definitely in a couple of days or so. Then, before we parted, and with some embarrassment, he said that

Panagoulis wished to have three thousand drachmas. He saw the disbelief in my eyes, and stammered that two or one would do if we could not give him three. I was sure it was not Panagoulis who had asked for the money. I looked at Kostas—his pleading eyes were saying, 'Please, please give him the money, we need him.' I gave the three thousand drachmas, which is about forty pounds in English money, to Bekakos, and once again, many days passed without any news at all from him. It was the end of February and the carnival was on. I remember saying to Kostas that either Bekakos was having a nice time with his girlfriend on my three thousand drachmas, or he had handed them to the military police for my fingerprints. At last he appeared again. This time he said that his brother, a sailor in the merchant navy, had drowned in one of the boats that had sunk; two boats had indeed gone down with many casualties, and the news had been in the papers. Because of the sudden death of his brother, his father was ill with a heart attack in the Evangelismos Hospital, and he himself had been given compassionate leave.

I was looking at his tie, which had red stripes. Any Greek would wear a black tie if his brother had died. He noticed my look, and explained that he had had no time to go home to change into civilian clothes, so he had borrowed clothes from a friend. This time he gave us two alternative dates for the escape. If it could not be done on the first date, it was definitely going to be done on the next. Once again he got some money.

Bekakos did not know my name; he did not know I was a doctor, he did not know that I could easily check at the hospital; he was after all only a boy of twenty-one. I checked all the entries at the hospital in the register of admission for the month and there was no patient named Bekakos.

I told Kostas that I definitely did not trust the boy any longer. I had to agree that it was not a trap, but could it perhaps be no more than a way of extorting money from us? All the same the appointment had to be kept, and was kept both times, and of course we saw neither Panagoulis nor Bekakos.

A few days later Kostas came to see me again. He gave me a note from Panagoulis which Bekakos, who had reappeared, had brought for him. I suppose that I forgot to give him Panagoulis's note back, and I must have put it in my handbag. That was the handbag I took with me to go to the police station where I was falsely told I was being taken on the day I was expelled from Greece. The note had escaped all the searches, and was expelled with me to London.*

I tried to persuade Kostas that in my view this note meant that Bekakos was deceiving both Panagoulis and us. He was telling Alexandros that we were not ready, or that we were wavering, while for us he had other excuses. Kostas's affection and admiration, and his faith in Panagoulis's judgment, remained unshaken and unshakable. If Alexandros trusted Bekakos, we should trust him too. He added that because of my doubts he had managed to let Alexandros know our fears, and he had got a message which meant that he should have no doubts about Bekakos. Kostas said that the note was a confirmation that the bars of Alexandros's cell window had been cut.

Actually we were both right. The bars had been cut before February 27th, 1971. Bekakos had indeed given Alexandros a file for

* 27/2/71. Any delay is unjustified. Everything is OK. Have no doubt whatsoever about anything. Takis [Bekakos] will explain by word of mouth. A. PANAGOULIS

the purpose. But from then on he did what I had guessed: deceived both Panagoulis and us. Why? What happened? Why did he go so far as to smuggle in the file, let Panagoulis cut the bars, and so put everybody, himself included, in great danger, and then stop and go no further? Carried away by Panagoulis's courage, did he believe that he should co-operate and assist him, only to discover that he did not dare go on?

Was it my fault? Did he waver when on the first day I said that it would not be possible for him to leave the country immediately after the escape? Was it our fault because we gave him the money he asked for? Was he after all a confused and unbalanced boy, unable to bear the responsibility of the role for which he cast himself?

Once again we found ourselves with new dates for the escape. This time I would not give in; I refused to believe Bekakos any longer. Once again Kostas said that if he had no other help, no money, and no car, he would go alone, on foot, and wait outside the camp to take Panagoulis away and hide him. He would not desert his friend. I knew Kostas, and I knew he would really do this. So I helped again, and yet again, but I refused to see Bekakos.

How long did this go on? How many times did Bekakos play this game, get some money and then vanish once more? How many times did the dangerous wait outside the camp take place? How many more lies in fact did Bekakos actually tell? How many impatient and reassuring letters did Panagoulis write, believing that we were afraid of a misfire? One day we shall be able to say.

In the middle of all this frustration we heard a wonderful piece of news. On the night of June 5th to 6th, 1971, Nicos Zambelis escaped from the prison on the island of Aegina. Zambelis, a cousin of Panagoulis, was serving an eighteen-year sentence for being a member of Panagoulis's group (see p. 72ff). According to what was said at the trial of his cellmates and the guards on February 14th and 15th, 1972, Zambelis cut the bars of his cell with a file, reached the roof of the building, walked to the edge which looked over the outside world, removed fourteen tiles, uncovered a wooden beam, slipped a rope around it and reached the street. He then pulled the rope after him and fled. He walked a couple of miles until he found an unguarded little harbour, jumped into a boat and started trying to reach Piraeus, the harbour of Athens. The engine of the boat did not work, and Zambelis must have rowed. He got lost, but fortunately a couple of miles from Aegina he met a fishing-boat which towed him for another mile in the right direction. An hour and a half later, once again lost, he met a patrol boat from Piraeus. Zambelis told the officers that his engine did not work and asked for their help. They towed him to Tourkolimano, in Piraeus. Zambelis escaped abroad successfully. So far we can rely on the information given at the trial.

If what Theophyloyannakos, the commanding officer of EAT ESA, told me while I was his prisoner is true, Stathis Panagoulis came to Greece in a yacht belonging to an Italian countess. The boat was left off the island of Zakynthos, and Stathis went to Athens. Travelling with friends on the car ferry, he took Zambelis to Zakynthos, from there to the yacht, and so to safety abroad.

After Zambelis's escape, all the windows of all prison cells in the country were checked, and Panagoulis's bars were discovered to be cut. Not knowing that they had been so since February 1971, the military police connected the two things and concluded that a resistance organization was trying to free all the Panagoulis group, possibly in order to kill Papadopoulos.

Alexandros's mother was due to see him when suddenly, brusquely, and without explanation, she was told that she could not do so. Then again, from inside the camp we learned that Panagoulis had been moved. We tried to find out where he had been taken to, but this time without success. In the meantime, in July, Androusopoulos moved house. He had to do so, and this worried us. Supposing that Panagoulis could find some way of re-establishing contact, how was he to be given Kostas's new address?

At about eight o'clock in the morning of August 23rd or 24th, I was on the terrace watering my plants when a policeman called and handed me a summons to go to EAT ESA on Thursday, August 26th, to be interrogated as 'accused'. I did not read any further, but left the summons on the table. The policeman was terribly polite and apologetic. He hoped he had not called too early, and that he had not unduly disturbed me.

I resumed my gardening. I had been expecting this summons since the beginning of the year, since I had been told that people under torture had admitted what they were asked to admit, that they had active resistance contacts with me. A friend who had spent the night at my home came out on the terrace holding the summons. She looked terrified. 'Did you read this?' she asked. I read it. It said that I was being charged with 'conspiracy', with 'having used bombs and explosives'. I said 'Nonsense!' Still, not unnaturally I wondered what might be behind this ridiculous charge.

The evening before the interrogation, on Wednesday August 25th, Kostas came again. He knew where Alexandros was. He was in KESA, the training centre of the military police, in the Papagos district.* A young corporal had brought him a message. The corporal was to help Panagoulis escape. It would have been done already but for the fact that the corporal had taken ten days to find Androusopoulos's new address. It had to be done within the week because Alexandros was about to be moved back to Boyati, where the military police had reinforced all their security measures to near exaggeration-point. Would I please take them close to the camp so that the corporal could show Kostas where to wait with a car to take them both to a safe place?

I showed him the summons. I said that I could not help them any more, and especially not at that moment. Most probably, according to usual practice, I was being watched and followed, even if only to see my reactions to the summons. It would be pure folly to take them in my car to a place that was to be their rendezvous if the escape succeeded. I suggested that he and the corporal guard should go to the Papagos district in a taxi; after all, it was a residential district. They could afterwards walk to the point where they had to meet. He said the corporal was terribly frightened and refused to go by taxi. I suggested postponing the whole thing. No, it was impossible, it had to be done that night; otherwise the corporal might lose confidence. The escape ought to be carried through within one or two days. He had a car and a driver ready for that; all he needed was someone to help that very night to take them to the place of the rendezvous.

I was expecting a friend for dinner whose wife and children were abroad on holiday. So I said I could ask my friend, perhaps he would agree to drive them. Kostas had left the corporal sitting at a café, about a quarter of a mile away. I told him to go back quickly to his corporal before my friend came, so that the two would not meet, and then to telephone later. But my friend arrived earlier than expected, and they met. Anyway, I did not introduce them, so Kostas never

* The Papagos district is situated three to four miles from the centre of Athens and its residential area is inhabited mostly by officers' families. Apparently a number of military camps had recently been installed there.

knew his name. After Kostas's departure I asked my friend without telling him anything more about the circumstances whether he would be prepared to drive Kostas and another friend to a secret rendezvous. He could not do so because his car had been smashed, but he did volunteer to go to the café and tell Kostas why it was impossible. We were back at square one: I could see no alternative to a taxi. My friend performed his errand and came back to tell me that Kostas had said again that a taxi would not do, but the young man he was with was able to drive, so would I let them use my car? He would phone to ask me, and if I said yes, would I leave the keys in the car for them to fetch? I accepted, and asked my friend to take the keys to my car, which was in its usual parking place, leave them there, and then go away before the others arrived at the car. My obliging friend did more; he waited for them, and took the car out of the open parking lot on to the street. He was wearing a red pullover. I was to suffer much over the question of who the 'man in the red pullover' was.

12. *Summoned for Interrogation*

On Thursday August 26th, 1971, at eight o'clock in the morning, I went to EAT ESA. To reach EAT ESA you must drive along Vassilissis Sofias, one of the main avenues of the city; you pass the Hilton, and shortly afterwards you turn left. On one side is the American Embassy; on the other, sloping lawns stretch for some hundred yards, with the statue of Eleftherios Venizelos in the middle of them, and the EAT ESA barracks is behind them.

At the gate stands a sentry-box with two soldiers; I showed the summons and gave my name, and a soldier took me in. As I was crossing the gate I saw above my head some three yards inside the courtyard a banner saying WELCOME TO EAT ESA.

We went almost to the far end of the courtyard and turned right. I remember that there are two beds of flowers outside a small building, and then offices on both sides of a narrow corridor. I was taken to the second office on the left. The man who had summoned me, and who was to interrogate me that day, was Captain Papaphilippou. He was a regular investigating judge of the military court. As such he should have been sitting in an office of the military court building, not at the Special Interrogation Centre of the Greek military police, but that is where he was. He was sitting at a desk, his back to the wall; I think he was in uniform. On the other side of the desk was a chair. I was asked to sit down, and would I take a cup of Turkish coffee? I said yes, and especially a glass of water, please. And how did I like my coffee? With a little sugar. Next to Papaphilippou's desk, a little further up the room, was another desk with a man in civilian clothes sitting behind it. He was to write down whatever I answered to my interrogation.

I showed the summons to Papaphilippou and asked him what exactly they meant by accusing me of 'bombs and explosives'. He waved the thing away. No, this had nothing to do with me. I was accused of belonging to the resistance organization PAK, and since PAK has a militant branch, all persons accused of membership were charged in this way.

The boy arrived with the coffee and glasses of iced water. Could I please have two glasses of water? Of course I could. Did the open window bother me? Was I cold? No, I liked fresh air.

Well, what about PAK? What is PAK? I said it was a resistance organization of supporters of Andreas Papandreou. And who was the head of PAK? I said that abroad I believed it was Andreas himself. And inside Greece? I did not know. What connections did I have with PAK? I said I had none. I did not belong to any resistance organization, but my ideology was that of the Centre Union party. If there were a free election, I would vote for Andreas Papandreou. Papaphilippou stiffened imperceptibly. Did I go to George Papandreou's funeral? Yes, I certainly did, and I sent a wreath. With my name on it? he asked incredulously. Of course with my name, I thought I had written 'with love and admiration', I said.

Papaphilippou remained silent for a moment. I was sipping the iced water. Then he opened a big folder. It contained statements of different people who had been held at EAT ESA, and the real interrogation started.

'Do you know X?'

'Yes I do.'

'How did you come to know him?'

'I have known him for about forty years. We were both members of an excursion club.'

He read from the statement. Was it possible that the man had really said what Papaphilippou was reading to me? Pages and pages of resistance activity I was supposed to have taken part in, or rather to have initiated. I said I could not believe the man had said all these things. He would not have said all that even if he wanted me arrested.

'Here they are,' said Papaphilippou. 'And this is not all.' He went on reading. ' "T. came to see me on behalf of Andreas Papandreou, I told him that he should see Lady Fleming, who is high up in the organization of PAK, and not me who knows nothing about it." '

I asked why, if I was so high up in PAK, did Andreas send the man to him, who knew nothing about it, and not to me? I had never heard of T. and never met him. Papaphilippou could not be telling the truth.

'Let us go further. "I gave Lady Fleming five thousand drachmas last Christmas for families of political prisoners." Did he give you these five thousand drachmas?'

'He did.'

'So you were one of the main agents who helped families of political prisoners?'

'I helped women and children in need.'

'They were families of political prisoners.'

'Most were. They were the ones who needed help more than others. Is it a crime to help children?'

For a moment Papaphilippou forgot his sweet manners. There was cruelty in his voice. 'You tell the men to join in the resistance and we shall look after your families.'

So that was it. I knew that helping the families of political detainees was a punishable crime. I knew that their neighbours did not dare approach them. They were supposed to feel rejected, as if they were suffering from some horrible contagious disease, like the lepers in the Middle Ages. But I had not thought of it in the way he was putting it.

He regained his composure. 'Let us go on.' And we did. He had a long list of names of people who had allegedly attributed a number of things to me. Had they really done so? The statements he was supposed to be reading to me, did they really contain all these accusations? As one after the other I refuted every charge, he remarked ironically that if I refused to admit having done all that, I wouldn't be able to claim a decoration when 'my side' came to power.

He went on. He seemed to enjoy his reading. Except for planting or handling explosives, every imaginable resistance activity had been attributed to me. 'Did I do everything?' I asked. 'The way you put it, PAK and all other resistance organizations have only one member between them, me.'

So far he was quoting the statements of people who, as far as I knew, had not been ill treated, at least not seriously, and who had been released since.

But we went further, as he put it, and names of people who I knew had been terribly tortured were mentioned. 'K. said this.' Among other things, K. had had three ribs broken from the beating.

'It is not true.'

'Why does he say it?'

'He may have suffered some painful pressure.'

'M. says that.'

'It is not true.'

'Why does he say it?'

'He also may have suffered painful pressure.'

'And Frangias?' Papaphilippou was holding a huge mass of papers, Andreas Frangias's statement.

'Don't talk about Frangias,' I said.

'Why? Are you also suggesting that Frangias was tortured?'

The man who was recording what I was saying at the other desk looked up and asked the same question.

'Please,' I said, 'please do, both of you, remember that Frangias spent most of his imprisonment in hospitals, and that I am a doctor.'

There was an uneasy look in their eyes, and they were silent. They never read to me what Andreas Frangias was supposed to have said about me. They believed that the doctors had told me what Frangias had suffered, and that is exactly what I wanted them to believe. But it was not the doctors, it was the police, and the officers, as usual, who had informed us.

Andreas Frangias, another martyr in their hands. Frangias, in his early fifties, had been arrested by the security police in October 1970. He was terribly beaten, especially on the head, and the beating continued for five days even after he had shown symptoms of brain injury. In spite of all this beating, Frangias did not speak; he had some experience of torture, being one of our heroes of the resistance during the Nazi occupation of Greece.

Eventually he had to be transferred to a hospital, to the Department of Nervous Diseases in the Polikliniki, where he was kept under strict guard. There he got proper medical attention, but before he had time to recover, and against medical advice, he was taken away by the military police. It was announced that he was going to be deported. Soon after that we heard he had been moved back to hospital again, this time to a military one. There must be a department in this hospital that cannot be medical; the terrible things that we have heard happen in that place are not medicine. Frangias was put for four and a half months with mad patients and treated accordingly, although he was not mad.

Frangias's wife, who had been allowed to see him when he was at the Polikliniki, was suddenly refused permission to see him. We heard that he was in a very poor state, that he could not take food, that he was continually sick, that he was in grave danger of death. What was happening to him? He was well on the way to recovery when he had been taken over by the military police. What had he suffered since?

One day his wife was called. They told her that her husband had a brain tumour and that he might die. If she would sign a statement to the effect that he had been suffering from something of the sort before his arrest, they would let him free.

There was something the military police could use to support this contention. Frangias, in order to be allowed out of the country some months before his arrest, had pretended to suffer from dizziness and other symptoms he had read about, making it sound like something very serious that needed diagnosis and treatment in specialized medical centres abroad. To have him freed, his wife signed the statement about the tumour, and as usual the military police did not keep their promise. He was not freed, and his wife did not see him for another two months. Instead his name appeared in an official list published in the newspapers of a number of people who had been released after months or years of exile in designated villages 'where otherwise they were living in freedom'.

Andreas Frangias's name was the last in this list, and it was obviously added at the last minute. Not only was he not freed, but he had never been in village exile; indeed, he had never since his arrest enjoyed the slightest freedom.

There were arrests that followed on these last months when Frangias was held in the military hospital. We learned that many times he was brought to the brink of death. We learned that the military police had made him sign a statement of hundreds of pages.

Eventually Frangias was freed. I had met him before his arrest, he was fifty-two, and fit and young-looking for his age. One day, after his release, I was visiting a friend at the Evangelismos Hospital. In the corridor my friend's wife pointed out an old man, thin as a skeleton, leaning on a cane. 'Andreas Frangias,' she said. It was as though we were looking at his shadow.

Later on I was told that when Frangias is confronted with things he is supposed to have said and signed, he does not remember them. What was done to this man in the military hospital? Was he given hallucinogens? Did they use narcoanalysis* pushed to the limits of endurance?

---

* Narcoanalysis, properly so-called, is a technique of psychoanalysis that utilizes drugs which take the patient to the brink of unconsciousness and enable the physician to get responses from him that have been long since repressed or forgotten by the patient, and which he cannot give when fully conscious. The technique can be abused by police interrogators to make a prisoner talk, since his resistance and will-power are diminished. For the benefit of prisoners-to-be, who may undergo such an interrogation, I wish to let them know that they can withhold information. It simply requires a greater effort and concentration.

They never told me what Frangias was made to say about me, and they must have seen from my expression that I knew quite enough about his suffering; whatever he may have said about me or other people does not make a lesser hero of Frangias.

It was about midday. On my right was the door, and it was open. A man in a brown striped suit had been standing there for a little while already. I felt that he was looking at me, but every time I tried to see his face, he would turn his back. Then he entered the room. He was about fifty, stout, with dark frog-like eyes and a skin deeply marked with smallpox. I recognized him from the description of some of his victims. He was Major Theodoros Theophyloyannakos, the commanding officer of the place and the chief director of torture.

He inquired about my comfort. Was I all right where I was sitting? Did the open door bother me? Perhaps I would feel happier in another room? I reassured him that I was perfectly all right. Captain Papaphilippou was looking after me and giving me the water I needed. I was on about my tenth glass of water by then; I drink a great deal of water, not only because I am a diabetic, but also because of serious gastro-intestinal problems.

Theophyloyannakos did not introduce himself, and I was not supposed to know who he was. He leaned against the wall, next to Papaphilippou, and started talking. First to Papaphilippou. 'We must not tire Lady Fleming, see that you finish soon so that she can go back home.'

'We are far from that yet,' said Papaphilippou firmly. 'We still have a lot of work to do.'

Then the smiling and the sweet Theophyloyannakos showered me with compliments. 'We know what a good person you are. You have done more for Greece than we officers have ever done.' And so on. As I watched him, I felt a cold shiver up and down my spine. Honey-smiling talk did not befit him, it made him look horrible. This was the man who had tortured Panagoulis. He had tortured the young chemist, Spyros Lucas, until he was a mass of bleeding flesh. With his own hands he had slapped his schoolmate, Major Constantine Pnevmatikos, before ordering and directing the tortures that followed. He had tortured Nikolaos Konstantopoulos and left him seven days without water, he had tortured Sartzetakis ...

'You should be on our side,' the honeyed voice went on. 'It is true you have strayed from the right path. We shall put you right again and

1. Sir Alexander and Lady Fleming in Athens in 1952

2. The torture room on the terrace of the security headquarters in Bouboulinas Street, Athens, formerly the washroom. The building was demolished in 1971. In the new building the tortures take place in the basement, no doubt in a 'scientific' specially designed torture room

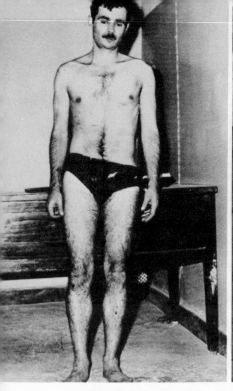

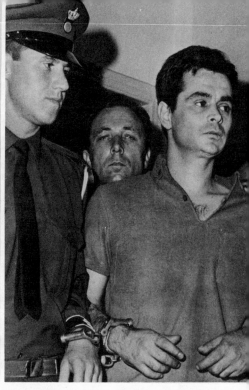

3. (*above, left*) Alexander Panagoulis, immediately after his capture following the suspected attempt to assassinate George Papadopoulos

4. (*above, right*) Panagoulis escaped from prison on June 5th, 1969, only to be betrayed and recaptured four days later

5. (*below*) Unexpectedly, at the funeral of George Papandreou hundreds of thousands of people flocked to express dissent from the regime. The former prime minister symbolized opposition to the Colonels

you will be our friend.' This theme with many variations was to come at me again and again after my arrest.

I suddenly reacted. 'Don't you think that you are a little egotistic? Why are you so sure that you are more intelligent than I am? What makes you believe that you know better than I do which is the right path for me?' The smile left his face, but it took him only seconds to compose himself.

'See that you don't tire Lady Fleming,' he repeated in a paternal way, and walked out.

Papaphilippou looked again at the long list of names he had written on a sheet of paper. I suppose they were those who had mentioned my name in one way or another or had simply admitted having met me.

'Did you ask Z. if he had a typewriter, and if he could type out Andreas Papandreou's speeches so that you could have a lot of copies and spread them around? And did Z. answer that he could neither type nor did he have a typewriter, and did he beg you not to mix him up in these things?'

'Don't ask me ridiculous things,' I said. 'Why would I go to someone who cannot type and had no typewriter? Don't you think that it would be easy for me to get hold of both? I have access to both.'

'But did you not tell him to join PAK, to help Andreas Papandreou? Did he not say, "Please, please, Amalia, don't mix me up in such dangerous things"?' He was imitating the voice of the man very successfully. It sounded so true that I was astonished.

'Supposing I did ask him, why should he "beg" me not to mix him up in such things? Could he not simply refuse?'

'That is what I told him,' he said, with intentional innocence, 'and he answered that I did not know you, that if I did I would have known that no one can resist you when you want something done.' His innocence was obliterated, and a certain slyness had taken its place.

It was two o'clock. We had been at it since eight in the morning — six hours. He said he had to go home for lunch, and would I care to eat the food of the place? He would be back at four. Until now, except for losing his temper momentarily about my having helped the families of political prisoners, he had been irreproachably polite. Naturally, he had tried on me some of the ordinary tricks of interrogators: if I said that I did not know someone, he would come back later with something like, 'So what did you say he told you?' and I would repeat, 'I told you I didn't know him.' But that was all. So I ventured to say that it did not seem fair that he should go home for lunch and leave me sitting in a chair waiting for him. I had answered his summons in the morning, and I would certainly be there again at four, or whatever time he wanted me.

'Let us see,' he said. 'Suppose we leave it for tomorrow; we still have a good deal to go through.'

'Please let us finish today,' I said, 'there is a lot I have to do tomorrow.' I was worried about Kostas and Panagoulis. Were they going to attempt the escape the day after?

'Don't be so sure that you will go home when we have finished,' said Papaphilippou. 'I may order you to be detained.'

I did not answer.

He asked me to follow him, and we started towards the exit, but he stopped at the office next to his own, the one which is the first on the left as one enters the building. It was the commanding officer's room that we entered.

Theophyloyannakos was standing there, all smiles. Papaphilippou brought up the problem of whether we should go on that day, or might it not be better to leave it over until the day after? I said again that I would much prefer to continue that day, and could I go home for lunch? 'Yes, certainly,' said the major, 'and I shall send you in one of our cars. You may accept,' he added, 'there will be no sign of ESA on it.' Then he showed me the photograph of a young man in uniform on a horse. 'You know who this man is?' he asked. I said no, I did not. 'Well, it is our prime minister fighting in the war, defending this country.' I thought all I could see was that he was on a horse—rumour has it that he never fought in the war—but I kept my thoughts to myself. 'I shall give you a photograph of Mr Papadopoulos to hang on your wall at home,' he said.

'Thank you, I don't want Papadopoulos in my house.'

'I shall ask the prime minister to inscribe it to you personally.'

'No, thank you, I am not having Papadopoulos in my house.'

Suddenly the peaceful atmosphere changed. Theophyloyannakos started shouting in anger, and I noticed that anger and shouts suited him better than honeyed conversation. 'We do all we can, we try our best for the country, we hold out our hand to you, but you refuse it. You will not help, you insist on remaining in your destructive opposition. We are the army.'

'Not the army,' I said. 'You are a group of officers. Where are the other officers?'

'We gave our lives and our blood in the wartime to protect the country.'

'Greek soldiers and the Greek people gave more blood than you ever did.'

His shouts suddenly became something hysterical. 'I shall send you to prison to rot for the rest of your life. I shall pull your teeth out one after another.' He picked up his name plate from the top of his desk. 'Do you know who I am?' he shouted. 'I am Theophyloyannakos. Have you heard of me? Do you know what I have done to people like you? I tread on their throats. I pull out their nails.' He was foaming at the mouth, and I must have been white with disgust.

I said, 'Shame on you.'

He said, 'Don't dare speak to me like that!'

I repeated it twice. His face became something monstrous, he came close to me, his terrible face almost touching mine, and his hand raised. 'Don't you dare say that again!' he howled. And I did not dare.

The major calmed down a little. 'I have a collection of teeth and nails here in this drawer, would you like to see them?'

'No, I do not want to see them.'

I saw Papaphilippou's hands in the air gesturing at him to stop. And all of a sudden Theophyloyannakos returned to calmness and smiles. He opened the drawer and took out a folder of papers. 'Here they are,' he said. Papaphilippou said that it was almost three o'clock, we had better leave things until tomorrow. 'No,' said the obliging major. 'Lady Fleming prefers it to be today. We shall send her home in a car. She will be here at four o'clock. Shall we send a car to fetch you as well?'

'No thank you,' I said, 'I will take a taxi.'

'Let us make it 4.30,' said Papaphilippou, with a sigh.

Suddenly I remembered that I had ten people coming to dinner that night, and I told them and asked whether they thought I would have finished by nine, in time for my dinner party.

'Who are these ten people?' asked Theophyloyannakos.

'I won't tell you,' I said.

It was as if thunder had struck him. I don't think anyone had ever dared answer him like this. The shouts started again. I was to tell him the names immediately.

'No,' I said, 'you are an efficient police state. You can find out these things yourself. And anyway, I am cancelling the dinner.'

Papaphilippou, who was obviously hungry, was looking desperately at his watch. And seeing that there was no way to change me, Theophyloyannakos generously sent me home in a car. As he had promised, there was no ESA sign on it. The EAT, in order to follow people, use all sorts of commonplace cars, sometimes with foreign plates.

Courageous friends were waiting for me at home. I gave them a list of the people I was expecting for dinner, asking them to phone from a kiosk or a café and say that to my great regret and for a quite particular reason, the dinner had to be cancelled. At 4.30 I was at Captain Papaphilippou's office again. They brought Turkish coffee, just as I like it, with three glasses of iced water.

'You should not have spoken to the commanding officer the way you did,' Papaphilippou said.

'Torturers are filthy beasts,' I replied.

He had a strange look and remained silent for a few seconds then. 'What kind of resistance do you think the people ought to put up against the regime?' he asked.

'You don't really expect me to answer such a question?'

'Yes, certainly,' he said. 'The people have the legal right to resist. It is absolutely legal. So what would you tell the people to do?'

I said that I would not answer his question.

He assured me again that according to every law resistance was a legal and perfectly non-reprehensible thing. How did I conceive of resistance? What did I believe people should do?

I said that even if I had something in mind, I was not prepared to tell him.

'Oh yes,' he said. 'You will tell me. It is part of the interrogation. You will have to tell me. Besides, I am very interested in your way of thinking. I am very interested to hear your opinion.'

'If you are interested in my opinions,' I said, 'we may discuss them one day, but not as we are now, with you from your grand position as an interrogator and me in the dock.'

'We have not finished with this,' he said, and his voice was hard. 'We shall come back to it and you will answer.' We moved to another subject.

'You have contacts with people abroad. How?'

'Is not the post available for that?'

The law does not allow letters to be opened. Letters of course are opened, and read, and if they are interesting, they are photocopied. But that of course is something the government will not admit to.

'Do you know Christos Sartzetakis?'

'Yes.'

'What is he?'

'A wonderful man.'

'Do you know Takis Touloupas?'

'Yes. For a very long time, since the occupation.'

'What is he?'

'Another wonderful man. A hero of the resistance during the Nazi occupation.'

'They said about you ... '

'No,' I interrupted. 'Don't say anything, because this time I shall not believe you.'

'And Evi Touloupas, his wife, do you know her?'

'Yes,' I said. 'She also is a wonderful person.'

'All the opponents of the government are wonderful people according to you,' said Papaphilippou.

'These people are my friends, and they are wonderful people.'

'What about Andreas?'

'I believe that he is the best man for Greece,' I said. 'I believe he would bring progress and development and social justice to the country.'

'He is also your friend?'

'Yes, all the Papandreou family are my friends.'

'Do you know Margarita?' (Andreas Papandreou's wife.)

'Yes.'

'Did you see her when she came for the funeral of George Papandreou?'

'Of course I did.'

'She rang Andreas and said "how wonderfully we organized everything".'

'No,' I said, 'she did not say any such thing. I was present when she spoke to Andreas. I heard what she said. She spoke with respect and emotion. And of course you know that nothing was organized for the funeral. You know that it was the outburst of an outraged, crushed people.'

He took a statement out of his folder. 'Here is what she said; here they say that she spoke triumphantly, about how well everything had been worked out.'

'I was present,' I repeated, 'and I heard what she said. Perhaps the person who told you does not understand English, but I do, as you know perfectly well.' I had indeed been present, and Margaret was crying; we were all crying, and were all happy that the brave Old Man had been given such a glorious farewell. Papaphilippou was trying to sully our emotions and feelings. 'Please, please stop,' I said. 'I am disgusted.'

He put the statement down and took another. 'K. said that you were to manufacture a false passport for him. He came three times in nine months to ask you if you had it, and at the end you said that you had not managed to get it.'

'If I had said that I could make a passport I would have done it,' I said. 'Please don't underestimate me.'

'And B. said you wanted to give him a passport, but he did not want to take one.'

'But I insisted?' I asked.

'So all this is not true?'

'No,' I said, 'it is not true.'

'Then why do they say so?'

'Perhaps they were made to say so?'

'Is it true', he said in a soft and quiet voice, 'that you said that if you were tortured you would say everything?' I did not answer. Slowly and sweetly he repeated the same question. I still did not answer. Suddenly this man with the irreproachable manners, this regular military judge, afflicted me with nausea. Was he threatening me with torture?

Months later, in January 1972, I was to read that a young man named Demetrios Kyrgios, who had been interrogated by Papaphilippou, had said at the military court,

At the ESA I said all sorts of things so that they would let me sleep. They told me 'Kyrgios, you will say this,' and I answered, 'Write whatever you like. Write that I killed my mother. But let me sleep.' Our life was hell in there. My hearing was impaired. Whatever they wanted me to say at ESA, I said it. Papaphilippou was there. The president remarked that it had been said in court that Papaphilippou was always very polite. Kyrgios replied,

Papaphilippou was all honey. His strong-arm boys did the beating. Papaphilippou was urging me to speak. 'Say this, Kyrgios, so that I can save you; say that, Kyrgios, so that I can help you.' And on Saturday he said, 'I shall leave now, we shall come back to this on Monday.' Which meant for me that they made me stand all the time from Saturday to Monday.*

Papaphilippou went on to me, 'N.A., the nephew of I.A., came to see you one day. What did he come for?'

'Listen,' I said. 'So far you have been reading statements to me. Why don't you read N.A.'s statement. I believe that this time we shall not differ about that, but I shall speak only if you tell me what he said.'

'N.A. said he came to you to ask you to give him his uncle's passport, which you had. I.A. was in exile in a village in the Peloponnese. N.A. and his friends were going to try and get him out of Greece. They needed the passport. N.A. said that not only did you deny any knowledge of the passport but you were horrified to think that he believed you had it. Is that true?'

'Yes, it is. It is exactly as he told you. And he also said if I had really not got the passport, it would be terrible. I told him it was terrible for me that he imagined I had it. What would happen if the security police got hold of him and tortured him and he was to tell a story like that? How could I persuade the police that I knew nothing? You see,' I said, 'I was a good prophet.'

'So you never had I.A.'s passport?'

'Look,' I said, 'you have been questioning me all day. You must have realized how I feel about political prisoners, that I would like to see them all escape to freedom. Do you believe that I would have ruined the possibility of an escape by withholding a passport if I had it? When I.A. himself was asking for it through his nephew?' He seemed to find my argument valid.

'Since this morning,' I said, 'you have been waving the shadows of false passports. Has one single person told you that he has seen such a passport or any passport in my hands?'

Papaphilippou did not answer. He had gone through his list of people who had spoken about me. It was 9.30 in the evening: six hours of interrogation in the morning, plus five in the evening, plus one hour of threats and oversweetness from Theophyloyannakos.

---

* From the defence plea of D. Kyrgios, *Bima*, January 1st, 1972, at the PAK trial.

'You have iron guts,' Papaphilippou said. 'I am a wreck.'

I suppose I managed not to show it, but I also was a wreck.

Papaphilippou was looking thoughtfully at me. 'I should send you to prison with the others. But I shall let you go. You are free.'

Perhaps it would have been better for me if he had sent me to prison that night. Instead he sent me home, once again in an official car.

A few of my friends were sitting in my house and worrying. They were delighted to see me safe and free. I told them some of what had happened, and especially about Theophyloyannakos's threats. I fell into an exhausted sleep.

The door bell woke me. It was one in the morning. I thought: Theophyloyannakos, the military police. It was Kostas. I said, 'For heavens sake, Kostas, why are you here again?' He wanted to know about me first, but then he also had a problem. 'What is the problem now?'

'The person who was to drive the car for the escape now refuses to do so. We must find a car.'

'Kostas, you will send me to prison.'

'I will,' he answered as usual, and as usual we laughed.

'Kostas, it is serious. Don't you understand that you must not come near me now, especially now? Kostas, it is one o'clock, I am exhausted. How can I find anybody to drive a car for you at this hour? Haven't you got a friend who can do it? Why don't you learn to drive?'

Kostas promised he would, but now he had to have a car for Saturday, which meant tomorrow, because it was already the early morning of Friday. He needed a brave man to drive the car and wait with him outside the camp to take Panagoulis and the guard to safety. He had no one he could turn to, so could I help?

I asked him to go away and let me sleep, and I would try to think of something or somebody the next day. Kostas left. I tried to sleep, but it was no longer possible. Although I could not desert Panagoulis if he was really to escape, I could not but realize that I was a potential and indeed an actual danger; it would be intolerable that I should compromise them by my presence.

On Friday, however much I tried, I could find no solution. The people I could count upon were away, nor could I decently approach friends and let out what I needed. It would have been safer to have two cars which would take one man each and leave in different directions. But there was no question of such a thing this time. There was not even one car or one driver.

Then I remembered John Skelton. He was a nice young American, a theology student. He was going to be a priest. He could not stand suffering any more than I could. When we were afraid that Professor Karageorgas might be sentenced to death and executed, John had gone out with a plea to the Churches to help save his life. Perhaps John would agree to help?

I rang Skelton and asked to see him. When we met I told him what I needed, without mentioning the name of Panagoulis. Skelton accepted. I told him that if there was any possibility of getting a second car, he would be in it.

Kostas came to see me again that day. I told him I had secured one car. We agreed that the two men would have to hide in the same house. I was to put Kostas in touch with Skelton. I still hoped for a second car with a Greek to drive it, with a Greek to be outside the camp. I could have found many ready to do it if I could speak, but that was ruled out.

Kostas either came or rang to say that our party was postponed until Monday. I don't remember what reason the corporal had given, but I now know the real reason.

Alexandros Panagoulis is the most courageous young man I have ever heard of. Alexandros has, as the people who heard him at the trial say, an intense and enormous intellectual power. As his poetry shows, he is a patriot and a pure ideologist, but he is not a very lucky man. The fact that Androusopoulos had moved house was to prove catastrophic.

Dimitris Staikos, the young corporal (I heard his name for the first time at the trial), took ten days to find Androusopoulos's new house. He managed to meet him only one day before my interrogation at EAT ESA. This interrogation had eliminated me as a potential helper. While I was at EAT ESA on Thursday, August 26th, Kostas, wanting perhaps to make another reconnaissance, made Staikos hire a car under his own name, and, as Kostas told me, this gave such pleasure and so excited the young man that he went driving about like mad. Perhaps Staikos boasted to some friend in the camp about the hiring of the car, or in some way became suspect to his officers. I imagine that Staikos was questioned and threatened, and at the same time shown this law which says that if anyone who has conspired to do a subversive act betrays his group, he is personally immune. Staikos, confronted with the choice of torture or immunity, not unjustifiably chose the latter. On Friday, August 27th, and only on Friday—one day before the planned escape—Staikos betrayed the undertaking.

Staikos was not an agent provocateur. He did not mean to betray; he was made to do so. In court he lied. He said that from the beginning he never meant to help the escape, that from the beginning he was laying a trap. There is no doubt that he had been instructed to say so. When asked why he took so long to report the plan to his superiors, he said something to the effect that he wanted to have first every possible piece of information.

Kostas and I, listening to what he was saying, knew that he was lying. At the time we let it ride, but now I can say it, since his superiors obviously know it and it can do him no harm. Besides, it saves him from the shame of being a traitor, of deceiving Panagoulis and giving away Kostas.

So from Friday onwards the attempt became a trap. Staikos knew Androusopoulos, he had his full name and address; and he had seen the 'man in the red pullover' handing them the keys of a car. The car had the steering-wheel on the right. That is all that Staikos knew. He did not know that I or Skelton existed. He did not even know the number of the car he had driven; he had not noticed it, since at the time he did not mean to betray the attempt.

The military police made him change the day of the attempt from Saturday to Monday, August 30th, so that Androusopoulos might be followed and something more be learned about the organization they believed we must be. An officer, Captain Demetrius Antonopoulos, was ordered to follow Kostas. Of course, I learned all this only at the trial, when I heard Captain Antonopoulos testify. He gave me the impression of being an honest witness.

On Saturday Kostas rang to tell me about the postponement, and I told Skelton. He had hired a car for the purpose and I told him to use it to have a nice weekend. How long had the car been hired for? Until Tuesday morning. That was all right, he would be able to return the car on Tuesday morning.

I kept hoping that someone would turn up to whom I could confide the story—a Greek who would be a good driver, who would have a good fast car and would do the waiting outside the camp with Kostas. If that happened Skelton could be further away, and could take the guard, not Panagoulis, in his car. But it was August, the hottest month in Athens, and everybody I could think of was away. Monday morning came, and I had still not found anybody else. So I rang Skelton again, and we met at 11 a.m. I told him that I would enormously have preferred that he should not be driving the car outside the camp. Was he sure he did not mind? He said, 'No problem.' I said again that it was much more dangerous, and again he said he did not mind. We arranged that I should take him and Kostas out for dinner, so that they could meet and talk things out.

Skelton spoke Greek, but not well, and Kostas felt safer if I was there for their first meeting. By then I was as sure as one can be that I was not being followed, and it was to be proved that I was right. The military police still knew nothing about my connection with Panagoulis's prison-break. I was still afraid, however, that I was a danger to the others; but it was Androusopoulos who was the danger – he was being followed.

I took Skelton in my car and we drove to Hagia Trias Church about a mile and a half from my home, on the way to Kifissia. That is where we were to meet in the evening, at 10 p.m., outside the church. I had told them that I was to take them to dinner, 'their last dinner in freedom', I had said. We would have plenty of time, since the attempt was not to take place until as soon as possible after 2 a.m. on Tuesday morning. The corporal was to be on guard from two to four, and he hoped to manage the getaway as early as possible, so that some time would have passed before their escape was noticed.

Monday August 30th was a very busy day for me. I had a number of important appointments. I had also to take a boy of nine called Petros to the airport and see him safely on to an aeroplane for Zurich, where the head of the Pestalozzi village school, which is near Zurich, was going to meet him.

The father of this little boy had suddenly died the year before, without leaving any money to his wife, who was partially invalided with a dislocated hip and poor eyesight. There were two small children, Petros, who was eight when his father died, and Maria, who was ten. There was not even any money for the funeral. I heard about it from a neighbour of theirs, a daily help I sometimes used. They all lived in a working-class district at Tourkovounia. Naturally, I tried to help them so far as I could.

When my daily came another day she told me that the priest of Tourkovounia and some good neighbours were strongly advising the mother to have Petros taken into an orphange, because he was an extremely lively little boy whom she could hardly control, and he might turn out badly. As far as I know, children are not happy in orphanages, so I was upset, and asked that she should come and see me and perhaps I could find a better way to help Petros. She came. Her name was Julia; I found her intelligent and sensible, and very distressed about the little boy. I made her promise that she would resist all pressure from the priest and the neighbours, and I on my part promised her I would see Petros went to a school where he would be happy and well educated.

I tried different alternatives unsuccessfully. Then I met another boy who had already been for a year at the Pestalozzi school, and he and his mother told me how happy he was there, how well looked after, and so on. I therefore arranged for Petros to go there too, and this critical Monday was the day on which he was due to go. A label with his name on it was hung round his neck, the air hostesses made a great fuss of him, and an excited and very happy little Petros left for his first journey in an aeroplane.

I kept all my other appointments, and did all I had to do that day. It had been a very busy one, and I was already very tired when I left my car on the street behind the church, a few yards from a police station, and walked to the front of the church where Kostas was waiting anxiously. I was a good quarter of an hour late. Unknown to us, some men from the EAT ESA, under Captain Antonopoulos, who had been ordered to shadow Kostas Androusopoulos, were waiting on the opposite side of the road.

A few minutes later John Skelton arrived, driving a Volkswagen. Kostas and I got into the car. Kostas wanted to approach the camp once more to show the place to Skelton. I suggested that we might have this 'last dinner in freedom' I was offering them in the Papagos district. Kostas laughed at the idea. The Papagos district was all military camps and nothing else, he said. The district, which I knew and had often visited, was a residential suburb with villas and gardens full of roses. Skelton drove where Kostas directed him, and it certainly did seem full of military camps. Perhaps the residential part I knew was further north. After showing Skelton the place they were to return to at 2 a.m., we left Papagos, and Kostas asked Skelton if he knew where Vouliagmeni Street was. Skelton said no. So we drove south towards Vouliagmeni Street. But when we arrived there,

Skelton said he did know it, it was the street which runs down to the airport and the sea. We started looking for a place to eat at what must have been 11 p.m. We wanted to find a certain taverna in Cholargos, which is north of Papagos, and we turned back again, got lost, and eventually found the taverna. It was late, and there was nothing to eat but veal cutlets.

During the dinner we remembered that it was Saint Alexander's day, Panagoulis's name day. I said what a lovely name-day present he would have if they succeeded. And Skelton said that it would also be a wonderful birthday present for him. I asked if it was his birthday. He said it had been a couple of days ago.

I was in a hurry to leave them because a close friend had rung me in the morning asking me to have dinner with her. She had sounded worried, and I wanted to go and see her but had to tell her that I would go after dinner and might be very late. She had asked me to go any time and even wake her if she was asleep.

We left the taverna. Skelton asked me if I thought they would be finished by ten in the morning, so that he might return the car. I said that the thing would be over by half past three whether Panagoulis had made it or not. I said the chances were ninety-nine to one that he would not come out; I didn't believe it was as easy as they said. But I supposed that one had to respond to him, even for the one chance in a hundred. They both agreed, and Androusopoulos said that he was confident that they would make it this time. I told Kostas that I would call him at his office in the morning to see how things had gone. He should not ring me during the night, much as I would want to know how it had gone, because my telephone was probably tapped. Any message at all so late on the night of Panagoulis's escape would be dangerous for both of us. They left me by the church, close to my car. Before they started I went back to them; anguish had got hold of me again. Through the open window of the Volkswagen I touched Kostas's arm. 'Kostas,' I said, 'before I leave you, I want you to know how deeply I admire your courage and your devotion to a friend.' And I thanked John for his help. I knew that Skelton was risking very little, and Kostas very much. But it was a Greek affair, and I felt very grateful to Skelton, who was an American, for the risk he was taking.

I drove to my friend's house, which is on the circular road round the shoulder of Lykabettus. It was one o'clock, and she was half asleep. We talked until almost three. I was restless, and although she had her own problems she sensed my state of mind. She had a fierce headache, and asked me if I had an aspirin with me as she had run out of them. I said I had none, but could go round to find a kiosk or a chemist's shop and get them for her. In Athens there are chemists' shops open all night in almost every neighbourhood. She said she would come with me, as fresh air might help her, and she knew of a kiosk nearby which was open late. If the kiosk was closed, there was a pastry shop opposite which was open all night and where she had been given aspirin once before. So I drove her there, to the little square of Steyi Patridos. The kiosk was closed; my friend got out of the car and walked to the pastry shop. She came back and I started driving her towards her house. After a little while she said she would rather walk. It was only a small distance by foot, and in a car it was all one-way streets. It was now after three in the morning. I started for home, but the anguish which had somehow left me while we were talking gripped me once again. Had Panagoulis made it this time? I would have to wait until late in the morning to know, and I felt miserably frustrated. Then it occurred to me that if Panagoulis had escaped, which ought to have happened by 2.30, almost an hour ago, patrol cars would be out searching for him in all directions. I knew that they meant to drive towards the sea, so I took the opposite direction, towards Kifissia.

The road was empty, with only a very few private cars with late-nighters returning home. No sign of any emergency. Once again Panagoulis had not managed to get out! I drove on, passed Kifissia and reached Ekali. The night was beautiful and calm. Although it was August, Ekali was green and fresh and cool. A wonderful feeling of well-being after the harassing day overtook me; all anguish left me. Dawn was breaking, and I turned round and started slowly returning to Athens. Everything was so peaceful and beautiful that I thought that I should do this often, drive out of town early in the morning. Whatever I did, I was generally awake very early. In this happy mood I entered my parking place.

13. *Arrest*

It was 5.40 in the morning. I parked the car and had put out one foot when three men converged on me. This parking lot covers the whole area between two parallel streets, Sekeris and Merlin, and has entrances on both sides. Both streets are perpendicular to Vassilissis Sophias, the main avenue which leads to Kifissia. I think that one man must have been waiting at each entrance and a third inside the car park. They were armed. One had a revolver which he stuck in my ribs, the other two had tommy-guns—at least, this is what I imagine tommy-guns to be. They pulled me roughly out of my car and ordered me to follow them. I managed to put down both feet and stand.

'Put that thing down, my boy,' I said to the young soldier who was prodding me with the revolver. 'What do you expect me to do, fight you? And anyway, who are you?'

'ESA,' they said with one voice, and produced identity cards which I did not even look at. I had no doubts about what they were. 'Follow us,' ordered one of the boys. I said I wanted to take my handbag and lock the car, but was not permitted to do so.

Although I realized that Kostas and John Skelton must have been arrested, my first reaction was to think how ridiculous the three young men looked with their weapons and their serious and important air. When one of them, who was also the driver of the ESA car, started driving at full speed, swerving madly to cover the small distance between my parking place and the American Embassy, I could not help thinking that he must have seen many James Bond films.

We entered the ESA courtyard and I was taken to a room. I have since desperately tried to remember which room it was. Was it in the building I had been in on August 26th for the first interrogation? If so it must have been the office which was on the other side of the corridor opposite Theophyloyannakos's room. But in the morning I was in another little building with two offices in front and the prison cells at the back, and much as I try I cannot remember being moved from one place to the other. It may be that at the beginning I was taken to this second little building and that my memory of a different room is due to the number of people who were in there waiting for me.

There were many; it seems to me now that the room was full, but as a good actor dominates the stage, and all the extras seem to be there to enhance his presence, Theophyloyannakos, the commanding officer of the Special Interrogation Centre, the man I had quarrelled with so violently less than five days before, attracted all my attention. He almost danced and jumped with evil triumph. He had been trying for over three years to find some evidence against me and now he thought that he had it.

'Lady Fleming in person,' he said, 'and in full battledress!' I was dressed up for dining out in a very pretty summer dress and jewellery. I had the impression of being in a madhouse, with everyone moving all round me and everyone howling something. At this moment I could have denied any knowledge of the attempt. I had realized that the others had been arrested, but that had surely been done miles from where I was found, and three hours earlier. Skelton must have given my name as soon as he was arrested. I knew that Kostas would not, and the corporal did not know me, nor did I know him. Whatever Skelton might have said, I could just say I knew nothing. Had I not, for twelve hours, five days before, refuted every charge supposed to have been made against me by so many people?

But this time I cared only about one thing: what had happened to Kostas, to Skelton, to Panagoulis, to the corporal? And this is what I said, and repeated again and again, 'What happened?'

'We ask the questions here,' said Theophyloyannakos, and I suppose he did ask something. But suddenly I was deaf to everything but my own thundering thoughts and voice.

'What has happened?' I remember that I was seated. I don't know how or who had invited or made me sit down, but I remember them being above me, standing around me with their lips moving. I could hear only one voice, mine, demanding to know what had happened.

Seeing that there was nothing for it but to answer me, Theophyloyannakos bellowed with enjoyment in every word: 'Panagoulis was killed. The others are arrested. One man is wounded.'

How many times had I said to Kostas, 'And what if he is killed in the attempt to escape? What if instead of saving him, we help them to kill him?' And so now it had been done. 'You killed him,' I said. 'You killed

6. (*above*) Andreas Frangias, a hero of the resistance in the Second World War. In November 1970 he suffered brain damage and internal injuries under torture, and was then imprisoned in a psychiatric ward, though he was sane, and 'confessions' were obtained by means of drugs. (*Left*) Frangias on October 5th, 1970, and (*right*) on April 22nd, 1971

7. Kostas Georgakis, a twenty-two-year-old student who on September 29th, 1970, burned himself to death in protest against the regime

8. Lady Fleming in the Black Maria on the way to prison after being sentenced.

9. Lady Fleming entering the court to obtain her release from prison on grounds of ill health

10. On her return home, Paschalis refuses to believe that Lady Fleming had been obliged to 'desert' him

him.' I had clasped my hands in despair, and I think that I must have sounded like Hecuba when she is told that her husband and her sons have been killed. 'You killed him. That is what you have always wanted to do, you killed him at last.'

Theophyloyannakos spoke again in another voice, soft, soothing, almost apologetic. 'Well, yes,' he said, 'that is the way it happens; when a prisoner tries to escape the guard shoots.'

I cannot remember what happened next. I think that questions were falling upon me from all sides. My recollection is only of despair that the martyred young man was dead, and of a buzz like flies buzzing near my ears, disturbing me in my distress. I don't even remember Theophyloyannakos telling me that it was not true, that Panagoulis had not been killed, that no one had been wounded. But he must have told me that, because my next recollection is that I knew it, that I had recovered and now I could think, hear and speak.

The first thing I said was that I wanted to take all responsibility for whatever Skelton had done, because I had asked him to do it. I said I had asked him to hire a car and to be with Androusopoulos at a certain place to meet two men, but that I never mentioned Panagoulis's name to him.

My mouth was dry. I asked for a glass of water. Theophyloyannakos said no. I replied that I could not speak without water. Water was brought.

I asked what were the circumstances of the arrest, and whether Panagoulis had come out of the camp; he said no, he had not. They arrested them because the ESA knew everything, they had always known everything, and ordered two soldiers to climb over the camp fence, pretending to be Panagoulis and the guard. Kostas and Skelton ran to meet them, and so they were arrested. Things had not happened in this way at all, but I could not know that at the time. Corporal Staikos had indicated the place where Kostas and Skelton would be waiting, and as soon as they arrived three carloads of armed men from ESA surrounded their car and arrested them.

Theophyloyannakos added that this was why I had waited in vain by the church to take Panagoulis away and hide him; he told me they knew what I had been doing all day, even the fact that we had all had dinner together at a taverna that night. By then I was sure that he was lying. Skelton had obviously mentioned the dinner at the taverna and that must be how he knew it, but I knew I had not been waiting near the church to take away Panagoulis, so I told him it was not true. He said it was, that they knew everything, they were close beside us everywhere, even at the taverna. They had overheard all our conversation, and they even knew what we had for dinner. I asked what. 'Shish kebab,' he replied, which is probably what one out of three people would eat at any taverna.

I said, 'Well, we did not.' He did not seem to mind that, he went on repeating that they knew what I had done and where I had been the whole day, but that they wanted me to write it down myself, to describe every single minute of my day, not for their own benefit, because they knew all that, but because that was the way they liked things done and I had to do it. It was an order.

Another man gave me a bundle of sheets of paper and a pen. Theophyloyannakos told me that the man's name was Petros and that I would meet him again. There was nothing very striking about this man which I could put into words. He was probably fortyish and I thought at the time that he could have been selling haberdashery or something of that kind. Another man attracted my attention. He was about the same age as Petros, though he looked more distinguished, and even handsome, except for a terribly cold and cruel expression in his blue eyes.

I pushed the paper away and said that I was not going to write anything. Petros did not look like a salesman any longer. He bent over me and shook his finger like a maniac. 'This proves you are a communist!' Bewildered, I asked why. He explained that communists knew how to do things like that, communists refused to write anything down because that is what they were taught in the schools of Moscow. It seemed a good piece of advice. If that was what the schools in Moscow were teaching, I had done very well to refuse to write, and I was not going to write. Communists know much better than I did how one ought to behave in such circumstances. Besides, I had very good reasons for not writing. I knew what I had done and where I had been all day and all night, and it was perfectly obvious that Theophyloyannakos had not the slightest idea.

Petros spoke again: 'How often do you change the number plates on your car?' What was he talking about now? I had not changed the number plates of my car since years ago when I had altered the English registration number to a Greek one. Theophyloyannakos joined in, and the pair of them shouted the same question antiphonally. Petros was on my right and Theophyloyannakos on my left, but the shouts seemed to come from every direction.

'There will be a beautiful story tomorrow in the papers about your car and the village in Euboea.' I asked which village, and what were they talking about, but they went on and on without explaining. Suddenly I remembered, and I said, 'Oh, the number plates of the car?' Petros answered with vicious grimaces, mocking my voice, 'Yes, yes, yes, the number plates of the car.'

I had just recalled that the rear lights had not been working one evening, and I had got a police summons. I was made to hand over the number plates to the police for three days so that I should not have the use of the car for that time. 'Police Division No. 3,' I said. Theophyloyannakos stretched out his arm dramatically. 'Check,' he said. Two subordinates ran out and soon came back. They nodded yes, it was right. Yes, I had told the truth.

Later I remembered the village in Euboea and ventured to ask him what all that was about, but he did not tell me. He kept asking me where I was going to take Panagoulis if the others brought him to me when I was waiting by the church of Hagia Trias, so I asked why they had not arrested me there, and at half past two, when they had apparently arrested the others, instead of arresting me at almost six o'clock in the morning in my own parking place at Kolonaki? He asked me where I had been, so I told him. I said I had not taken an active part or accompanied the two boys, as he very well knew, but I was involved in the plan, I would certainly have helped if I could, and I had asked Skelton, who knew nothing about Panagoulis, to drive the car, so that naturally I must take complete responsibility for him.

Theophyloyannakos was listening attentively. Then he said, 'Do you know what we do to our enemies? We circumspectly fill up a bag full of filth, and then we drop it on them when we think the time is right to do so. You wait and see what will be in the papers about you.'

I felt as if my heart was shivering with apprehension. Calumny is terrible, and I could rely on their filthy imaginations. It is an easier matter if one is not restricted by any basis in reality. They could write what they wished; I would not be allowed to disprove it.

I drank some more water, and with a firm voice and a superior air I said, 'Mr Theophyloyannakos, my life is crystal clear. I advise you to be careful lest your bag of filth turns and covers you. This is what

Tsoukalas* tried to do to Sartzetakis, and the supreme judges of the French high courts reduced him to dust.'

A thoughtful expression appeared again in his eyes. I think he did not know much about the French answer to Tsoukalas, but he took my advice, and there was no filth about me in the papers.

Actually there was nothing at all about our arrest on Tuesday September 1st in either the morning or the afternoon papers. I couldn't have read it anyway, since it was thirty-two days before I was allowed even to see a newspaper.

The last thing I remember in this room was being told to stand up against the wall. Flashes went on and off while someone photographed me. He must have been an expert in his field, since I have never seen anything so terrible; when thirty-two days later I saw the photograph in the paper, it was the face of a criminal, which seemed to have been photographed after the head had been severed from the body.

Then comes a blank in my memory. Was I still in the same room, or had I been transferred to another building? Perhaps it was the same and looked different because it was now broad daylight, and Theophyloyannakos with his supporting cast had disappeared. I cannot remember being taken to another place, but perhaps I was. Before, I had been seated in the middle of a room with all those people around me, but now I could see the room I was in; there was a desk with one chair behind it and a wooden bench with a back, which looked most inviting, as I was very tired. But the dozen or so young conscripts, most of them in civilian clothes, in whose care I had been left, did not allow me to rest. I was told to sit on the chair at the desk. I was feeling very sick.

I always want to vomit when I am upset, but I also get diarrhoea; both conditions put me in desperate need. I asked the young boys to let me go to the lavatory, which could not be very far, one could smell it from the entrance of the building. They refused. I said I wanted to vomit, and they laughed. A uniformed N.C.O. came in. I told him that I wanted to vomit and would he let me go to the lavatory. He walked out and came back with a bucket. 'You can vomit in here,' he said, and they all laughed. I would have vomited in spite of their presence, but there was the diarrhoea as well. So I folded my arms on the desk, put my head on them, and tried to control my needs. Then some soldiers took hold of one side of the desk and some the other, and they started

* Minister of Justice.

to rock it, while one or two more of them pulled open the drawers and banged them repeatedly on my stomach. I don't know how long this game lasted. To me it seemed an eternity. At last they all got tired, it did not amuse them as much as they had hoped because I did not complain; I did not even speak. All my will was concentrated on my stomach. They left, and only one young man remained in the room. He stretched comfortably on the wooden bench and asked if my name was really Fleming. I said, 'Yes, let me go to the lavatory.'

'Did you live in England?'

I said, 'Yes, but let me go to the lavatory.'

'Where in England?'

'London, let me go to the lavatory. I must vomit,' I said.

'Where in London?'

'Do you know London?'

'Don't ask questions,' said my new master.

'Take me to the lavatory,' I begged.

'Where in London?'

'Chelsea,' I said. 'Were you in England?'

'Yes.'

'Take me to the lavatory.'

'No.'

I could not get angry with the young boy. I felt sorry for him for what he was made to do, and also I was much too physically distressed to have any strong feeling about anything else but vomiting. 'Where were you in England? Did you study there?'

'Yes,' he said, 'but don't ask questions.'

'All right,' I said, 'I shall not ask, but please let me go to the lavatory.'

'I was studying in Newcastle,' he said suddenly. He got up, peeped out of the door, and said, 'Come.'

The lavatory was almost directly across the corridor, at the head of the 'T' formed by the two corridors. It was divided in two. One was the actual lavatory, in principle a hole in the floor, and this had a door one could lock; the other part had a dirty basin with running water. Both places were unbelievably filthy. I locked the door of the lavatory and was immediately violently sick. The Newcastle boy started banging on the door, calling me to open it. I could not, since diarrhoea alternated with vomiting. He kept banging and shouting that if I did not open he would break down the door. Perhaps he was worried that I might faint or be ill or something while he was responsible for me.

I came out, washed my face and drank some of the tap water. The sight of the dirty basin made me feel sick again. I was taken back to the office. My watch had stopped. I did not know the time. Another young soldier, also in civilian clothes, was guarding me now. I asked the time. He said it was none of my business.

I was called into the office opposite the one where I was sitting. Theophyloyannakos was there, seated at the desk. He invited me to sit in the chair opposite him. Thirst was tormenting me, and my mouth was dry. I thought that it was dangerous to show weakness, that if he knew how much I needed water he would see an easy way to torture me. But I knew that without water I would not be able to speak. My mouth was getting drier and drier, and he might think that I was afraid of him. I said, 'May I please have some water?'

He considered it for a moment, looking thoughtfully at me. I think that he realized what a good weapon he had against me, but that it was too early to use it. So he said, 'Yes, of course,' and water was brought.

The interrogation started. I had not written anything. Why? This meant that I had things to hide.

Well, didn't they say that they knew all I had done on that Monday?

They knew, but they wanted me to write it myself. This was how they liked things done, and I would be forced to do it just like everybody else. He told me I was responsible for all the people who had been arrested the previous night. I was the main culprit, but he would not keep me in prison because he knew of a much better way to punish me. He had his information, he knew what kind of a person I was and what it was that could hurt me most. He would send me home—not immediately, though. He would keep me a couple of days until I had told him a few things he wanted me to tell him, then I could go home. I would be free, he said, and the others would be in prison, and every half hour he would send their mothers to me to tell me it was because of me their sons were being tortured and imprisoned. Every half hour, he repeated. And he would send the small children of the woman, because I was responsible for her arrest as well.

What woman, I thought. What was he talking about? I drank a little water again, and I asked 'What woman?' He did not tell me, but went on shouting ferociously about her little children who were going to come crying to me, blaming me for being deprived of their mother, and Androusopoulos's mother would come ... I was extremely tired, as it must have been over thirty hours since I had got up on Monday morning.

Suddenly I heard myself shouting hysterically. 'You have got me wrong. I don't care about the others. I care only about myself. I don't mind what happens to the others. I don't care if they are tortured.'

He was taken aback. He stopped me. 'Why are you speaking ill of yourself? I know all about you. You cannot deceive me. Evi Touloupas has told me what you are.' Evi, dear Evi, you did not know what suffering you were to inflict upon me by saying nice things about me!

It was evening by now. Theophyloyannakos called two soldiers and told them to put me in a cell, to give me a little table, a chair, paper and a pen, and to see that I wrote. 'Everything,' he thundered at me. 'Everything you did at every single minute from Monday morning until you were arrested.' And he left.

The cell I was taken to, where I was to remain for the thirty-one days until October 1st, was about five feet wide and seven long. It had a cement floor. The walls were dirty and damp and literally covered with the corpses of mosquitoes. The ceiling was high, and high in the wall there was a window. It had iron bars on the outside, a metal mesh inside that, and a glass window innermost, which was closed. Originally it must have been a normal window, but most of it had been blocked with large stones. The cell smelled horribly of lavatory and mould. It was hot and stuffy. A strong electric bulb added heat. But for the little table, the chair, the paper and pen there was nothing. The soldiers closed the door. It was a wooden door with a vertical observation slit about one inch wide and six inches high, for the guards outside to watch the prisoner. A thick iron bar was put across the door outside and locked in place by a big metal padlock. In my flat the entire front wall is open glass; it is a french window giving on to a terrace full of plants and flowers. I keep this french window open almost the whole year round, except for some very cold days, and even then it is partly open, because I cannot live without fresh air and coolness. What is more, I suffer from claustrophobia. When the cell door closed I felt as if I was suffocating.

I sat in front of the table with my elbows on it and my head in my hands, and a thousand thoughts struggled for priority. Why did we fail? What had really happened? They were not following us, at least, not me; so much was obvious from what they had said. They knew nothing of what I had done that day or where I was. Perhaps the corporal was a trap, prepared because they had found Panagoulis's bars cut after Zambelis's escape. How was Panagoulis now? Was he being beaten? Was Kostas being tortured? Skelton, I trusted, would not be, he was American. But Kostas?

How happy I would have been if they had succeeded. This time Panagoulis would not have been re-arrested. Kostas and Skelton were to take him somewhere, and without their knowing it, another person was to move him on immediately so that neither Skelton nor Kostas should know where he was. Kostas was Panagoulis's friend, he was visited by Panagoulis's mother; even if the escape had succeeded, he could still have been taken in the day after for interrogation. Kostas ought not to know and did not want to know. I was the only one who did know. And now, suffocating in this dirty cell, thinking of Panagoulis ill treated again, perhaps lying handcuffed on the bare cement floor, which was the punishment he often suffered, I saw in my mind the beautiful villa where he might now have been hiding. The soft bed with clean linen sheets, the french window on to the large veranda that overlooked the sea. After all these years in a tomb, he would have had the immensity of the sea to look at, and fresh sea air to fill his lungs. I knew that soup was being kept hot for him, and there were prawns and fillet steak and fruit of all sorts and champagne to celebrate his name day and his freedom. After so much unkindness, solitude and suffering, he was to feel again the warmth and care of a nice family.

Then I remembered that it was the one Tuesday in every fortnight when my daily did not come. Since I was not taking any active part in the escape I had not made any arrangements for the cats to be fed. I had no reason to believe that I would not be at home. Had the military police announced my arrest? Usually they did not; perhaps no one knew.

The sound of the key turning in the padlock and the bar being moved made me jump—Theophyloyannakos. Interrogation again! Then I realized that for every evil there is a worse one: the closed door, well secured by the iron bar and the big padlock, which would be hell for anyone suffering from claustrophobia, was now a blessing; it represented protection from the interrogation, which I found that I dreaded more.

The door opened and two young conscripts walked in. They looked at the paper which I had not touched. 'You have not written,' said one. I said that I was not going to write (instructions from Moscow!). He shrugged his shoulders. They opened both panels of the door and pushed in an iron bed. It had once been painted white, but the colours had gone, leaving black patches everywhere, which made it look very dirty. There was a mattress on it covered with a dark grey blanket. I was allowed to go to the lavatory, and to wash my face over the dirty basin, and rinse my mouth, which was dry and bitter. I also drank some water in the palm of my hand. Then I ventured to ask for some water for the night, and the guard gave me two plastic cups which I filled with water.

I was taken back to the cell. Before locking me in, one of the soldiers pointed to the switch inside the cell and told me to leave the light on.

Together with the bed they had brought my white linen summer coat which had been left in the car. It must have been past midnight; I had not lain down for about forty hours, I had not eaten anything for over twenty-four hours, but I felt no hunger. I laid the coat, well spread out, on the bed, and threw myself on it, face down. The thought of the suffering of others was useless now. I could no longer hope to help them. 'Now I can think of myself,' and I was asleep. In the morning the guard told me I had never moved all night.

It was the only night they let us sleep, the only night they did not bang on the door or the padlock. My bare arms and legs were all mosquito bites, but I had not felt anything. The summer dress I had slept in, as I had nothing else to wear, was drenched in sweat. It was very hot, and the big electric bulb which burned all night did not make the room any cooler.

I knocked on my door and asked to go to the lavatory. Once again I was able to wash my hands and face, though nothing more, because, for a reason which I never understood, I was not allowed to close the door of the place where the basin with the running water was. It had to be kept open and a guard was usually standing by. I felt that the filth of the cell had spread over me and entered inside me. I asked the guard would he please open the window. He said no, only on the commanding officer's orders, which meant Theophyloyannakos.

In spite of the closed windows, the number of mosquitoes in the cell was something unbelievable. One would think that EAT ESA were especially breeding them as assistant torturers. The mosquitoes seemed

to know that they had been given extra powers, surely on the orders
of the commanding officer. A mosquito started eating me up, and when
I pushed it away it settled again an inch further on, and went on with
its breakfast. I looked at it and thought I could see it looking back at me
with an air of superior contempt. 'Hey you,' it seemed to say. 'Don't
you know that I am an EAT ESA mosquito?' The mosquitoes had also
acquired the cunning of the military police: they attacked one without
warning, they did not buzz.

Through the slit in the door I was asked if I wanted tea. I had seen
some cups of tea on the bench outside my cell, but I thought that by
now the tea must have absorbed the smell of the lavatory, so I said,
'No, thank you.' I was not hungry, and when I had gone to the
lavatory I had filled my cups with water again; it was all I needed.

By now it was Wednesday morning, my second day in this terrible
place, although to me the time had seemed much longer. My anguish
for Kostas was very great, and I was very worried about any discomfort Skelton was suffering, since I felt responsible for him. And I
worried even more about the others, because there were others, but
thank the Lord I was the only one to know them.

Theophyloyannakos's shouting was something horrible; he created
the effect of huge waves breaking inside my head and body. The day
before, with his shouts and his threats to torture others and to send their
mothers and children to blame me for their sufferings, he had managed
to bring me to the edge of breakdown. Now that I had had a little rest
I felt ashamed of myself for having allowed him to see that he could
make me suffer. And anyway, who was this woman whose children
would come to me to cry for their mother and blame me for her arrest?
Another bluff?

I had already started learning something from my experiences. For
example, their bluffs in the style of 'We know everything, we have
been following you everywhere.' I realized how right I had been in
telling friends the police knew very little, and that most of what they
did know we were telling them ourselves because we believed they
already knew it.

Theophyloyannakos had said he would send me home in a couple of
days, but only after I had told him a few things. So that was it; his
howling and his threats had but one aim, to break my resistance. He
did not want to torture me physically because it might cause too much
of a stir, but he had other ways of persecuting me which would show

no scars. At this moment I understood one of his main characteristics: the man was acting. Throughout all this angry howling and threatening, Theophyloyannakos was an actor playing a part.

The door opened, and a soldier ordered me to follow him. I was taken to the front office where I had suffered the rocking of the desk. Theophyloyannakos was waiting there. He said they had changed their minds, they were not going to release me. I had a mixed feeling of apprehension about myself and of relief that I was going to share the fate of the others. He told me to make a list of the few things I would need, and to give them the telephone number of someone who could be called to bring them to me. I was reluctant to bring him into contact with any of my friends. But I said thank you, I would do it. He was not shouting yet, and I soon realized that this was the routine; he seemed to need a little time to work himself up. He started by telling me something that I was to hear almost every second day, that he was an honest officer and a patriot.

I said that I had no objection to believing him. But would he agree that the enemies of his party could also be as honest and as patriotic as he was? He considered this for a while, and reluctantly said yes.

In that case, would he also agree that we should behave like honest and civilized opponents? If so, we could talk. 'But', I said, 'if it is to be like yesterday, we cannot talk.'

He accepted it, and the interrogation started. I asked for water, and it was brought. Soon we came back to the same old questions: why I had refused to write down where I had been and what I had done on Monday. Where had I met Androusopoulos? I had met him years ago at Kastri, at the house of the prime minister, George Papandreou. 'He says the same thing,' said Theophyloyannakos, 'which proves that you have prearranged your answers.'

I said it could also prove that it was true. Why did I want to free Panagoulis? I said because he was being tortured and because they had deprived us of all legal means of dealing with the matter. My answer had him shouting again. The questions fell upon me like hailstones. Who else was involved? Who had given my car to Androusopoulos on the night of August 25th? I said, 'I don't believe that he took my car.' He described to me how it had been done, that a man in a red pullover had taken the car out of the parking lot and had given Kostas and the corporal the car and the keys. I did not answer. Somebody had obviously talked. I was thinking of my friend who had given them the keys of the car. Would I be able to protect him? No one but me knew his name. How are people made to betray their friends?

'Everyone talks in this place,' he went on. 'They are demoralized from the moment they pass the gate. Don't hope to be an exception. You will have to speak.' Who had put us up to this? Andreas Papandreou? What was the name of the organization? Who were the other members? I was silent. Who was Skelton and who was behind Skelton? I repeated that Skelton was innocent, that he knew nothing, that I had asked him to drive a car and that was all, that I wanted to take complete responsibility for him. I said there was nobody else, just Androusopoulos, who was Panagoulis's friend, and me, who was sorry for him. The shouts went on and on. I was thinking of the man in the red pullover. What methods were they planning to use on me?

It must have been midday when he stopped. He called the guard and told him to take me to my cell. On the way to the cell the guard started trying to persuade me. 'Don't go against his will. You will not manage. Strong men have to speak at the end. Why suffer unnecessarily?' And he asked me for the list of things I needed, and the telephone number. I was not willing to give it, and I said I would try to remember. I did not want them to worry the young woman who helped clean the house. I did not know that they had interrogated her already and had taken her to open my apartment and that they had made a search. They had taken music tapes, papers, my address books, and both my Greek and British passports, and had made the young woman sign a statement that they hadn't taken anything.

There was more interrogation in the afternoon, and more in the evening. If I did not speak they would torture people in my presence. They knew everything and everybody involved, they just wanted to test my willingness to help them. I said that I was not going to help them. I believe and hope I seemed cool and composed, but in fact I was terrified in case they might really know the others and be going to arrest them.

During the night we were not allowed to sleep. The young soldiers would throw themselves against the door, or just bang on it, or shake the padlock and the bar. I did not mind. I could not sleep anyway, I was too worried, too hot with the closed window and the big bulb shining and the mosquitoes making such a good meal of me. By Thursday I had been there three and a half days. I had eaten nothing for fifty-eight hours, but I was still not at all hungry. Theophyloyannakos's shouts and threats and my own anguish about the people he might get hold of made me feel continually sick.

At about ten o'clock, Theophyloyannakos called for me again, and this time he had an offer to make. 'We have discussed with the prime minister how you can do the least harm to your country, and he has decided that you will do less harm by going away. So give us a list of a few things you want put in a suitcase, and we shall take you to the airport. You will probably write an article or two, you will probably speak a little, and afterwards you will join the tramps, Helen Vlachos and the others.' I asked him if by this he meant that I should relinquish my Greek nationality, and he said yes, of course.

I sat back more comfortably in my chair. I felt strong now. I said, 'Voluntarily, never.' He was astonished. He described to me all the ordeals I was to suffer at EAT ESA, the days and weeks of interrogation, of which I had as yet no idea, and after that a long sentence which would leave me to rot in prison. 'I strongly advise you to accept this offer now, when it is being made to you. Believe me, you will be spared much suffering.'

I said, 'It seems that the price of being a Greek is high, but I accept it and I will pay it.'

He said, 'You will bitterly regret this.'

I thought he was right, and I told him so. I said, 'I know I may regret it. I know that when you do all the things to me you have just promised to do I shall think that if I had had more sense, I could have been sitting in a theatre in London enjoying a marvellous play, and I love the theatre. But I am not leaving Greece. You are a sadist,' I added, 'and you are inhuman. But you are a Greek, and I am a Greek, we will fight it out between us. I promise not to ask the protection of the British Embassy. Anyway, you know that if one has two nationalities, inside Greece only the Greek nationality is valid. You have a Greek in your hands, treat me as you like.' Eventually I was sent back to my cell.

14. *In the Interrogation Centre I*

I thought that I could not possibly go on forever sleeping like a dirty animal, in my only dress. I also thought that by now my friends would be frantic at not knowing where I was. So I wrote a note asking for a few things and strongly underlined '*books and Katol*', a mosquito repellent. And so from the fifth day my life became in some ways more comfortable. I had sheets and a pillow, a toothbrush and a night-dress. I could change my dress. Food also came from home, but I could not touch it or even look at it. The most important things were the Katol, which drove the EAT ESA mosquitoes out of my cell, and the books. I had something to take my mind away from my sad thoughts during the long sleepless nights.

I think that it was on the fifth or sixth day of my detention that I received Theophyloyannakos's first offer of a position as a Cabinet Minister. He was in a good mood, and pleased with himself. Had the doctor he sent come to see me? He had received a report from my own physician that I was a diabetic and also suffered from a number of other disorders, and that it was dangerous for me to be deprived of my drugs. I replied that the doctor had come, and that he was very nice, and he had given me my drugs, thank you.

Theophyloyannakos was definitely pleased. There were times when I thought there might be something human in him. At these moments I felt tolerant and sorry for him, because of the brainwashing he had perhaps himself undergone to become what he was. At such moments I felt I could talk to him.

'How is Kostas?' I asked. 'Please let me see him.' I was worried about Kostas. Somebody had talked, somebody had spoken about my car and the man in the red pullover. It must have been Kostas, and Kostas would not have spoken without strong persuasion.

Theophyloyannakos was affable. 'You are fond of Kostas,' he said. Yes I was, how was he? 'He is all right,' he replied. And then he said that I cared about people, that he knew I did care sincerely, but I had chosen the wrong ones. He knew all about me, and he was still studying me and gathering information, and everything he had heard was good. But I was naive, and people were exploiting my kindness.

'Come on to our side,' he said. 'Come and help us. We are honest officers trying to do our best for the country and the people. Why don't you help us? For five years you have done nothing but fight us. Stop it, join us, help us to do things the way you like them to be done. I shall take you to the prime minister, you will tell him what you have against us, what you think is wrong. You care about the people's welfare, don't you? Well here is a way to satisfy your inclinations. Join the government. Take the Ministry of Welfare.'

For a moment I was speechless. Then I said, 'No, thank you. I shall never join you. You may not know it, but you are ruining the country.' And then, seeing that the storm was soon to fall upon me again, I added quickly, 'Will you give me something which is much more important to me than a ministry?'

'What?' he asked.

'Will you allow your soldiers to open the window of my cell?' The order was given.

When we walked out of the office, before handing me over to the guard to take me to my cell, he said, 'You are our friend, you will join us.' I replied loudly and clearly so that the soldiers would hear me well, 'I am not your friend, and I shall never be your friend.' The major had said similarly misleading things before. A friend of mine had been arrested, ill treated and eventually released. A few days after his release, Theophyloyannakos summoned him to his office at EAT ESA and warned him not to dare to indulge in the slightest anti-regime comment or activity, threatening to re-arrest him and send him to 'rot in prison', one of his favourite expressions. When my friend was allowed to leave, Theophyloyannakos accompanied him into the corridor where soldiers were standing about and two women were waiting for permission to see their imprisoned husbands. Theophyloyannakos, all smiles, patted my friend on the back and said in a loud voice, so that everyone present could hear him, 'Well, dear Mr X, it was so nice of you to come. Come and see us whenever you want to tell us something.'

So whenever the building was not shaken, as it usually was, by his shouts, when for instance he was offering me ministries, he would always try to give the impression as we emerged from his office that he had broken down my resistance. He repeated with monotonous predictability that I was or I would be their friend. And equally monotonously I would answer that I was not and never would be.

The doctor was a very nice young man. He was a laryngologist, and he felt rather embarrassed to be treating a diabetic at all, since the disease was not in his field, and a diabetic who was herself a doctor was worse still. He asked me what drugs I had been taking, and he gave me the ones I mentioned. So I ventured to tell him that I was also taking Valium (a tranquillizer), and could he give me some Valium? Of course, what strength? I said 5 mg in the morning and 5 mg in the evening, and he gave them to me. The truth was I had never used a tranquillizer in my life before, but I certainly needed it then. I added that I was also taking four Bellergal (another calming drug) every day, and he prescribed the Bellergal as well. I shall always be grateful to that nice military doctor.

My cell window was opened. Some fresh air came in, but bringing with it more of the foul smell from the lavatory, which was close by.

After half past two in the afternoon there was usually no interrogation. The masters of the inquisition were having a rest. I would also try to get some sleep to make up for the sleepless nights. Also in the evening after ten interrogation was not to be expected, so I could sleep until almost midnight, when the battering of the door and the shaking of the bar and the lock would usually start. Sometimes there would be no banging on my own door, but there certainly would be on the cell just to the left of mine. Later I learned that this was Kostas's cell.

Still, it was not always easy to have this afternoon nap. The young soldiers seemed to choose these afternoon hours to play what I thought was a game of football or something of the sort. It started like a wild charge of cannibals all shouting at once. There were also screams and moans, and I thought that it was rough playing. There were bangs on my wall which I thought might be caused by kicking. The shouts and screams seemed to come in through my window, which looked out from the back of our small building. I wondered whether there was a football field there for the soldiers, although from what I could guess of the geography of the place, there was no room for one. After the window of my cell had been opened the shouts and screams were louder and clearer.

In the middle of one night my door was opened with bangs and shouts and three soldiers barged in. One was in uniform. They stood threateningly there without speaking. I did not speak either, I just looked at them quietly. After a while they walked out, replaced the bar and locked it. Their sudden appearance was a chilling reminder of the statements of people who had been tortured. Day and night, soldiers walked into their cells and punched and kicked them and banged their heads on the wall or the cement floor. They had not dared hit me, they wanted only to frighten me. I tried to sleep again, but a horrible suspicion had gripped my heart. The shouts, the screams, the moans — were they just a rough game of football? The next day when it happened again, I concentrated all my anxious attention on listening to these sounds, and then clearly and unmistakably I recognized Kostas's voice in the screams and the moans. His voice has a very special timbre; when he spoke to me on the telephone he never needed to tell me his name, I always recognized his voice. How was it that I had not done so all these days?

I don't know how many times I heard him scream or for how long it lasted. Now if I heard the soldiers even talk loud I froze with horror, took Valium and blocked my ears. What was the need to suffer since I could not help?

The first time I saw Theophyloyannakos after I had recognized Kostas's screams, I pleaded, 'Please don't torture Kostas.' He said that they had never so much as touched anybody in the place. Major Theophyloyannakos is the greatest liar I have ever met, and it does not bother him at all to be found out. He said quite blithely that they never touched anyone, even though he had threatened so many times either to torture me personally or to torture others in my presence. I asked him again to let me see Kostas, and he laughed a cunning laugh; he told me to be patient and I would see him.

With this new terror in my heart, the strong light all the night, and the interrogation at all hours and on almost the same pattern, I had lost my sense of time. I no longer knew the date or the day of the week. I think it was on the seventh day that I heard rushed steps, the door was opened with great clangs, and a furious Theophyloyannakos came in. He said that he had just been told that the food which was brought from home was being sent back untouched, and that I had also been refusing any other food. He was thundering. If I did not eat he would forcefeed me with a tube himself. Not the doctor, he insisted, himself. I tried to persuade him that I was not on a hunger strike, that I simply could not eat because the sight of food brought on nausea. Also, it was better for me not to eat, it was a magnificent cure for my diabetes. He shouted and roared, then he went away, and the nice young doctor came in and begged me to eat. I said I could not. Food was brought, I think from a restaurant nearby and left on the table. It was meat and salad, just right for a diabetic. The doctor must have got it. I asked the guard to take it away. He said, 'Commanding officer's orders, it has to be left there until you eat it!' I felt three years old. I buried my head in the pillow in order not to see or smell the food.

Some time later, after a bad moment, I told Theophyloyannakos that one day I was going to write the story of my stay in EAT ESA, and that the more he did to me the better, because I would have more to say. He said, 'Your interrogation? Flowers!' I agreed, I said that I had even thought of a title: 'V.I.P. Treatment in EAT ESA.' They certainly seemed to care about my being kept well and fit. They did not hit me. I did not dare say that I could hear Kostas's screams, and that this for me was perhaps a worse agony. I was afraid to speak about it at all. They might take him somewhere further away and hit him more.

I think it was probably about the eighth day that Skelton was released. This was denied, but Skelton was in the cell next to mine on my right, and I heard him very clearly saying goodbye, and through the slit in my door I saw him leaving with a bundle of his things in his hand. He was brought back one or two days before the trial. The American masters of our Colonels must have ordered his release. It was a happy day for me; one less worry on my mind.

The doctor came almost every day. He took a sample of blood, and of course after seven days of a diet of water, my blood sugar level had fallen, although not to normal. But I had ketones, which is the worst of the symptoms of diabetes.

Immediately Theophyloyannakos told the government spokesman to issue a communiqué that I was not suffering from diabetes and that I was perfectly well.

Actually this was nothing compared with the official communiqué of the same government spokesman, two days after my arrest. It stated that I had been arrested with the others in my car, driving it outside the KESA camp and waiting to take Panagoulis away; in fact, of course, I was arrested in my own parking place about three miles from where they said I was. But of all these communiqués I knew nothing as I was not allowed to see the newspapers.

The day Skelton left was a doubly happy day for me. I had persuaded the doctor that I would get an infection if I did not wash, and so on the eighth day I had my first shower. After, of course, obtaining permission from the commanding officer, the doctor told the guards that I should be taken to the showers every morning. This meant not only the unbelievable luxury of washing, which made me feel human again, but also a walk for a few yards in the open, where I could breathe fresh air and see the real light of the sun. I remember how I blinked on the first day.

The route from my cell to the showers went out of the front of my building, behind some barracks and the office building where Papaphilippou had questioned me, and then turned towards the front of the camp and the wide lawns along Vassilissis Sophias Avenue. The shower building was at right-angles to the lawn, and when I was a few yards away from the entrance, I saw my little car. She had been forced to follow me into captivity, and there she was, standing desperately lonely under the bright sun. I knew that when I was arrested there had been nineteen tins of cat food in the car. It amused me to think that the military police had probably believed that they were some sort of explosive device. At the same time I could look out across Vassilissis Sophias Avenue, full of cars going up and down, full of people who were not imprisoned in EAT ESA, unattainable.

Aside from the big masters, there were the lesser ones as well, the military guards. My drugs had to be locked in a cupboard in the corridor and the guard had the key. Most days the same young man was on guard, and although not particularly nasty—he was not yet, as I learned, in the beating squad—he could not resist flaunting his power over me. Every single morning we had to play the same wearisome game. 'Why two pills of this?' he would ask. 'You should take one.' He did not know how many I had to take, but then he had the keys. He could give me the tablets or not give them. He knew he was annoying me, and he enjoyed it. Nothing that.the doctor told him when I complained would change things. Or he would examine the Valium and say, 'This is a tranquillizer, is it?' And I would say, 'Yes, it is.' And I would read in his eyes the thought, 'We are trying to break your nerve here and we give you tranquillizers?'

The same kind of thing happened over my shower. I would start begging them from almost seven o'clock in the morning to escort me to the shower. The begging usually lasted till ten. By then the water was cold, so they would say that the water was cold and I could not have a shower. And I would retort that I did not mind, I would rather have it cold than not wash at all. And they would say they would have to ask the doctor if he allowed me to have a cold shower. And if the doctor was not to be found, I had no shower.

There was a small test which made it easy to distinguish between the nice young soldiers and the ones that had already become sadists. When I knocked at my door asking to go to the lavatory, some of the guards would shout, 'Wait', and I could see them through the slit in my door sitting quietly and reading a newspaper while diarrhoea was tearing at my insides. There was one who was very nice. He never spoke to me; being kind, he was more afraid than the others. Whenever he took me to my cell after a stormy interrogation, he would urge me, just as the others did, not to go against the will of the commanding officer, saying I would have to talk in the end, no one had succeeded in holding out against him, so why suffer unnecessarily? He spoke according to his orders, like the others, but when I asked him for a match for the Katol, he gave me three.

One morning Theophyloyannakos seemed particularly happy. He asked me whom I had rung up on the Monday morning the day before my arrest. I said no doubt many people. He asked me if I knew N., and I admitted it. He told me that N. had taken Zambelis, the man who had escaped from Aegina Prison, on the car ferry to the island of Zakynthos. He gave me all sorts of details. He also told me that I had taken part in this as well, that I had moved Zambelis from one house to another in Athens. He asked me if I had gone with N., a girl called S., Zambelis and others to Zakynthos, or if I had met the Italian countess who had taken Zambelis out of the country in her yacht. I said no, I had never been to Zakynthos in my life, and I knew neither the Italian countess nor a girl called S. And he said, 'All right. It was a trap that I laid for you. I know that you did not go with them. N. and the girl told me everything and confessed everything like nice, brave people. And they also admitted that I knew everything myself. So why not confirm their confessions?'

I said I knew nothing about all this curious rigmarole, and if other people said that they had done it, why ask me about it? He said it was for my benefit, so that I could help the interrogation just for once. People who helped the interrogation had a better deal. He said he had my friend N. and the girl S. there, would I like to see them? Stupidly I said I would not. It was a bluff. Neither N. nor S. had been arrested. He also asked me if N. had ever met Kostas. I said yes, I had put them in touch with one another when I had asked N. to help find a job as a typist for Kostas's sister, which N. had in fact done. 'Yes, I know,' he said, 'and I know she works for the Lambrakis newspapers.' These are *Vima* and *Nea*, the two liberal newspapers. Then he changed his tone, and asked, with an air of candid curiosity, 'Has Lambrakis anything against you?'

'Why?' I asked.

'Because', he said, 'there was not one line about you in his newspapers, not one! Have you ever quarrelled with him?'

I said I had not, and asked if there had really been no mention of my arrest at all. He said, 'Nothing.' He was jubilant. 'And we thought that there would have been such a fuss, with the BBC and the foreign press.' He said 'BBCs', making it plural in Greek, covering all foreign broadcasts.

I persisted, 'And there was nothing?' And I believed him! I was sent back to my cell. So no one had cared to speak up for me. I felt more lonely and more helpless, I felt tired and weak. I had hardly eaten anything yet. It must have been the eighth or ninth day, I no longer knew. I tried to have a bite of lunch, fearing that Theophyloyannakos might forcefeed me *himself*, which would have been a nice way to torture me. But I could not eat, and surreptitiously threw the food sent from home into the big dustbin which was next to the basin in the washroom. I was sorry about that; I thought that the other prisoners in there might need it.

There was a girl who wept and screamed every evening. She was in the cell next to the lavatory on the other side from mine. But I was sure that the weeping and the screaming came from anguish, not maltreatment. According to whether they were nice or not, the soldiers would either open her door and try to make her stop crying, or they would shout, 'Stop that or ... ' When Theophyloyannakos told me he had arrested the girl S. I thought that it must be her. But S. was never arrested, and I never learned who this girl was. One morning I told Theophyloyannakos about a girl who was crying and asked if he could not do something to help her. He replied that I had hallucinations. But a couple of days later the crying stopped. Had she been released or moved elsewhere?

One afternoon I was taken back to the front office for interrogation. This time there were two more men with Theophyloyannakos. One was Petros, the man who had been shouting at me about the number

plates on the night of my arrest, the one who might have been selling
haberdashery. The other one was the man with the cruel blue eyes.
He had been in and out a number of times while Theophyloyannakos
was interrogating me. His face was so hard and cruel that I had
wanted to find out who he was, and had asked for his name.
Theophyloyannakos always refused to tell me. 'You will know it in
time,' he would say. This time had come.

The two men had been given the best seats, the ones between the
wall and the desk. Theophyloyannakos sat on a chair on the other
side of the desk, on my left. He gestured first at Petros and then at the
other man, and said, 'This is Mr Petros Babalis, and this is Mr
Evangelos Mallios, of the Security Police Headquarters.' They were
Mallios and Babalis, the renowned torturers of the Asphalia of
Bouboulinas Street, the Security Headquarters, whose infamous
names I had heard so many times. Sentences from Panagoulis's letter
came back to me, and I remembered things he had shouted in the
military court. 'The principal torturers were Major Theophyloyannakos, Police Officers Mallios and Babalis,' said the letter.
It was their victim I had tried to save, and I was in their hands. In
court, when Evangelos Mallios went up to testify, Panagoulis had
shouted, 'You have no right to testify. You have tortured me, you
were the specialist in the sexual tortures.' And in the letter he had
written, 'Burns with cigarettes, on my hands and genitals. Insertion of
a long metal wire into my urethra and heating of the extended part of
the wire with a cigarette lighter.' So this was the man who had
excogitated these subtle and horrible devices. How did he do it?
Did he bend quietly and coldly, like a surgeon, over the genitals of the
young man whose body and head were already all wounds and
blood, whose feet were swollen from the beating, and who already had
broken ribs and a broken heel? How many police officers were
holding down the agonized body? Was Babalis one of them? He had
most probably done the beating which had broken the bones.

Babalis started speaking, while Mallios's steel-cold eyes were fixed
upon me. Babalis said they knew I had planted the bomb which killed
a policeman in the attempt to blow up the statue of President
Truman,* a bomb which had blown off the arm of a worker at the

---

* A bomb was found in position at the statue by a policeman; he phoned emergency
services and was told to leave it alone until the special squad had arrived. But he was
curious, he took it and unwrapped it, and was killed by it.

PX, and another which substantially damaged the building of the newspaper *Hestia*. I remained silent, still in the grip of horror at the memory of Panagoulis's tortures. 'Answer!' shouted Theophyloyannakos. I looked at him and he pointed at the other two. 'Answer them!' I looked at Babalis and told him not to talk nonsense. He repeated the same things and asked if I had done them. I told him again not to ask me idiotic questions. He shouted 'Answer!' So I said no, I had not, and moreover I had never seen explosives. He asked me why I had visited the PX. I said I had never been there. He asked if I knew what the PX was. I said yes, it was the special store for Americans. He asked why I had gone down Syngrou Avenue (the main avenue which leads to the sea) with Kostas and another slim, dark, tall man from the Ministry of Interior called Kyriazis or Kyriakides, who was working in the passport department and forging passports for me. I said I had never gone down Syngrou Avenue with Kostas and had never met or heard of the man they were describing; in fact I later discovered he did not exist. They went on and on about this; I had gone with Kostas and Kyriazis-Kyriakides for a reconnaissance of the PX to arrange the place where we were going to put the bomb. I asked where the PX is, and they told me it was on Syngrou Avenue.

Then Mallios spoke. Quietly, coldly, without raising his voice, he said that the charge I was under at EAT ESA was nothing compared to the evidence against me they had at the Security Police. When Theophyloyannakos was finished with me, they would take me there. And they had their methods of making people speak. There is the straight interrogation, he said, and the zigzag one, and he added suavely, 'In interrogations, *everything* is allowed.'

Then suddenly, without altering his expression or changing his tone of voice, unbelievable abuse poured out of his mouth. I had the peculiar impression that he was not a human creature, but a robot who had cold cutting steel eyes and a gutter for a mouth. There was nothing Greek about him, even considered as a robot, no Greek hands could have manufactured him.

Babalis spoke again. 'Who is Amy?'

I said I did not know. I wondered if it was this woman with the children they kept telling me about.

'Who is Vanghelis?' asked Babalis. I said I did not know that, either. He went on and on about these two names. Accustomed to being interrogated by Theophyloyannakos for all these days, I turned to him every time, and he would shout, pointing at the other two, 'You answer there.' Babalis said, 'On your honour, you don't know who Amy is and who Vanghelis is?' I said that he had no right to ask a person who was being interrogated to answer 'on his honour', but that just for this one question I would answer him, 'Yes, on my honour, as you put it, I don't know any Amy or any Vanghelis.' He asked by what name I called N., and I said that I called him by his name, which was N.; what did he expect me to call an old friend? Babalis suddenly became nasty. He bent over me, and 'thouing' me, which is very rude in Greece, said with a horrible grimace on his face, 'Thou art old and diabetic and thou wilt die.'

The door opened, and Kostas Androusopoulos walked in like an automaton, followed by a young soldier in tears. They stopped. Kostas looked straight at the wall that was in front of him when he entered, without turning to look at us. Babalis asked me if I knew the soldier who was crying. I looked at him and did not recognize him, so I said no. Kostas then turned around and without being asked, without looking at any one of us, speaking very slowly in a completely expressionless low voice, a voice which seemed to come from beyond this world, he said, 'Yes she does know him.'

I looked at Kostas in amazement. What had happened to him? Then I looked back at the soldier. It was Bekakos, the guard at the Boyati Military Prison who months ago had helped Panagoulis cut the bars of his cell but had not gone any further. I had seen him only three times, and then when it was dark and he was in civilian clothes. Besides, now he was grimacing, half crying, and I had not recognized him.

'You must give the name of Yannis,' said Kostas to me in the same faded voice. 'Otherwise they will sentence us for using bombs.' Yannis, the taxi driver who had taken us to Boyati on the night of the great storm, was completely innocent, but how was I to prove it. I felt my knees changing into cottonwool. They would find Yannis, I would not be able to save him. And what were these bombs? 'Kostas,' I cried, 'Kostas, you are mad.'

'Yes,' repeated Kostas, and one could see that he had to make a great effort to talk even in this slow and faded voice, 'Yes. If you don't give Yannis's name, they will sentence us for planting bombs, for having killed people, and for the explosives and the bombs which were found in the house at Hagios Sostis.'

I could not understand. What was he talking about? Above all, what had happened to him? What had they done to him? I was speechless. For over two hours now they had been questioning me about bombs, about people I did not know. They had abused and threatened to torture me. And now Kostas's condition and the things he was saying as I was looking at him bewildered me and made me feel completely lost.

At that moment Theophyloyannakos gave one of his best performances. He went over to the two young prisoners and started shouting, 'She is rich, she will get out of it, you will rot in prison. She is blaming it all on you.' Although, on the contrary, I had tried to shoulder all the responsibility I could, I did not answer. I was speechless, trying desperately to understand what had happened to Kostas. My mind seemed to have stopped working. The guards were told to take Kostas and Bekakos away. In the same automaton-like way, Kostas turned around and started for the door. Then I woke up. 'Kostas,' I shouted, and they stopped. Out of the corner of my eye I saw Mallios and Babalis ready to pounce, and Theophyloyannakos's outstretched hand stopping them, to see what I was going to say. 'Kostas,' I asked softly, 'did you plant bombs?'

'No,' said Kostas's dead voice.

'Kostas,' I asked again, 'this house in Hagios Sostis, this house with the explosives, does it exist?'

'No,' said the same voice.

'Then why do you worry about it?' I exploded. And then I knew. Kostas was under the influence of hallucinogens, under the very definite and strong influence of the drugs.

The two of them were pushed out of the door, and I turned around like a fury. Theophyloyannakos came first into my orbit, and I shouted, 'What have you done to Kostas, what have you done to drive him mad? We were supposed to talk like honest and civilized enemies, but you brought these people here,' and I pointed at Mallios and Babalis. Then with contempt and frenzied rage I shouted, 'The official state which is lying, the official state which is calumniating, the official state which is forging false evidence: that is what you are!'

I sat down, with my arms folded. 'Well, from now on I have got amnesia, and not only from now on but also for whatever I have said so far.' Theophyloyannakos paled. I had admitted that I knew of the attempt to achieve Panagoulis's escape, I had admitted to having helped it, and having wished and still wishing it success; I had taken on myself responsibility for Skelton's actions, I had said that I was the one in a position to act, that Kostas had nothing to offer but his love for his friend and his own self-sacrifice. But I had not written anything down, and Theophyloyannakos might have to start all over again.

Babalis spoke, but with less assurance than before. 'You have lied,' he said. 'You are Amy and N. is Vanghelis.'

'Grant me a little more originality, if you please. Since my name is Amalia, I think I would have chosen something more dissimilar.' It was true that I had never heard that anyone called me Amy or called N. Vanghelis.

They left the subject of bombs and explosives but continued their questions. Who was Yannis, what was his name and address? I said I would not tell them. What had N. done? I did not know that N. had done anything. 'He was waiting with Kostas outside Boyati camp to pick up Panagoulis.' They said they knew that because N. had admitted it. Why didn't I admit it as well? I said I did not know anything about it. Who was Kyriazis or Kyriakides? What did we go to Syngrou Avenue for? I did not answer.

Bekakos had made a statement that I had him photographed in a wig to make a passport for him. Where was the passport, where was the wig? Had Kyriazis made the passport? I said I had amnesia, and I had no idea that complete passports were made by one person in the passport department. I thought passports went through many hands. On and on they went, and I was either silent or repeated that I had got amnesia, until they became quite wild and suddenly I had the three of them on me. One grabbed me by one shoulder, another by the other, the third put his hand on my knee. 'Take your hands off me,' I howled, and they did.

But Theophyloyannakos put an ugly face within inches of mine. 'Be careful,' he said, 'I am under great pressure to use other methods on you. Be careful. I may use them.'

'Use them!' I said, and I felt that at that moment I was so angry that I could stand any torture.

15. A Detainee's Life

The guards were called to take me to my cell. I was distressed. Kostas
was not only being tortured but also being given drugs. What drugs?
Was it LSD? Would it harm him? He had given them Yannis's name.
They would get him, it was easy; Yannis was a driver I often used.
They would find out who he was and they would arrest him. Yannis
had nothing to do with us or with our wish to see Panagoulis free and
help him get that freedom, Yannis was just a driver; and yet how could
I convince them of that? I was exhausted by all these shouts, all these
threats, and, more than anything, by the memory of Kostas in the
condition I saw him in.

The door opened. Theophyloyannakos came in, and the door closed
behind him. I jumped up from the bed where I had been lying, my
face buried in the pillow, and put on my shoes. 'Never mind,' said
Theophyloyannakos. 'I cannot receive you in slippers,' I said. I will
not let him see that I am distressed, I thought. I will not let him
believe that he can break me.

He looked around, took the book which was on the bed and
examined it. He picked up from the little table the writing-pad I
used to write the simple notes I was allowed to give to my maid, which
usually ran: 'Bring me books, bring me Katol.' He turned the pages
to see if there was anything written. These visits of the Master who had
the right to search and touch my few belongings always enraged me.
I feel very strongly about respect for human dignity, and of course
in that place no such respect exists. I suppose that was why he did it.

He dropped the writing-pad, came opposite the bed where I was
seated, and leaned on the wall. 'You will tell me', he said calmly, 'the
name of Yannis.'

I said I would not, and that anyway Yannis knew nothing. 'You
should not waste your time trying to find him,' I said. 'Honestly, truly,
Yannis has nothing to do with this. He was just a taxi driver on a
job.'

He said, 'Then if he is innocent, why don't you give me his name?'
I said I was afraid he might be ill treated. Not if I gave his name, I was

told. I still refused to give it. It was late, and Theophyloyannakos left.

That night there were no shouts, no screams, just the banging of the bars and locks for the amusement of the young soldiers. In the morning I was called to the front office. Babalis was there alone; he said good morning. I did not answer, and he started again about the bombs. I would be accused of having planted them when they took me to the Security Headquarters. He told me that what I would suffer there would make me think my life in EAT ESA was paradise.

I had heard many people who had been arrested by the security police tell me their stories. I knew that they were threatened with being sent to EAT ESA, where their life would be hell. Actually no one can say which is better, or rather less horrible, because it depends on the individual case. There is however one fundamental difference: in the Security Headquarters the torturers have experience: they know how to torture and beat and how to cause excruciating pain without leaving scars or breaking bones. Panagoulis was one of the few exceptions to this policy, for they had an absolutely free hand with him and were not obliged to leave him unmarked. In EAT ESA the beating is usually done by the young soldiers, and until they get the hang of it, they can do too much damage. I have a friend whose spine was dislocated for good. I know of another man whose arm was broken in such a way that it could not be properly set.

Babalis was still talking. He said he was in the special branch whose task it was to exterminate communism; that was his job, and he did it. I was a communist, I had contacts with the underground of international communism. He went on and on and I got tired and bored.

'Why waste your time', I said, 'telling me things that I know you do not believe? You know very well that I have never even seen any explosives or any bombs and that I am not a communist. If communism is your department and you don't know that I am not a communist, then you are not very good at your job. Use your tactics', I added, 'on the young boys you arrest and torture and terrorize. Don't you see that you cannot impress me?'

'Well,' he said, 'I know that you are not a communist. Sign the "statement of condemnation" against the communists and I am finished with you.'

'I won't sign anything,' I said.

'Why, since you are not a communist?'

'Because it is beneath my dignity,' I said. Babalis sent me back to my

cell. Which of the statements did he want me to sign? The one which
said: 'Do you acknowledge that the communists rape women, kidnap
children, slaughter old people and destroy their property? ... Or was
it the one that asked:

Does any member of your family belong to ... communist
organizations, or reside in countries which have a communist
regime?

Do you acknowledge that the [Greek Communist Party] with
its variously named organizations has through its activities and
actions betrayed the national interest and has sought by every
means the destruction of the social order, the seizure of power,
the mutilation and enslavement of the country to the Slavo-
Communist camp and the removal of the Greek People from
Helleno-Christian ideals, causing monstrous catastrophes to the
country and unheard-of crimes at the expense of the people?

Do you condemn the Greek Communist Party and its variously
named ... organizations?

Or was it one like the new Declaration of Loyalty?

A few moments later I was summoned again. This time it was
Theophyloyannakos. Before he had time to speak, I poured all my
bitterness over his head. In my anger against Mallios and Babalis I felt
as if I belonged in some way to EAT ESA; they had arrested me, so
they were responsible for me!

'Why did you call these tramps,' I demanded, 'these liars, these
forgers of evidence, these common slanderers?'

On and on I went, and eventually he answered, 'Well, this is the
interrogation method, over-accusing so as to get the truth.' And
suddenly he started howling, 'You are much cleverer than I thought.
You are much more of a conspirator than I thought. You were
raging at them just to get that out of me.' I was bewildered by his
anger, and I think he realized that I had not had the cunning intention
he had imagined. Nonetheless, I was thankful for the information.

Whatever I do or think or write after all these months in exile, it is
all tuned like radio waves to Greece and the Greek people, to those
who will be arrested after us. I would like to help them through my
own experiences. Let them know now what Theophyloyannakos told
me that day, and not be afraid, when their turn comes, if the police

or the ESA accuse them of much more than they have done; this usually means that the interrogators know nothing, or very little, and that they are trying to put the prisoner they interrogate into a panic with some heavy charge to get him to confess the little he has actually done. 'No, I did not plant a bomb, I only passed on a pamphlet,' they want him to say. Let them know that what the interrogators say is mostly bluffs and traps. The things they claim to know by having followed him about and listened to his conversations, they do not know. All they have to go on is what we tell them because we believe that they know it already. Let them know that the shouts and howls and ferocious threats are frequently mere theatre, that Theophyloyannakos is a magnificent liar and a much less good actor, but that he has a strong dramatic sense and acts continually.

If they feel strange, if they have hallucinations, if they see weird images or wild animals on the wall, this means that they have been given hallucinogenic drugs. They must understand that and not panic, but use all their will power to resist believing anything they are told then and anything they think they see or hear. It is better at such moments to refuse to believe even the truth in order to escape being led to believe false rigmaroles. Finally, let them try as hard and as long as they can to show they are determined not to talk and are not afraid. It may be that in this way they will escape torture. If, however, torture does come to them, then it is up to the resistance of every individual. I have not been physically tortured. I cannot know. But I believe that if they are really angry, and feel for their torturers that contempt which torturers deserve, that may help them. The day that I felt in this way against Mallios and Babalis, I believe I would have been able to stand much ill treatment.

When he had calmed down, Theophyloyannakos returned to Yannis. He must have Yannis's name. I said I would never tell him. But I had no hope, he could find Yannis.

In the evening he came into my cell. He was triumphant. He leaned on the wall again and asked, 'Who is Helen?' Helen is Yannis's wife, so I knew Yannis had been found. Still, for what it was worth, I did not answer. He repeated his question. I said she was a woman who embroidered tablecloths for me. 'How do you find her when you need her?' I said she used to ring me up to ask if I wanted anything.

'But otherwise, if you should want her?'

'I ring her.'

'And what is her telephone number?'

I said I did not remember. I knew that he knew all that, that he had Yannis, and that he was just enjoying a cat and mouse game. At last he said it; he had arrested Yannis. So I told him again that Yannis knew nothing, that he was just a taxi driver on a job, directed to go straight ahead or right or left by his customer. He knew nothing of where we were or why we were there or what we were talking about.

No, he said, Yannis must know a lot, and he would be made to spill everything. He would be tortured until he did. Theophyloyannakos said Yannis had a bigger house than my own. Why? How? Who had given him the money? The organization, no doubt. He was going to ruin him, shut his house, and send him to rot in prison.

I begged and pleaded, and cried, 'Why don't you hit me? Why do you strike at poor people? Yannis's wife has been working since she was eight years old to have this little house. Why don't you hit *me*; I have had everything put into my hands since I was born?' Actually it was not difficult for anyone to have a house bigger than mine, since my flat has only one room.

And then, seeing that he had achieved his intention of distressing and upsetting me, he added, 'And it was Yannis who drove Bekakos to have him photographed wearing a wig.' Having nothing but Yannis's safety in mind, I answered quickly, 'No, it was not Yannis, it was me.' I saw the triumph in his eyes. The day before, frenzied with rage, I had said that I would have amnesia. I had then refused to answer any question, and this had included questions about Bekakos, the photographs, and the wig. Now Theophyloyannakos had my admission on these subjects. He left, very pleased with himself. I did not mind. I had no intention of denying it, since that might have meant more torture for Kostas.

I could not sleep. What would Theophyloyannakos do to Yannis? What about Helen, the young woman I was so fond of? She would be frantic with worry. I heard moans and humble pleadings coming from the corridor, then rough talking, 'I told you not to move!' then a bang and more moans. Some quiet would follow, and then the same things again. My guess was that someone had been made to stand or sit very uncomfortably without being allowed to move. Was it Yannis? I never learned.

Next morning I was summoned again. Before Theophyloyannakos

had time to speak, I said, 'I want you to admit one thing: that last night I told you about Bekakos and the photographs of my own free will. I want you to understand that if you use the methods you used the other day, I shall not speak. You know that I have never tried to protect myself since the first night, and that I took on responsibilities I could have denied. Will you admit that?'

As usual, he considered things for a moment, and then he said, 'Yes.' Then I said that I had asked for the photographs to be taken, that I had given the soldier the wig, and that Kostas had nothing to do with it. Theophyloyannakos asked if the photographs were to be given to the man in the passport department for him to make a passport for Bekakos.

I said no, that was not the method, I did not know anyone in the passport office nor did I believe that one man could accomplish such a task. Did a passport really not go through many hands, I asked.

'Then what were the photographs for?'

'I will not tell you. Perhaps at this moment other people are using the same method to escape from the country. I cannot tell you, and even Kostas does not know, because I did not tell him. There may be other ways, perhaps people do use forged passports, but I don't know how to make them, I wish I did.'

He did not insist, but went back again to the man in the red pullover. I had thought he had been forgotten. My guess now is that Theophyloyannakos had been interrogating Kostas the rough way, and that eventually Kostas had broken down under the beating and had said that I was the only one who knew this man's name, which was true. So now he was grilling me; he said he wanted the name of the man who had handed over the keys of the car, the man who had taken the car out of my parking place and given it to Kostas and the corporal on August 25th. I told him I would not reveal the name.

He shouted and howled and threatened. He said that he would find him. I told him that this man was yet another who had nothing to do with the escape. He had just obliged me by taking the keys to Kostas.

Then Theophyloyannakos had a brilliant idea: he said, 'Yannis is the man in the red pullover.' I cried out, 'No, he is not.' He said he was. He would bring Yannis here, in my presence, and he would torture him until he admitted he had handed over the keys. He saw my distress, and was jubilant. I asked him why he didn't bring Yannis face to face with Kostas and Corporal Staikos and ask them, since Yannis was really not the same man nor did he look at all like him. Theophyloyannakos insisted it was Yannis, and that he had no need of me any longer. Yannis would tell him, Yannis would be made to admit it. On this dreadful note he sent me back to my cell. We had spent the whole morning, and it was lunch time. Again the guards gave me the basket with the food from home, again the sight of food made me feel sick, and once again I emptied the boxes into the dustbin.

At six I was summoned. Theophyloyannakos said that I was to tell him the name of the man in the red pullover. If I did so, on his word of honour as an officer he would have the man brought in and tell him he knew all about him, that he just wanted to warn him to keep quiet in the future, and that would be all. That would last about a quarter of an hour, after which he would release both him and Yannis.

I knew what his word of honour as an officer was worth. The first morning of our encounter, in Papaphilippou's office, had he not given me his word of honour that no one had ever been tortured in EAT ESA? I said I would not give the name. He threatened to use other methods on me, methods which made people like me talk. He threatened to bring Kostas in and skin him alive in my presence. He was shrieking. Then he started to make offers again. He would not have the man arrested at all, he would go himself to see him and warn him, and that would be all. Would I accept that? He said that I knew he would find him, that I knew how efficient they were, and that no one had ever managed to escape arrest. If I gave the name, he would not touch the man, but otherwise he would arrest him and torture him, and then he would get the names of others as well. I remained silent. He said, 'All right, I shall not go to see him. I shall only speak to him on the telephone in your presence. What about that? I shall ring him and warn him, and that will be all, on my word of honour as an officer.' I was still silent. He said, 'Look here, see how good I am with you. I make you an offer. Suggest how you would like me to deal with this, and I shall do it in whatever way you suggest. But I must have his name, and I will have it, no matter what means I have to use to get it; so think about that. At present I am offering to accept your terms. In a little while that chance will be gone.' He bent still closer towards me, and the terrible expression of a monster I had seen on the first day in his office was back on his face. 'Accept my offer,' he repeated, 'don't make me do what I prefer not to do. Accept my offer now, while there is still time, otherwise it is with humiliation that you will beg me to let you tell me the name.' It is an unjust truth that although it ought to be the torturer who feels humiliated, it is in fact the victim.

I had been asking continuously for water, and water was brought to me, and I was drinking all the time.

There was a sudden light in his eyes. 'The garage men,' he said, 'they must tell me; I shall have the four garage men brought here and they will say who they allowed to take your car away.' He was calling my open parking space a garage, even though he knew very well from his own inquiries that when Kostas had taken the car no one was there but one old man. Nevertheless, he insisted he was going to have the four men brought in, close the garage, torture the men in my presence, and bring in their wives and children.

I said, 'Major Theophyloyannakos, when you arrested me I made an oath, a very great oath that I should never give you the name of any person. You are a Christian,' I added, 'you will understand that I cannot break my oath.' I saw the fury flash in his eyes. He knew what I meant. Ever since the Junta took over there have been banners and placards all over Greece proclaiming 'Greece of the Christian Greeks'. It had created some annoyance among the Moslem and Jewish minority, let alone among the Christians.

Theophyloyannakos went on with his threats to arrest the four garage men. He called a captain in and told him to go and arrest them. Then he told him to wait a little longer, and went on alternating between threats and offers. Every quarter of an hour or so, in a voice which I wanted to be firm but which had started weakening, I would just say, 'I cannot break my oath.' Theophyloyannakos asked the captain to wait outside. He realized that my resistance had started failing me; perhaps alone, without witnesses of my defeat, I would speak. He kept shouting. I was exhausted, I put my elbows on the desk and covered my face with my hands.

'Take your hands down,' he howled. I took them down. 'Look me straight in the eyes,' he howled again, and I did. He kept telling me how much better it would be for the man if I gave his name; he would not touch him or do him any kind of harm, but otherwise he would find the man, even if he had to put the entire military police force on to the job; he would find him, and then he would torture him with his own hands.

I started getting confused. Perhaps it would be better for the man himself if I did tell his name? And then I realized that I had too rich an imagination ever to betray anyone. I saw the man they were after sitting in my chair and taking my place, being interrogated. I saw him being tortured. I thought of his sons not allowed to go abroad to the universities they had chosen. I saw him dismissed from his job, ruined. No, I could not speak. And with a fairly firm voice I repeated, 'I cannot break my oath.' Again he bent across the desk. 'Give me the name,' he howled. 'Don't you understand? I am an interrogator. I must, I must have this name.' Then like a wounded tiger he roared, accentuating every word, 'How am I to explain that I can get anything I want from the others and nothing from you? How am I to explain it?' Then more clearly than ever before I realized that they had one kind of power over us and only one: the power that comes from the exercise of torture. Without his claws, Theophyloyannakos, the terrible Theophyloyannakos, was nothing. And I felt sorry for the despair of the man for his frustration because he could not torture me. He took me to my cell and asked the captain to wait outside. He was giving me fifteen minutes to decide, to call from my cell and to give the name. Otherwise the captain would bring in the four garage men and torture them until they had spoken. I said he was going to torture innocent people to blackmail me. And I said again, as I had done earlier about Yannis, 'Why don't you torture me? I am in your hands, why torture poor innocent people?' He said they were not innocent; they were responsible for the car. If they had given it, that meant that they were part of the organization. He would wait fifteen minutes for me to call and give the name, no more. I said, 'Don't wait. I shall not call you.'

I was locked in the cell. I was distraught and exhausted. I felt that I could not stand this any longer, but also that nothing could make me give away another man. He could arrest and torture people, but he would not do it with my help. I must sleep, I thought, whatever happens I must sleep. I had hidden three Valium, that is, 15 mg, and three Bellergals, just for such a moment of great stress. I took them all and went to bed. I covered my head with the sheet and folded my arms to protect my eyes from the light, and soon I was asleep.

Immediately, the door opened, and the guard told me to get up. I froze. Was I to witness the garage men's torture? I was taken into the front office again, where an officer in civilian clothes whom I had never seen before was waiting for me with paper and pencil in his hands. He asked me to sit down and give the name and address of the man. I said I would not. He insisted for a while, and then walked out, leaving me guarded by a young soldier.

I sat waiting, wondering what was to happen to me. The young soldier was looking shyly at me. 'Do you remember me?' he asked. 'Do you remember me from the first day of your arrest?' I said no, I did not. 'Don't you really?' he insisted, and then, 'Don't be angry with us,' said the soldier. 'We are obeying orders.'

'I am not angry with you, my dear boy,' I said. What had he done to me that first day? Perhaps he was the one who had pushed the drawer of the desk on my stomach? I asked him, but he did not tell me. I waited for a time, and then I asked him who we were waiting for, and he said, nobody. I was to spend the night there, without sleep. I had already been exhausted when I had gone to bed; now with the 15 mg of Valium and three Bellergals, my eyes were closing and I could not keep my head up. I tried to support my drooping head with my hands.

'Please,' said the soldier, 'put your hands down. I am not allowed to let you do that.' So I put my hands down and smiled, as I had not the strength to laugh at the thought that I had taken all those drugs which were going to make the night without rest that much more difficult. The guard said with admiration, 'And you can smile!'

I asked if he would give me a cup of water, since the use of a glass was forbidden as a potential weapon. He said yes, with shining eyes, happy to be able to do something for me, to make up for what he had done the first day. He asked a soldier to guard me, and went out and brought me a cup of iced water. He started talking to me, asking a lot of questions; he asked if I had travelled to many countries, and I said yes, and if I had always been very, very happy in my life, and I said no.

At about two in the morning he was replaced by a brutal one. He had had to get up from his sleep to guard me, and he thundered and shouted that because of me, because I would not do as I was told and speak as everybody else had done, soldiers had to suffer. When he stopped to breathe, I looked at my watch and said soothingly that it was half past two already, and that in four hours it would be time for everybody to get up and the ordeal for both of us would be over. 'Four hours?' he said. 'You will stay without sleep for days and nights till you do speak.' A little later the telephone rang, and a soldier came to say something or other to my angry guard. 'Would you like to sleep?' he asked me.

'Let me be,' I answered.

He said, 'Come, or I shall drag you.'

I assured him that he need not use force to make me go to my cell to sleep. At the door he said, 'In half an hour I shall make you get up again.' I thought that he needed the half hour for some business of his own, and lay down all dressed. Then I changed my mind. I put on my nightdress, and went properly to bed. In a minute I was asleep. I was not made to get up.

In the morning the door opened again suddenly, and Theophyloyannakos walked in. He took the writing-pad from my table and said, 'I shall write here, and give my signature, that if you give me the name of this man, I shall only summon him here for a few minutes to tell him in your presence to keep out of all resistance activity from now on. And then I shall release both him and Yannis. I shall sign it and give you the paper to keep.'

I said, 'I told you that I cannot break my oath,' because I dared not say, 'How can I trust you?' And so it went on and on all over again, with shouts and threats and the offer of the signed guarantee. He managed to make a wreck of me again, but I did not speak.

My resistance to the powerful master, and especially the fact that I had spent the nocturnal ordeal smiling, had somehow impressed the young soldiers. Some of them said to me, 'And you were smiling.' Unfortunately, the same night I lost any reputation for courage I may have got. As the diarrhoea was bothering me, I called during the night for my door to be opened so that I could go to the lavatory. But as I was entering the place, a huge rat which was in there got a good look at me, ran to the hole, and dug his head in, leaving most of his body, with the tail waving, sticking out. I screamed and jumped back and said pitifully to the young man, 'A rat!' He roared with laughter, and I begged him to do something about it, as I did not dare go near it. He flushed the water, and the rat went further in, but it was with the greatest apprehension that I approached the dirty hole.

Next day was another day. I was called again to the front office, and found a human Theophyloyannakos. I told him about the rat. I said they were going to get the plague or something of the sort in there with the filth and these rats. He said, 'Oh, you mean Rocky? He belongs to ESA.'

He said he had released Yannis, and, what was more, he was not going to indict him or mention his name. I thanked him and told him that I would always be grateful for that. He said, 'Do you know why I did it?' I said, 'Because you understood at last that he was not involved at all.'

'No,' he said. 'He was very honest and he told me everything, and then he said that he owed you a debt of gratitude, that you looked after his father and mother and his wife Helen, who adores you. He said he could not refuse you a favour if you asked him, and then he asked me, "Mr Commanding Officer, what would you have done in my place?" and I said, "Yannis, I would have done what you did." ' Liar, I thought.

However, when I was released from prison I asked Helen, and she told me exactly the same story, adding that Theophyloyannakos had asked whether I could lie, and Yannis had said no, I could not, that there was no cunning in me at all. This was something he had been inquiring about from anyone who knew me. Being such a wonderful liar himself, he found it difficult to believe that I was telling the truth— at least, as often as I could.

This monster who has tortured so many of my friends puzzles me in some things, and the case of Yannis's release is one. I thought I could see something human in him, and this is why, to the great anger of a friend whose young son he had inhumanly tortured, I cannot manage to hate him.

I asked him again if he had really released Yannis, and he assured me that he had done so. So I thanked him, and again he said that it was a pity that I was so naive and believed the wrong people, and he started his usual recording once more, the one about 'all information we get about you is good. But you have strayed; we shall bring you back to the right path and you will be our friend. Of course,' he added, 'you have to be punished first, everybody who strays has to be punished.' Then, relishing every word, with a cruel light in his eyes, he said, 'And you *are* being punished. This suffering here, you have never had to experience anything like it in your life.' Usually, when I went for interrogation, I would brace myself up to face whatever was to come. But this time, with the emotion of Yannis's release, and the exhaustion of the two last days, he found me unguarded. My scream rose from the deep dark pit inside me, from that area of unbearable suffering which I thought I had locked and made watertight: 'This is nothing to me!'

He stopped short. I saw the shock in his eyes, the start of amazement.

Then I saw the girl in the hospital bed. She was twenty, and so beautiful. She had a smile on her pale face, and a small dictionary in her hands. Beside her sat her brother, a boy of twenty-five, who had not left her side, day or night, since they had come to England.

He had rung me from Lamia, a town in central Greece. He was coming to London in two days, bringing his sister who had leukemia; would I please find a doctor, a hospital bed, an ambulance, and go to the airport to meet them, as they did not speak a word of English? Thanks to my dear friend, Alex Haddow, it was arranged for her to enter the Royal Marsden Hospital, and there she lay now. But no one could help her; she was dying.

Later that day, her brother rang me. He had had a letter from his mother saying the Virgin had visited her in a dream to tell her that in such and such a place there was a well of holy water, a well where her icon had been found some years before, and if her daughter drank some of this water she would be cured. She had known nothing of the icon story, she had never heard of the well, but yes, it did exist in that place, so the vision must be true, and she was sending a bottle of the holy water by aeroplane to arrive that evening. The young man asked me to find out how we could get hold of this bottle.

I rang the airport, and said we were expecting a drug and that it was most important we should have it immediately. I was lucky to pick an extraordinarily nice man; he inquired, and told me that there was no drug anywhere. So I had to tell him that I was the widow of the man who had discovered penicillin, and then the whole story of the holy water, and that the girl was dying and that at least for the mother's peace of mind she should drink the holy water. The man asked me to hold on, and that even if he was a very long time he would come back with an answer. After a considerable time he did come back; the bottle had been taken by one of the crew to Richmond. I told the young man and he drove immediately to Richmond, found the bottle, and the girl drank the holy water. One hour later she was dead.

At the undertaker's where she lay in her coffin, the brother gave me a gold chain with a little gold cross. 'Please,' he said, 'fasten it around her neck. She loved it.' He lifted the dead girl's head, and I bent and fastened the chain, my face near her lovely face.

I had seen so many people dying, I had seen so much sorrow. I had seen the people I loved go. To bring them back to life for one second, to see them smile just once more, I would happily stay years in his

horrid cell and bear his shouts, his threats, and my own fear. Theophyloyannakos was still looking at me. Did he realize that I had known
suffering far deeper than anything he could inflict?

I think it was the morning after this that he called me again. He told
me he was resigned to the fact that I was not going to talk; nor was it
his intention to continue pressing me to do so; the interrogation was
finished and closed. He then sent me back to my cell.

I felt wonderful. I had won; I had not spoken. The basket arrived
from home. I no longer felt nauseated, and I opened the boxes, and
found just what I liked best, minced meat in vine leaves, *yaprakia*. I was
ravenous, and ate with delight what was meant to make both lunch
and dinner. Then, like a sated animal, I lay down with a book on the
bed.

The door opened, and I was summoned back to the office. Theophyloyannakos, Babalis, and Mallios were there. Again, the two
security men were given the good seats behind the desk, and
Theophyloyannakos was on my left. And the interrogation started all
over again.

Greeks who will be arrested after us, remember that they will do
this: encourage you to relax, and then pounce on you before you have
time to be on your guard again.

They wanted the man who had been in the car with me and Kostas
and Bekakos when we drove down Syngrou Avenue, the man who
worked at the passport department. I said that I did not know any such
man, and that we had never driven down Syngrou Avenue in the way
they were saying. I have never driven there in my life with Kostas
and Bekakos. They went on and on.

Then they came back to the man in the red pullover. Oh Lord, I
thought, not again. I repeated my little verse, that I had sworn never
to give a name and I could not break my oath. Then Mallios spoke:
'This man Yannis, I must have him.' In deep anguish I turned and
looked at Theophyloyannakos for help. He said, 'No, Mr Mallios, we
shall keep Yannis out of this.'

'That is not possible, Commanding Officer,' said Mallios. 'You may
have finished with him, but Security wants him.'

'Now, look here, Mallios,' said Theophyloyannakos. 'Surely we are
not going to quarrel about this. I have released Yannis, and I don't
want his name to be mentioned.' For a while this went on, and I got
more and more distressed, when suddenly I realized that once again

this was a theatrical performance for my personal benefit only. I leaned back in my seat, relaxed, and enjoyed it. I found that Theophyloyannakos's acting that day was beneath his usual standard. Meanwhile, Babalis did not speak; indeed, he remained so silent that I had to remind myself he was there at all. Eventually I was handed back to my guards and locked up in my cell.

By now the Katol, which was burning all day and all night, had added its own disagreeable smell to that of the lavatory and the mouldy dampness. But none of this bothered me, nor did the bars, nor the lock, nor the claustrophobia. That cell was my place of refuge.

In the evening, Theophyloyannakos came in to see me again, and as usual he leaned on the wall and I sat on the bed. 'Do you remember what I said that day when you gave me the chance of leaving and being spared all this?'

'Yes,' he said hopefully, imagining that I was now going to ask him to let me go.

'Do you remember', I went on, 'that I said I love the theatre?'

'Yes,' he said again.

'Well, it is true, but I am used to theatre of a very high standard, and to a very high standard of acting.'

'Wasn't I good?' asked Theophyloyannakos.

'No,' I said, 'not by my standards.' But, I thought, at least he *is* intelligent.

16. The Psychology of a Torturer: Theophyloyannakos

It must have been the fourteenth day after my arrest when I was called early to be taken to the shower. I was pleasantly surprised; why was it they did not make me beg for it until ten or later? When I came back, I was told by a soldier to change into my 'good dress', not the one I was wearing to go to the shower, and to be ready because somebody from the British Embassy was to come and see me. I knew that the American Consul had seen Skelton on the seventh day, but I thought that it was perfectly proper for the British Embassy not to have bothered, since only my Greek nationality was valid in Greece. Also I had said I did not want the British Embassy to interfere, in fact I had promised Theophyloyannakos that I would not ask for its protection. I was Greek, and I wanted to remain a Greek, whatever that might entail.

Soon I was summoned to the commanding officer's office where the British Consul-General was waiting. Oh dear, I thought. I knew him, and he was a reserved, cold Englishman. After fourteen days in isolation I felt that I needed somebody warmer. When I entered, Theophyloyannakos, a corporal, and another EAT ESA officer were there and the British Consul-General was standing in the middle of the room looking like somebody on a duty visit to hell. We sat down, myself next to the British Consul, Theophyloyannakos at his desk with the corporal interpreter beside him. The other officer sat a little further back. Both Theophyloyannakos and the other man could speak English, but I could hear the interpreter translate every word we were saying.

The British Consul-General had a very determined expression on his face. With drops of sweat on his forehead, due, I am sure, to the effort of speech, he first told me that he had been trying to see me ever since he had heard of my arrest, and asked me whether I had been told that was so, as he had been led to believe I had. I said no, no one had mentioned it. He asked me about my health, my drugs, if I had medical care. I said yes, a very nice doctor came to see me almost every other day, and I had been given my drugs. Then he asked me how I was in there, and I whispered, 'Don't ask me that.'

Theophyloyannakos thundered, 'You whispered something.'

Then firmly, almost stubbornly, the British Consul-General said that he wanted me to know how concerned the British government and the British Embassy and all my friends all over the world were. He was bringing me greetings and good wishes from all my friends in Athens, and I was to know that the British Foreign Secretary was to see his Greek counterpart in London, and one of the subjects they were to discuss was me. He then asked what I wanted him to tell my friends, and I said, 'Tell them not to worry—about me. Tell them that I have found out that I have more courage and greater strength than I thought.' And then again I repeated slowly, 'Give my friends, give all my friends, this message: they need not worry.' I stopped again, and then added, 'about me.' I hoped that the word would go round, and would reach those who ought to know, that I had not spoken and that I did not intend to do so.

Suddenly Theophyloyannakos banged his fist on the desk. 'From now on you speak Greek' he ordered. Unfortunately, the British Consul-General speaks Greek. 'This communist paper the *Guardian* ...'

'Tell him it is *not* a communist paper,' I said.

' ... says that you went on a hunger strike. Tell him, tell him, were you on a hunger strike?'

'No,' I said, 'I was not on a hunger strike, but I would not eat; I could not eat for about ten days.' 'Why?' 'Because of the horror of the interrogation,' I said. Theophyloyannakos gave me a bad look, but continued, 'But now you eat?' I said, 'Yes, I do, because you said the interrogation is over and because you threatened to forcefeed me *yourself*.'

At this moment I felt I wanted to tell the consul about the offer of a post in the Cabinet, but I thought that it would make Theophyloyannakos look such a fool that he might jump on me and physically tear me to pieces. So I asked him whether he would allow me to tell the British Consul-General that he had offered me the post of Minister for Public Welfare, and Theophyloyannakos bent forward, hands outstretched, all smiles, and said, 'Yes, of course, who could we have better for the job?'

I can still remember the puzzled look on the consul's face. He asked me if there was something special the embassy could do for me, and I said no, thank you, I was a Greek citizen as he knew, and he could not do anything for me. It was just very nice of him to come and see me. He agreed that my Greek nationality was making things very difficult for them. I said I knew that, and this was the way I wanted it to be. I added, 'I know you cannot help me, and I don't want you to help me.' He asked. 'You would not give up your Greek nationality?' I laughed and said no, I would not.

Then the British Consul-General started all over again saying in Greek that all my friends were thinking of me and were sending messages, that all over the world there was a great interest in my arrest. 'Stop!' shouted Theophyloyannakos, 'Don't make her stronger, she is strong enough.' Nothing he could say could have pleased me more!

The consul said, 'I brought you some books. They are outside in the car,' and a soldier went out and brought the books. 'I shall come again, what can I bring you?'

I said, 'Books, please.'

'May I come again to see Lady Fleming in a couple of days?' asked the consul.

'Of course, certainly,' said Theophyloyannakos, 'come in two days' time.' The consul asked, 'Do you want me to come?' and I said, 'Oh please do. It's so nice to see a human being!'

Theophyloyannakos announced that the visit was over, and the consul left, promising to come back two days later. In spite of innumerable efforts, he was allowed to see me only the day before my trial, that is, fourteen days later.

I was getting more and more confused about dates and days. There was so little change from one day to the next. Sometimes, when I had no interrogation in the evening, I would lean against the wall opposite the window and look up. There was a big block of flats behind the little building where I was, and I could see the top floor with its veranda. I used to think how nice it would have been if the people living in this top floor came out to sit on the veranda with their friends and have a meal there and talk, and I would be able to imagine that I was with them, that I had company. But throughout the thirty-one evenings I was in that cell, they never sat out, although there were many hot evenings.

Also, once at the beginning of my imprisonment I heard some lovely music coming from there, and it was so soothing that it seemed to bring me back into the civilized world. But it never came again. So I thought that when I was free I would go and see the people on the top floor and ask them to come out on the veranda to keep the prisoners company, and also to have some nice music for them.

The interrogation went on for several more days. It seemed that much as he had tried to 'put the whole military police after them', Theophyloyannakos had not been able to get either the man in the red pullover or anyone else involved in the case. Kostas under drugs and torture had said all he knew, and what I knew I would not say. His threats and shouts continued, but it was obvious that he did not have permission to use physical torture on me. One evening, after another long and unsuccessful interrogation, he took me to the cell and left me, shouting, 'I shall make your life harder, I shall make everybody's life harder.' My opinion was that it was hard enough.

I was locked in, and then the door opened again, and the guard said that on the commanding officer's orders, he had to take everything out of the cell. I was to keep the bed, one dress, one nightgown, and one pair of shoes, and that was all. He took everything else away, fortunately forgetting the Katol which was burning in a plate on the floor. I put my cup of water, which I had also kept, on the floor and lay on the bed. In the fear that they might take my books away one day, I had one hidden under the mattress. I took it out, and started to read. The sound of the door opening again made me jump up and hide the book. Theophyloyannakos entered and looked around like a general inspecting the battlefield after a victory; then he looked at me with triumph in his eyes. I was furious. I felt like slapping him. I smiled a broad smile, and remembering the French history I had been taught as a child, I said, 'Vae victis, as Vercingetorix remarked.'* For a moment Theophyloyannakos seemed to wonder, 'Now, who is Vercingetorix?' and then he retreated.

Two days later the young doctor came to see me. He looked around and said uneasily, 'Didn't you have a little table and a chair?' I said yes. I had, but they were taken away as a punishment. He went away and came back and said it was a mistake, and the table and the chair and my other belongings came back. From the beginning this poor man had not known what to do about me. The trouble had already started at his second visit. I had just been through all the shouting and threats from

* *Vae victis* means 'Woe to the vanquished'. He was a Gaulish general of about 50 B.C. who fought against Caesar. After defeating the enemy in battle, he arranged a ransom in gold for the liberation of some generals. When the scales of the balance rested even with the gold that the defeated put in, Vercingetorix threw his heavy sword on the other side, shouting, 'Woe to the vanquished.'

Theophyloyannakos when he happened to ask me how I was, and I answered angrily, 'How do you expect me to be with all these shouts, and these threats and the conditions here?' And he had answered shyly, 'Under these conditions, which I can do nothing about, how are you?' Ever after, he always used this formula when he inquired about my health. I was fond of my young doctor. He certainly did whatever he could for me, and the most important things were the tranquillizers he had allowed me and the chance of a wash! He had also provided a big water-jug as I needed to drink water all the time.

The interrogation continued, but alternated with quiet days, or rather quiet moments, which I tried to keep going as long as possible, because I simply could not get used to the threats and the shouts. Every time they upset and frightened me. During the quiet moments there were two topics, and usually one led to the other. Theophyloyannakos would start with the favourable reports he had had about me from all quarters, and go on to complain that I had strayed, which was a pity, because I could be of such good use to the country if I had stayed on the right path. But they would see to it. I should come back to the right path, and then I would collaborate with them. Why, if I loved my country as I seemed to, did I not do everything possible to serve it? How could I fail to realize that this could only happen if I helped *them*? They were honest officers, good patriots, working hard and trying to change the whole people into useful, honest, Christian Greeks. They themselves came from poor families, they understood the problems of the poor, they would put everything straight. Why were we fighting them, why were we not helping them? This plea for help came again and again, and in itself was a proof of the passive resistance of the Greek people. In this way I got my second offer to take up the Ministry of Social Welfare. Again I declined it, and tried to explain that, according to me, and to the overwhelming majority of the people, the only good they could do for Greece and the Greeks was to step down, allow the country to return to freedom, and to free and genuine elections. At this point the shouts started again: the people were not mature enough for freedom or elections. They had to be taught the right things to believe, and that was something only *they*, the military, could do.

'How can you believe such a thing?' I said. 'You have put Greece back fifty years. You are ruining the country. Mind you, I have no resentment against you. I am sorry for you. As boys of fifteen you entered the military school and this is how you came out. When you are overthrown, which you will be sooner or later, it is not against you that I shall turn. I will demolish the military school, not the walls but the spirit of the place, so that the new officers will not be like you, so that they will not dream of taking power or ruling this country by force. How did you come to believe that you can rule a country? What do you think it is, a regiment?' In spite of the words I used, he could see that I was deeply unhappy, not aggressive. He was no longer angry, just curious.

'Who would you put in charge?' he asked.

'I don't know,' I said. 'I have always lived with intellectuals, I am biased. I believe that education would make all the difference in the world.'

He said, 'All right, come and help us, join us. Become Minister of Education.'

Another evening, he was going on as usual about this wrong path I had strayed on, not because I had a bad nature, my nature was good, but because I was naive and had been misled, and so on. They would put me on the right path and everything would be all right for me again, but before that happened, he said, 'You have to be punished because everybody who strays must be punished. I do it to my own daughter,' he added. 'If she does something wrong, she has to be punished.'

'How old is your daughter?' I asked, and he said she was two and a half. At one time she had got into the habit of wanting to sleep in her mother's bed, and she cried until her mother took her into bed. So one night he left her to cry for two hours, and that was that: she never asked to go into her mother's bed again. People must learn discipline, he said, everyone must learn it. It was late, and he allowed me to be taken away to my cell.

The life in EAT ESA, with the continuous shouting, the threats, the screams in the night, the fear, the diarrhoea which had exhausted me, and the insufficient food, since I could not eat after a wild interrogation, had shaken my nerves badly. That night, when I went to bed, I could not rid my mind of the thought of the little girl crying for two hours to be taken into her mother's arms, without any response, except perhaps the shouts of this terrible father. I thought of how frightened and desperate she just have felt, not to dare cry for her mother in the night. I thought that being only a little child she could not help but do other things which would anger her father, and at such moments he probably had the horrible expression on his face that I had seen there often enough. Would the child ever be able to forget that face?

However I tried to reason with myself, I could not help being obsessed by the revelation. Next day, when Theophyloyannakos had me brought to him again, I told him that I had enough of my own worries without his adding the thought of his daughter to them.

'My daughter?' he asked.

I said, 'Yes, your daughter. Don't ever do that again, let such a small child cry for two hours. She may never forget it, she may have a psychological trauma that may mark her for ever, so that she will never be able to grow up into a balanced, happy young woman. I do accept that discipline is needed in the upbringing of children. But at that age she must feel adored.' I remembered that educationalists say that the character of a child is formed by the age of five, but I thought I had better give one more year to the daughter of a torturer, and added, 'Yes, a child must have discipline, but after the age of six; till then she must be made to believe that she is everything to her parents, that if she cries you will comfort her, and if she calls you will run to her. She must feel that you love her.'

He had a pitiful expression, and said, 'But I do love my daughter.'

And this again is one of the reasons I could not hate this man. When I have repeated this conversation I have been told 'So what? Even tigresses love their children.' Yes, but what is wrong with tigresses? They do not torture.

The interrogation continued. One day I asked the date. It was September 19th. Moussmouss, my cat, was due to have kittens between September 21st and 25th. I added that to the note I was sending to my maid, and asked that a friend, whom my cat loved, would please be there all the time until Moussmouss had had her litter, because Moussmouss had never had kittens before without my holding her paw. Also, she should see that the other cats were put out on the terrace, in order not to disturb Moussmouss. Speaking of the terrace, I remembered the flowers and the plants and my worry that my maid would not water them. So I also added, 'Please look after the flowers.'

I admit it was an unbelievable message to come out of an EAT ESA prison cell. It was, as usual, read before being sent, found to be very suspect, and was shown to the commanding officer. He ordered that the note should not be handed over but that instead my maid must come to see him the same evening at six o'clock. She came, quite worried and frightened. Theophyloyannakos was very polite; he asked her if she wanted coffee. She declined. All she cared about was to know why she had been summoned there. He asked her who Moussmouss was, and she said, 'One of the cats.' He said, 'How many are there?' and she said, 'Five.' And what was supposed to happen between the 21st and the 25th? She had no idea. And what were the flowers, and she said, 'Flowers.' He asked her to answer my note in his presence, which she did, promising that somebody would be there all the time to hold Moussmouss's hand. Her reply was not given to me. I kept on repeating my request but never got an answer.

Another two days of interrogation passed, with threats that I was going to stay and keep all my friends in EAT ESA for ever, or else until I spoke. On the evening of September 22nd, when I had returned to my cell terribly tired of it all, I decided to go to bed early. Anyway, the seance with the commanding officer seemed to have ended. I asked to go to the lavatory, and got ready to sleep. I saw my two cups full of water. I did not remember having left them full, but I took them to empty and refill with fresh iced water from the jug I had had for some days now, thanks to the doctor. But when I came back and was locked in, the jug was not there. I looked through the slit of the door and saw my nice guard, the one who used to give me three matches, and asked, 'Did you take the jug?' He said yes. I said, 'Won't you bring it back?' He said no. I said, 'Can I get some water from the tap, then?' He said no. I said, 'What do you mean no, aren't I allowed to drink water?' He said no. I asked why.

He said, 'Please don't ask me, you are not allowed to drink water.'

Was he the one who had filled the two cups before taking the jug away? I had not been allowed water for about twenty hours when the doctor came again. As usual, he said, 'Under these conditions, which I can do nothing about, how are you feeling today?'

I exploded. 'How do you expect me to be? I have had no water for twenty hours.' He said, 'What?' So I explained, and he opened the door to go out. I said no, I did not want him to do anything about it; if Theophyloyannakos wanted to leave me without water, let him do it. The doctor said, 'Listen, I am not doing what I want here. I am only a junior doctor. The commanding officer gave me orders to keep you fit, and I cannot keep you fit if he deprives you of water.' So he ran out and came back saying again 'It was a mistake,' and the two most wonderful cups of iced water were brought to me. I think it was then that I was sent to Captain Zissis, who, like Captain Papaphilippou, was a regular investigating magistrate of the military court. The time had come for me to make my deposition. Theophyloyannakos had given up.

I had seen Zissis before. About the third or fourth day of my arrest, an officer had come into my cell and, holding a telegram, asked me who was 'Petros, who had arrived safely'. I was happy. Petros was the little boy I had 'posted' to Zurich, with a label with his name on it round his neck. I said so. A little later I was taken to an office next to Papaphilippou's, the man who had interrogated me on August 26th. Zissis was holding a paper that I could not see. He asked me, 'What is "bin"?' I said I did not know. He insisted, and his expression seemed to say, 'We've got you now.' I asked to see the paper he was holding, saying I might understand what he was asking if I could see it, and I asked him what language this 'bin' was written in. Eventually he handed me the paper, asking me who Petros was and who was the signatory. It was the telegram saying in French, 'Petros bien arrivé.' The 'e' after the 'i' had been omitted. I put the 'e' in and returned the telegram. I said, 'Petros is a boy of nine I sent to the Pestalozzi school, and the signature is that of the director who met the child at Zurich airport,' and I gave the date and flight for the police to check.

So here I was again, asked to make a statement about the accusation. As before with Papaphilippou, another man was behind another desk next to Zissis to write down what I was to say. He was Captain Doumas, of the security police. I told Zissis that although I had not taken any active part in the escape attempt of August 31st, I knew of it, and had done whatever I could to help it. But I said, 'I wish to start with the reasons why I desire so much that Panagoulis be freed. And these reasons are the tortures that Panagoulis suffered and is suffering.' I said that I wanted what I was going to say about these tortures to be recorded, and asked Zissis if he would allow that.

'Let me explain,' Zissis said, and gave me a talk about the danger of speaking of things I could not prove. I said, 'Please leave this to me. I am just asking you if you forbid me to say these things.'

He said, 'Let me tell you … ' and I got another speech.

So I said, 'Listen, Mr Zissis, I do not want you either to explain or to tell me anything. All I ask of you is please to tell me yes or no, do you forbid me to talk about the tortures, which is my motive, and if you do forbid me, have you the legal right to do so? Please answer in one word, yes or no.'

Zissis did not answer. He folded his arms on his desk and buried his face in them, and there he remained silently while I was describing some of what Panagoulis had been through.

Doumas was writing, and every time I mentioned something striking, he would turn to the motionless Zissis and say, 'Mr Zissis, I am writing.' Zissis never answered or moved.

When I reached the few things that I knew Panagoulis had suffered after his recapture, after the first and the only successful escape, Doumas said, 'Oh no, I was there, they were giving him orange juice and everything.'

I said, 'I can give you details of what was happening to him then for at least five days. He was on the cement floor, hands and feet tied, and five men were around him who were not caressing him nor were they giving him orange juice.' Doumas looked cunningly at me, and said nothing. When I had finished making the statement, I signed it. Then Zissis produced three printed papers for me to sign. One was the confiscation of my car, and I asked why I should sign that, *they* had confiscated the car. He said it was a mere formality. So I read it, and it said that the car had been confiscated because I had initiated a conspiracy to commit a felony, or something like that, and I said, 'I have done that?' and I refused to sign.

The other was the report of my arrest, and again I asked why I should sign it, they had arrested me. Again Zissis insisted, so I read the paper, and it said that I had been arrested 'red-handed'. So I said, 'Red-handed? Surely you know that I did not even take part, and was arrested in my own regular parking place about three miles from the camp?' He agreed that of course he knew all that, but once again it was a mere formality. I refused to sign. There was a third paper, but I do not remember what it was about. I only remember that I refused to sign that as well, and so all three papers, instead of my signature, had written on them 'Has refused to sign'.

17. *In the Interrogation Centre II*

The trial was fixed for Monday September 27th. Three days before, on September 24th, I was allowed to see my maid for the first time, and have an official visit from my lawyer. My maid told me that Moussmouss had had three lovely kittens; she had sent me numerous notes with this news, but not one of them was handed to me.

I say 'official' visit from my lawyer because about three days before, Theophyloyannakos had summoned me to his office saying that as a special favour, and although the time had not yet come for me to see my lawyer, he would allow me to do so in his presence for a brief moment. A few minutes later he had started shouting at me and called the guards to order them to take me away. He was not going to allow this meeting. Eventually all was calm again and I managed to speak with the barrister, George Mangakis, who was a very old friend and a man who I knew would keep my defence on the high level I wanted it to be fought on. However, he was politically conservative and an opponent of Andreas Papandreou, and I wanted to tell him that I had three requests: that if Andreas's name were mentioned, he would say that I had the greatest esteem for him (Andreas was the man the military court tried to get everyone to condemn); that we would not attack the communists; and that in defending me he would not attack any other defendants. At the first two conditions Theophyloyannakos had jumped up in horror, but my barrister assured me that his duty was to speak my mind and not his.

Now at last, on Friday September 24th, I was to see him alone and discuss the brief. My maid came first for a minute and asked me if I was ill because, she said, I was very pale. I said I was perfectly well. But as soon as I started speaking to my counsel I had to go to the lavatory, and I passed pure blood instead of water. The deprivation of water, which had started forty-eight and ended about twenty-four hours ago, had caused a haemorrhage, I suppose. It became almost impossible to speak about my trial. I had to leave Mangakis every five minutes. Where was the blood coming from, the kidneys, the bladder? I felt exhausted, and had to go and lie down. Before I did so, both my lawyer and I told the guard to call the doctor. The guard that day was the young man who used to give me my drugs only after frustrating remarks like 'Why two and not one of this? Why this today?'

I kept going to the lavatory, bleeding continuously. There was a glass container for me to leave a sample of urine for the sugar test. I used it, and it was almost pure blood. This went on for the greater part of the day. After a time I could not go on knocking at my door to ask for it to be opened so that I could go to the lavatory, and filled instead all the plastic containers in which my food was brought from home. Towards the evening the big haemorrhage stopped and changed into cystitis. Every minute or so I felt the very strong need to pass water, and a few drops of blood came out. Then this also started to subside, and I could be calm for periods of fifteen minutes or half an hour. I knocked again at the door and went to the lavatory and asked the guard if he had done anything about calling a doctor. I said, 'You have been playing at doctors with me, why don't you cure me now?' He walked into the lavatory, saw the glass full of blood, and ran to the telephone to call the doctor. At this moment Theophyloyannakos ordered me to be taken to his office.

When he saw me, he asked me what was wrong. I told him I had been passing blood the whole day. He asked if the doctor had come to see me, and I said no, he had not. He inquired if I had asked for the doctor, and I said yes. Then he gave hell to the young guard. I felt sorry for him and defended him, and said that he had tried all day to ring the doctor and had done his best to help me. Nothing would calm Theophyloyannakos. I felt like the turkey which must be kept in good condition to be slaughtered and cooked for Christmas. He said he would have me sent to the military hospital, and I cried out, 'No!' He looked at me: 'Do you believe the things they say about military hospital 401?' I said, 'Yes.'

The doctor was called and arrived after 10 p.m. I asked him to give me antibiotics and a hot-water bottle, and to see that the soldiers brought me as much water as I could drink. 'I must be able to attend the trial,' I said. The next day, after my efforts to defend him, the young guard had changed into a sweet little lamb. I stayed in bed as much as I could, with my hot-water bottle, I took as many antibiotics and drank all the water I could, and I recovered. Before the trial I saw Theophyloyannakos twice more. The first time was on Saturday evening.

He summoned me again to his office, and this I liked, now that the shouts were over, because it meant walking a few yards in the open, breathing some fresh air. He asked me to tell him what lies Bekakos, Panagoulis's guard, had told. He said that he knew now that Bekakos had been lying. By then I knew it also. I had been given the deposition to read, and what Bekakos had written was all lies. He had talked about and even described the man in the department of passports and this man, so far as I knew, and as it turned out, did not exist. He had said that I had driven this man and himself down Syngrou Avenue, which I had never done. I remembered with resentment the number of exhausting interrogations I had suffered about the real name and address of this figure who had been created by Bekakos's imagination. But what pressure had been used on the poor man to make him invent all these stories? So I said, 'Listen, Bekakos is a story-teller, but then what made him tell these lies? I have nothing to tell you. Bekakos does not interest me, you will have to disentangle the mess for which you are responsible.'

He did not answer.

I asked him why, now that I had signed my statement and the interrogation was over, I was not sent away from this horrible place to Korydallos Prison, according to the regular procedure. He put on his most innocent expression and said, 'I have tried to do that, but there is no room in Korydallos.'

The day after, when my lawyer asked him the same question, he answered with equal innocence and goodwill, 'Lady Fleming does not want to go. She asked me to keep her here until the trial is over.' He knew my lawyer would tell me, and that he could not possibly believe him, but he did not mind, he just enjoyed telling lies.

As I was seated in his office, pleased with the fresh air coming from the french windows, through which I could see the flower beds, the telephone rang. Theophyloyannakos answered, ending as usual with a word which, coming from him, always made me jump: 'Kisses'. The first time I had heard him interrupting his shouts and threats to talk like that, I had the impression of hearing a huge, horrid, black, hairy, poisonous spider called a tarantula, saying 'Kisses', with a tender wave of its frightening legs. I had seen one in the zoo in Cuba, and I had never been able to forget the horror it had caused me. Now I was used to Theophyloyannakos, and even to his way of closing a telephone conversation. I no longer saw him as a horrid hairy spider. However, this word 'kisses', coming from the same mouth that had uttered all the terrible threats, still made me jump.

Before sending me back to my stuffy cell, Theophyloyannakos did something which embarrassed me deeply. He rang his home and asked for his daughter, and, without warning, handed me the receiver. I heard the childish voice, and asked him what the child's name was. He said, 'Maria', and at that moment he was a father. I spoke with Maria.

The last time I saw him before the trial he was his old self. He came into my cell at midday on a Sunday, the day before the trial. He was wearing an open-necked pink or mauve shirt, but with the same striped brown trousers that he always wore. He leaned against the wall as usual, and as usual I was seated on the bed. He said, 'I strongly advise you not to go against us at the trial, or you will pay for it. I shall come again to see you tonight.' When he said 'against us', he hit his open left palm with his right fist. I did not answer. He did not have the face to return to threaten me again in the evening.

In the afternoon I was called once more to an office in the front building. The British Consul-General was there, with an ESA officer I did not know. The consul asked me what I wanted the embassy to do for me at the trial tomorrow, and I said, nothing. He insisted, and I said that I could not think of anything I could wish at that moment. He was astonished. He asked whether I had not been told a few days ago to think about it and tell him. I said no, the first moment I knew I would see him was when I actually saw him. He said he had been trying to see me again since the day of his first visit, but had not managed to get the commanding officer's permission.

On orders from the ESA officer, we were speaking Greek. Just to tease him, I said, 'Well, if I were American you would not only have seen me but you would have got me out. Skelton was visited on the seventh day of his arrest and was out the day after.' The ESA officer said, no, this was not true, and I said it was, because I both heard him and saw him go away. And the officer said, 'No, the authorities tell you it is not so.' Can one tell the 'authorities' they are lying when one is a prisoner in ESA?

Yet while speaking of torture and policemen, there is one I want to remember. It was in the middle of the clash between the ELAS* and the regular Greek Army, who were helped by the British forces under

* The Greek Popular Liberation Army.

General Scobie in December 1944. Fighting was raging in the street where my house was. There were no taxis or private cars available, and usually lorries took passengers from outlying districts to the centre. One such lorry full of people was just passing my street when a bullet hit a young man on the lorry and cut the artery in his leg. Blood spurted as if from a fountain. Time, short, precious time, made it a matter of life or death for him; the Red Cross first aid hospital was a few yards further, round the corner; that was where the driver should have rushed at top speed. But self-preservation, ugly as it may be, is a natural reaction, and the other passengers, ignoring the wounded youngster, and most probably not understanding the urgency of the case, shouted to the driver to stop so that they could get down and hide behind the lorry. The driver stopped just opposite my house, and then a very young policeman leapt up on to the lorry and, standing in the middle of the shooting, revolver in hand, ordered the driver to go as fast as possible to the first aid station, threatening to shoot whoever dared do anything to stop the lorry, which disappeared at full speed round the corner.

Theophyloyannakos, Mallios, Babalis, police torturers, I want to forget you. You must disappear from our memory and our lives. From our police I want to remember just this one brave young man who stood up while bullets were flying round, in the middle of the cowering passengers, and risked his life to save the life of another man.

18. *Trial*

On the following day, I got up at five and managed to have a shower at six o'clock. I put on the best dress I had with me, a navy-blue Indian silk with long sleeves, but it hung on me like a sack: I had literally melted in this horrible place, and in one month I had lost a terrific amount of weight. Even the soldiers noticed it this time, and asked if I could not wear anything else: I said that all my dresses would look the same. Their answer was, 'Of course you will want to show how much you have suffered to have lost so much weight.' What mattered to me was something more important than my appearance. I felt utterly exhausted, and the question was whether I would last out the trial.

We were searched before leaving EAT ESA by an apologetic woman. In the Black Maria which took me to the Extraordinary Military Court, the only company except the police was another woman. She looked fortyish and attractive. She told me that her name was Athena Psychoyou, and in this way I met for the first time the young lady who, I had been told, had been arrested in the car with Kostas Androuso-poulos and John Skelton outside Panagoulis's camp. Hers were the children that Theophyloyannakos had been threatening to send me every half hour, to cry and blame me for their mother's arrest.

If I remember correctly, we were searched again on entering the building of the military court. The courtroom was on the sixth floor, and it was full. There were a large number of policemen in uniform and in plainclothes and some young men in plainclothes whom I recognized as soldiers from EAT ESA. Why were they there? To report to their commanding officer whatever we said, or to make us believe that they might do so and frighten us into silence?

Filling the room with police had a further advantage. The trial was 'open and free' to anyone who wished to come, always providing there was room. And, of course, there was no free space left, so only a very few relatives or friends were allowed in – only those who had the courage to insist and wait for room to be found. A large number of foreign press correspondents and photographers had been waiting for us outside the building, and they followed us up, squeezing into the courtroom. We exchanged signals of love and encouragement with whoever we even slightly knew. Then there was silence, and the judges entered. There was the secretary who was to keep the official record, the crown prosecutor, four army officers, and the president.

My lawyer, supported by almost all the other lawyers, said that the military court was not competent to try us, and that according to the latest laws and the declarations of the prime minister, we should go before a civil court. Their plea was rejected, and the lawyers said they would come back to it later. A demand that Panagoulis himself should be brought as a witness was also rejected. Then the trial started. First came the witnesses for the prosecution. They were all security officers or military policemen. The first to speak was Evanghelos Yannikopoulos of the headquarters of the security police. He said that I was a communist. My defence counsel challenged him, asking him to produce evidence of this. He said he could not do so for reasons of national security, but he did claim that I had helped families of communist political prisoners. Asked by the president of the court if they were families of political prisoners in general, he said no, they were all communists, I specially chose the communist families to help. He said that the security police had evidence of my involvement with communist underground organizations since 1967. Once again he was unable to answer my defence counsel and tell him what the evidence was, because this also was a 'danger to the security of the nation', and he went on and on about my connections with the international communists and the British communists who had given us the money to arrange Panagoulis's escape. I remembered the lovely old silver I had sold to find money to mount these unsuccessful attempts and to help needy families. And I remembered Mr Babalis of the headquarters of the security police telling me during interrogation, 'Well, I know that you are not a communist; sign the document condemning the communists' (see p. 156). Was it Mr Babalis, Yannikopoulos's superior, who sent him to testify that I was a communist by way of vengeance because I had refused to sign this revolting declaration?

Yannikopoulos was lean and extremely dark, with wicked, coal-coloured eyes. Suddenly he seemed to multiply. There was no longer one Yannikopoulos, there were fifteen or twenty, all dark, all exactly the same, all dressed in long, black robes, and they sat around Galileo pointing an accusing finger at him, threatening him with eternal fire in hell and with a shorter but very effective burning on earth; and

Galileo, under this overwhelming argument, was admitting that the earth did not turn around the sun.

Then came the turn of Captain Demetrios Antonopoulos. He started with a few lies: he said, for instance, that at the beginning of July they had information that Panagoulis was trying to escape, while the truth was that they had found the bars of his cell cut after Zambelis's escape when they checked all the cells and window-bars. He also said that Corporal Staikos, the second and last guard, as far as I am concerned, who was to help Panagoulis escape, had been laying a trap for us from the start. But the truth was that Staikos had betrayed the plan only two days before the attempt, and even then only because he was found out. However, apart from these lies, which he was obliged to tell, he gave me the impression of being an honest witness. Only one thing amused me. When asked where Androusopoulos, Athena Psychoyou, and Skelton were arrested, he said in the car driven by Skelton, some hundred yards from the KESA camp. But when he was asked where I was arrested, he said that he did not know. What could the poor man do? Could he say that I had been arrested hours later, while parking my car in my own parking place, in the middle of the smart residential district of Athens some three or four miles from the camp? How could he give the lie to the government's official spokesman who in his official statement to the press had said first that I had driven the three others in my car to the camp, and was arrested redhanded with them, had changed this story later to a second version, in which I was arrested at a place a couple of streets away while waiting for them, and a little later still indulged in a third version, that I had got tired of waiting and returned to the first rendezvous outside the camp, in an attempt to find my accomplices and whisk Panagoulis away to hide him, and was arrested there. All this of course I learned later, when I was allowed to communicate with people and see newspapers.

During our last two days, after Staikos had already betrayed the plan, Captain Antonopoulos had apparently followed Kostas, and saw us meet at the church of Hagia Trias; this was the first time he saw me. From what he said, it was obvious that at the time he did not know who I was, and that none of the police knew where I had been that whole day and night.

The third prosecution witness was Demetrios Staikos, the corporal guard who had been obliged to choose between betraying the whole group and being skinned alive, one of Theophyloyannakos's favourite threats; naturally enough, he had chosen to speak. He recited his lesson in a strong, assured voice, telling the court how he had laid the trap for us from the very first day. Only Kostas and I could follow the whole performance as if we were all characters together on a stage. The president did ask him why he had waited so many days to report to his superiors, but the answer was all arranged, and Staikos walked proudly away, a free man—at least, as far as I know.

Then came the witnesses for our defence. After the witnesses for the defence had finished, the speeches of the accused started. The first to be called was Bekakos. His defence plea was disgraceful. He pretended to cry, calling Panagoulis a monster who tried to kill 'our father, Mr Papadopoulos'. Even the president of the court got disgusted with him and asked him to say either 'Mr Papadopoulos' or 'the prime minister'.

In spite of the terrific speed of the whole proceedings, we had some short intervals. During one of these I tried to reason with Kostas Androusopoulos. From the very beginning of 1971, when he had asked me for help, I had told him that he had my permission to blame on me whatever he needed if he was tortured, as I hoped that I would be less ill treated. Androusopoulos was beaten for twelve days and twelve nights. I knew that, and I personally heard his screams at least a couple of times; his voice was unmistakable. He had been given hallucinogenic drugs, and, as I have described, I saw him with my own eyes under their influence. He had made three depositions. Two days before the trial, my lawyer had brought me the depositions of all the accused to read, and I knew what Androusopoulos had said. There was nothing at all against anyone in the first; there was very little in the second; there was definitely more in the third, and almost all charging me. I did not mind most of the things he had said, but I had reason to refuse to admit two of them: first, that I was to take and hide Panagoulis myself, and second, that I had provided the sleeping-tablets the corporal was to give Panagoulis's second guard so that he would be asleep at the moment of the escape.

Why did Theophyloyannakos insist so much? Why did he torture Kostas so badly to make him incriminate me further? In spite of the physical hardship, the appalling mental torture, he had inflicted upon me, in spite of everything I knew about him—about how horribly he had tortured others, so many others—I did believe that there were moments when I had seen something human in him. I knew that he was the greatest liar I had ever met, that usually he was acting, but I thought that I could see through his lies and his acting. Had he managed to deceive me? Was he a still better liar and actor than I thought. Whatever the truth of that, he seems to have hated me so much that to obtain evidence to damn me he tortured people, many people. He had wanted to arrest me for a long time. He had been trying to extract evidence against me by torturing others. Now that he had arrested me, he had to have such evidence, and only Kostas could, under painful persuasion, give it.

It is hard to know how the mind of a torturer works. What actually lies behind the tortures? Do torturers inflict unbearable pain because it gives them pleasure? Or is it simply a professional need, to obtain results, to be a successful interrogator? Bank robbers and train robbers do not want to kill; they want the money that someone else has, and they try to get it, whatever the cost to the one who has it. If they have to kill to get the money, they will kill. Is it the same with an interrogator like Theophyloyannakos? Success for bank robbers and train robbers is to gain possession of the money. Success and promotion for Theophyloyannakos depend on his obtaining the information he seeks. It has nothing to do with any ideology. Just as the bank robbers and train robbers will stop at nothing to get the money they want, Theophyloyannakos, in order to get the information he thinks useful to his career, will torture to the brink of insanity the person he believes may be withholding it. It is the same thing, the same motive: success. There is only one difference: the robbers display courage, they put themselves in great danger, while the torturer performs his function in security and even comfort. Yet there is no excuse for torture. It is an admission of failure. A really efficient and intelligent interrogator can get the information he needs without using torture. Sartzetakis disentangled the most difficult case, the murder of Lambrakis, under unbelievably difficult conditions and adverse pressure, without using torture.

So in the interval, in the presence of the police officers who were guarding us and were listening to what we were saying, I told Androusopoulos that I knew he had been tortured, that I knew he had been forced to say certain things, and I asked him please to take back these two statements only. He said he could not. In the despair I read in his eyes I could guess how much he had been tortured, and that it was exactly these things that I had reason not to wish to shoulder that he dared not retract. Had he been specifically threatened with more torture if he did? I shall know only when he is free to tell me. Again and again I told him, and the guards were listening, 'Kostas, they will not dare beat you again, Kostas, speak, say that you were beaten, or I shall say it.' He told me that I could say it, but that he would not support me.

We were sent to our jail for lunch, and almost immediately brought back. Each time we were searched, and I hated this violation of my privacy.

It must have been eight in the evening when Kostas made his address to the court. I think that Athena Psychoyou spoke before him. Or did she speak after me? I don't remember. While Kostas was speaking in a low and monotonous voice, I did not even try to hear. I was looking at my watch; it was about ten o'clock in the evening. I had been up since five in the morning, and only two days before that I had had this haemorrhage which had completed the exhaustion that the almost continual diarrhoea and generally unhealthy conditions of life had brought on.

Kostas finished. Surely there would be a break for the night; surely they would let us sleep. Instead I was called. I was so tired that it did not occurs to me that I could have said, 'Mr President, I am not in a position to speak.' Instead, I obeyed. I must have looked so pale that the president invited me to sit. I did so gratefully, because I thought that I was going to faint. In order to finish as soon as possible, I said that I had the greatest esteem for Androusopoulos, and that I accepted all that he had said, although I had not the slightest idea of what he said. I said I accepted everything with the two exceptions that I was not to take Panagoulis and hide him myself, nor had I given the sleeping-tablets. I was asked why Androusopoulos said that I had done these things; I replied that they appeared on his third statement, and they had been beaten out of him. 'How do you know that he was beaten?' asked the president. 'You were isolated, you did not communicate with him.' Instead of saying that I had heard his screams, I said, 'I have seen him today' and turned to Kostas and looked pleadingly at him, hoping that he would change his mind and speak; he gestured 'no' with his hand. The crown prosecutor said, 'Lady Fleming looked at Androusopoulos and he gestured negatively.' 'Well,' said the president, 'we shall ask him.' And they asked him to get up. 'Have you told Lady Fleming today that you were beaten?' 'No,' said Androusopoulos, 'I have not.'

'What have you to say to that?' asked the president, turning back to me. And I said that I had nothing to say. 'Have you been tortured?'

they asked me, and I said, 'No, not physically, except that they did not let us sleep and I was deprived of water when they knew that I could not be without it, and it is perhaps because of that that I had the big haemorrhage.'

'Why didn't they torture you if they torture others?' one of the officers asked, and I said, 'Don't you think that there are reasons why I was not treated like the others?' The judge nodded assent, but added, 'Now that Androusopoulos has behaved like a coward and denies what you said and does not disclose that he has been tortured, do you still esteem him as greatly as you said?' 'Of course,' I said, 'yes. I had and still have the greatest esteem for him. Androusopoulos is a young man of great courage.' 'Then why does he not speak?' said the president. 'Is he afraid of us?' I said, 'No, we have absolute confidence in you, but tonight we shall be back in the hands of EAT ESA. Tonight Androusopoulos will be at the mercy of his torturers again. I suppose you have never been tortured,' I added.

I was still tired, but at this moment sleep cleared from my eyes and my exhaustion dropped away. 'Please,' I said, 'do not misunderstand me. I refuse to admit only these two things that Androusopoulos said, but I declare that I wished and I still wish with all my heart that Panagoulis be freed, there being no legal means to put an end to his miseries.

'I am against the death penalty,' I said, meaning that Panagoulis had sentenced Papadopoulos to death, and that was the only reason I was against his act. I stated, and it was true, that my motive for trying to free Panagoulis was non-political, that I would have done the same thing for someone who had tried to kill *me*, if I knew that he was being tortured. And I asked the president to allow me to speak of the tortures Panagoulis had suffered and was still suffering, as this was my motive. I said wisely that I was not in a position to prove what I was to disclose, I was not personally present at the tortures, and could not disclose my sources of information; that I had sure information, which I had cross-checked, and that in my mind there was no doubt that what I had been told was true. 'What are your sources of information?' asked the president. I told him I could not say; if I did so they would ask me for the names of the persons, and I had not given one single name during the interrogations at ESA, in spite of great pressure, so please would he not ask me. 'We shall not ask you for names,' he said, and I told him that if he did not, they might ask me at EAT ESA where

I was again to spend the night. No one asked me what was so terrible about being asked in EAT ESA.

So I started a statement that Panagoulis had been tortured *inhumanly*, not only during interrogation, but the president interrupted and said I could leave the 'inhumanly' out. Did he believe that there were tortures which were not inhuman? I went on, but was soon interrupted again with 'Enough.' I pleaded that as this was my motive I should be allowed to go on, but was told that they were willing to accept that I believed in these tortures and therefore that this was my motive, but that if I said one more word about them, 'it would be held against me'. I thought, the foreign press is here, they are not supposed to hear any more. So I had to stop, but throughout my speech, I managed to put in one sentence here, one sentence there, and give an almost full picture of what I knew Panagoulis had been going through for three and a half years at that time, and now for four years. I also tried to deal with my two other great concerns, Skelton and Kostas.

I had asked Skelton, who was an American, not a Greek, to take part in this attempt, and the unfortunate young man had been arrested driving the car while I was not with them, nor anywhere near them. Still, I felt more responsible than him, and very rightly. For this reason I asked to take on myself any responsibility Skelton might be charged with and to answer for it, as I had done from the night of my arrest. And then there was Kostas, the young man whose courage, modesty and integrity I had learned to admire. Although Panagoulis had not even attempted the escape (but had remained waiting in agony behind his locked door), and therefore the crime intended by our alleged conspiracy had not been committed, I thought that Kostas was in great danger of a heavy sentence. He was Panagoulis's friend, it was to him that Panagoulis had sent both guards, and through them exchanged letters with him. It was Kostas who had made all the arrangements with the soldier and the corporal. All contacts with Panagoulis's mother, brother, and guards had been made by him. And to make matters worse, Kostas had already been sentenced once before for anti-Junta activities. So naturally I was especially worried.

I had to save Kostas, to say something to lighten his case. So I said that all he had to give was his love for his friend and his desire to sacrifice himself to free him, he possessed nothing else, no means, no possibilities. It was on me that he had relied, because I was the one who could help. And as the president was trying to find out the extent of my guilt I asked him not to bother, since I declared that if I could have gone to the camp to take Panagoulis in my car, I would have done, that if I could have hidden Panagoulis, I would have done. That it was for Panagoulis's safety, not mine, that I had not done so, since I had been interrogated a few days before and thought that I would probably be a danger to Panagoulis and the whole group.

I think that the logic of the thing was so obvious that the president and the officers believed me, and knew that I was not and could not be the one who was to hide Panagoulis. But what would have happened in my adopted country, they asked, in a case like this? I did not hear the 'adopted'. I thought the president had said, 'in your country', and I said, 'My country is this one here.' So he repeated the 'adopted', and I said, 'In England, if a mother believes that her son is being tortured she has the possibility of approaching her M.P. who will take the matter to Parliament. Parliament would appoint a commission to investigate the case and justice would be done.' I think that the court decided not to proceed on this slippery subject of parliamentary life and turned to another subject. Had I helped the families of political prisoners? asked one of the officers. Knowing that this was a punishable offence, I tried to avoid the answer. I had helped, I replied truthfully, whomever I could. But the question came again, clear and definite. 'That was not my question. Have you helped the families of *political* prisoners?' I said that I knew my answer would count against me, but yes, I had helped families of political prisoners. And, what is more, I had never asked the children I helped what the ideology of their fathers was. And suddenly, remembering my arguments with my communist friends and my bitterness against the false testimony of the security man Yannikopoulos, I added, 'Don't make a present of me to the communists. They will be very happy and also they will laugh a good deal. I could never, absolutely never belong to a party which accepts dictatorship and totalitarian governments. But I respect every ideology and every idealist, provided they do not force their ideology upon us. I don't ask my friends what their political views are. I don't choose them because of their political beliefs nor according to the colour of their skin.'

'And so,' said the officer, 'if communists came to power through elections, would you accept them?'

'Through honest and free elections,' I said, 'of course!' And I knew that they had got what they wanted. I was not a good citizen. I was not ready to exterminate communists, nor give them away to the police, nor would I let their children starve.

The interrogation was over. I call it an interrogation because this is what my defence plea had become. I had completely disregarded my own defence, and anyway, defence against what? I was proud of what I had done, and only sorry that I could not have done more, that we had failed and that Panagoulis had not been freed. I got up and started walking towards my seat. And then once more the dark Yanniko-poulos, the security man who had given false evidence, came to my mind. I stopped. 'I want to add one more thing,' I said. 'Listening to what Mr Yannikopoulos was saying this morning, I realized that five hundred years separate us. I live in 1971, and what Mr Yannikopoulos said reminded me of the Dark Ages, of the time of the Inquisition, when broadminded people were burned as witches.'

'Well, not five hundred,' said the president. Then Skelton was called.

At last we were allowed to go to sleep; it was, I think, two o'clock in the morning. When I had sat down near Androusopoulos after my speech, he had told me that my defence plea was so extraordinarily good that if only I could read what I had said I would understand how astounding I had been. 'You will get the severest sentence,' he added. At the time I did not believe it. I thought it was wishful thinking on his part, not of course that he wanted me to get the severest sentence, but that he hoped he would not have it himself. I, on the other hand, was sure of the opposite. I believed that personally I was hardly involved. I certainly expected to receive a prison sentence because I had known the plan and had been willing to help it all along. I had given the money that I was asked to give for the purpose; I had asked John Skelton to join Kostas and drive the car which would take away Panagoulis and the guard after these two walked out of the camp by their own means. I wished with all my heart that Panagoulis could be freed, so that his endless miseries would be at an end. But I thought the most I would get would be a few months, perhaps a year, which might mean a suspended sentence, so that I should be freed and able to go home. And I was longing to go home.

The next day, after the closing arguments by the crown prosecutor and our defence counsels, the judges retired to deliberate and decide our fate. When they came back to the courtroom they wasted still more time in allowing the photographers to take more photographs, and then at last read the sentences. The court had accepted that I had not taken an active part in the attempt, that is, that I was neither in the car with the others nor waiting anywhere to take Panagoulis in my car, and they ordered that my car, which had been confiscated by the military police, be returned to me. However, I was indeed given—if only by one month—the severest sentence. Hearing it, I was struck dumb. I was given sixteen months; and the four months over the year meant that I was not going to be allowed a suspension of the sentence, but that I should serve it, and that I was not going to go home but to prison.

I did of course realize that the sentences in general were very light, and I thought that this was perhaps due to the presence of the foreign press and of some legal observers. I was very pleased, especially for Kostas's sake, for whom I had feared such a severe sentence. He received fifteen months. I was pleased for Skelton, who was given seven months with suspension, which meant that he was to be freed at once. At the time I thought that the verdict was unfair to me.

Soon after, though, I remembered what I had said in court, that I wanted to shoulder Skelton's responsibility, and that I claimed the first role in what Kostas and I intended to do by saying that I had all the possibilities and that Androusopoulos relied on me. When I had said these things, my only intention was to help the two young men. Now that the tension was over, now that I had had some sleep and my mind was clearer, I realized that what I had said was actually the exact truth. After Panagoulis, I was indeed the most consciously responsible person in his attempt to escape. Besides, I had admitted two other major crimes: that I had helped families of political prisoners, and that I respected any pure ideologist, even if he was a communist. Both these things could not but shock an Extraordinary Military Court, which was competent under the present state of law to judge the *intention* to commit a felony, while the conspiracy, once committed, was judged by a civil court.

The bitterness which had overwhelmed me when hearing the sentence had in fact lasted only a few moments. I soon accepted the sentence as right, well deserved, and very lenient according to the Junta's laws and habits. When the foreign correspondents rushed up to me and asked if I were again given the choice of leaving Greece by relinquishing my Greek nationality, and so spare myself the hardships of imprisonment, would I accept it, I answered with one word:

'Never.' I was resigned to spending my months in prison, and so when at last I was taken to the Black Maria, the photographs that were taken of me behind the metal mesh showed a smiling face. I had done what I thought it was my duty as a human being to do. The judges had done what they thought was their duty. I had no ill feeling or any regret.

Athena Psychoyou and I were taken back in the police car to EAT ESA. We hoped that at last we were to be transferred to the proper prison, but we were kept for another two days. Punishment for me because I had spoken about the tortures? While in EAT ESA I kept asking the guards about Kostas, and tried to catch a glimpse of him through the slit in the door whenever I heard his cell being opened. I was still afraid that he might be ill treated. He seemed all right, and I suppose he was just going past my cell to the lavatory. I heard no screams on these two days, or shouts, or banging on the doors. And I did not see Theophyloyannakos. I learned that he was furious with me and had threatened to implicate me in every trial to come, in the Zambelis escape and in the PAK trial (which took place in March 1972), but he did not summon me to his office, nor did he or anyone else come to my cell.

I remained for forty-eight hours locked in my small smelly cell with only the lavatory for recreation. Even the doctor did not come; I had not seen him for five days. Eventually, on October 1st, Athena and I were taken to Korydallos. I asked about Kostas, and was told that he would also be taken in another car; he was in fact kept at EAT ESA for another five days. Before leaving EAT ESA I was again subjected to a body search, and my few belongings were also searched. This was the third search I had suffered in five days, and it always annoyed me immensely. Even more strongly than the locking of the cell, it gave me the feeling of deprivation of freedom, of being a slave with no right to privacy or ownership of possessions or even of my own person.

Athena and two police officers were in the car. Outside the closed door, which had a wire mesh at the top, sat two more police officers. Another policeman sat beside the driver, who was also a policeman. As usual, I sat near the mesh and looked out, and saw the people in their private cars look at me with interest. Most recognized me because of the photographs in the papers, and I got numerous smiles and friendly nods.

Korydallos is between Athens and Perama, the place not far from Piraeus where one boards the ferryboat for the nearby island of Salamis. On the way I tried to comfort my new friend, Athena. I said, 'You are American, you will soon be expelled to America and will join your children,' and added that I would stay and serve my sixteen months' sentence. It was the opposite that happened.

We arrived. Korydallos Prison consists of a row of well-spaced gloomy buildings, all with barred windows. The front entrance looks more cheerful; it has flower beds. We got out of the car, were made to pass through some gates with iron bars, and were taken first to some offices and then to the director. He had someone else in his office, so I waited outside for a few minutes.

Entering these gates with iron bars made me realize fully the meaning of 'prison' and my heart sank. I had lost an enormous amount of weight in EAT ESA, had had little sleep, lost much blood, and was pale and haggard. Also, as no one was there to see me, I had abandoned the pretence of strength and cheerfulness, and I suppose I looked what I was—deeply distressed. Suddenly I felt that someone was present. I looked up, a couple of yards away stood Sartzetakis's brother. He was looking at me with an expression of deep sorrow. Neither of us dared speak. He was there to ask permission to see his brother and so, a few minutes later, the men prisoners heard that I had arrived, looking tired and unwell.

From the director's office we were taken to another room, once more passing through iron barriers. All these gates had one peculiarity, they had no handles, only a lock which was opened by a guard with a huge key. In this office we were again searched, both we ourselves and our belongings.

While we were being searched, a nun came in. I recognized her as the young nun of the war years who had been a warder at Averof Prison, where I was during the Nazi occupation. For a moment I forgot that I was a prisoner and that she was now a high official in the hierarchy of prison guards, second to the deputy director, and I greeted her warmly and said, 'Well, as you see, here I am again. I seem to be in prison every time the country is occupied.' Soon however I remembered our relative positions, and saw to it that Sister Hierothea need not fear that I would try any sort of familiarity with her.

When the ordeal of this new search was over, we passed through one more iron-barred gate and started going up. Each floor was divided into two wings. There were iron barriers on both sides of every staircase landing. On the first floor some young women crowded behind their closed iron gate and shouted to us, 'We are the political prisoners!'

'Make room for us,' I said. 'We are joining you.' The woman guard who was at the gate interfered, shouting at them to shut up, and Athena and I were told that we were not allowed to talk to them. We were taken up one more floor. At the head of the stairs a number of women, old and young, some carrying small children in their arms, were waiting for the VIPs to arrive. They had been waiting for us for days now. The iron gate on the left was open; we were taken in, and as I advanced a tall young girl rushed out of her cell and embraced me. She was pulled away from me and I was locked in a cell at the far end of the corridor on the left side. I felt lost and downhearted. However, when I looked round I cheered up: my cell was large enough, something like three by three metres, and it had a big window which started at the height of my face. It had bars, of course, but I was able to open the glass window at will and let the fresh air in. The cell was clean and white-washed. There was a bed, a little table with a chair, a clean basin with running water, and a *clean* lavatory. It was again the Turkish type, that is, a hole in the floor, but the hole was not level with the place where one placed one's feet but some fifteen inches down and the footplates were white, clean porcelain, so one could sit. The flush would continue to operate as long as one was pressing the lever, which helped to keep it clean, and there was a piece of wood to cover it. Compared with where I had come from, the cell looked like Buckingham Palace, and this is the name it has now for my mates in this wing.

For an unknown reason, certainly frightfully wrong from the psychological point of view, the newcomers, although no longer incommunicado, had to be locked into their cell for the first day. There was a little spyhole in the iron door through which I tried to see out into the corridor. I could see three of the cells opposite which were open.

I made my bed with my own flowery sheets, and started making a home of my cell, happy to find it clean and comfortable. I also tried to fill my lungs with the clean fresh air. I was just beginning to feel relaxed when a terrible uproar started. I looked through the hole in the door and saw that the woman who had the cell opposite mine was throwing all her furniture and buckets of water out of the cell, screaming hysterically. More screams came from other cells; the women guards arrived. Some other strange creatures, I suppose inmates, joined in and were also screaming. It was hell.

I felt distressed. Where was I? These women were certainly not political prisoners. At last the screams stopped. The woman opposite stopped throwing things out, but instead sat on the floor saying that she was not going to go into her cell again. Now that she was speaking instead of screaming, I realized that she was a foreigner. I knocked at my own door and the guard came. I told her that I wanted to speak to her, and she opened the door. I asked what the woman had done, and she said that she had killed her lover. So I asked her please to tell the director to transfer me to the floor below with the political prisoners. She said that they were communists, and I said I did not care. She went to the director and came back with the message that he required me to write down that I wanted to be with the communists. I was given a piece of paper and a pencil, and I wrote, 'Please put me in the political prisoners' wing. I do not care what their ideology is, but as far as I know they are students and scientists, and at least we have that in common.' The director came up. He spoke in a very severe tone in German to the woman who had made all the fuss, and saw that she went into her cell. Then he turned to me, and equally severely he asked me what I wanted. I told him, and asked why I was with the common-law convicts. He said 'Because you are a common-law convict. Political prisoners do not exist in Greece.'

So we were all common-law convicts. I asked him what the women on the floor below were, and he said they were communist common-law convicts. So I said, 'Please let me be with them.' He said that I had to write and sign a statement that I was a communist. If I did, he would have me transferred there. I said I had done so already. He said no, I had not, he had read my note; it did not say I was a communist, it said that I did not care what the ideology of the others was. What he wanted, he said, was my signed declaration that I was a communist. Then I could join them.

Suddenly I was angry. All the bitterness about Yannikopoulos, the security man who claimed I was a communist in court, knowing that I was not, came back to me, and I was infuriated and disgusted that we were denied the status of political prisoners. 'All right,' I said, 'I will sign a declaration that I am a communist,' and I did so, and handed it to him. But he did not take it. He said no matter what I signed or said, he was the one to decide what I was, and he refused to believe that I was a communist.

I said, 'How can you? The official state has declared it in court, and here I give you my own signed assurance that I am a communist. How can you doubt it or deny it?' He said he did not care what the official state or the security police or I myself might say, he was the master here, he was the only one to decide, and his decision was that I was not a communist, and that I was to stay where I was and that nothing I could say or sign would make any difference.

I said, 'Listen, if you do let me join the political prisoners you will have no better prisoner than me, but if you insist on keeping me with the common-law convicts I shall not be a good prisoner.' He answered that he knew how to deal with bad prisoners as well as good, and I was locked up again in my cell.

The night came and I could put out the light, another magnificent luxury. From my window I could see a yard, and then another gloomy building with barred windows; on the adjoining terrace roof a guard with gun in hand was walking; at intervals another guard patrolled the yard. In the building opposite, I could see men prisoners. They were the real common-law convicts. My friends the political prisoners were in the building behind this one. I could not see them. Although all sentenced were together, there was one part for the ones who had already been sentenced, where Kostas would be, and another for those awaiting trial, where Sartzetakis, Touloupas and the others were; one group could not have any contact with the other.

Again I felt relaxed and happy. The harsh behaviour of the director did not frustrate me. I thought that being a prison director must be a very difficult job, and he had to use this sort of tone to be obeyed. How else could he deal with women getting hysterical and throwing out buckets of water, and others who wanted to sign statements that they were communists when they were not? I was in prison, and I had to accept the rules of the prison.

I had openly fought people who were far stronger than me, who had the power to crush me, to impose hardship on me, to put me in prison. I knew this when I started fighting them. It was with full consciousness of the danger that I had done what I believed it to be my human duty to do. What is more, I was still proud that I had done it. This time what I had wished with all my heart had not succeeded, and Panagoulis had not been freed; I had hoped I would help stop his sufferings, but on the contrary, most probably they were now going to be worse. This time we had been defeated. Panagoulis and the guard had not come out of the camp; the failure was their responsibility, but however the plan had failed we were defeated and had to pay. I was ready to do so without complaint.

I was happy that I had managed to endure without submission the terrible mental tortures and the physical miseries I had been subjected to in EAT ESA. I was pleased that in spite of my utter exhaustion I had stood up well in court. Now I needed a little more patience, sixteen months' patience—no, not sixteen. One third of the sentence could be remitted for good behaviour, that is, five months and ten days. I had already been detained for just over a month, so that made it six months and ten days out of the sixteen. With a little luck I would be only another nine months and twenty days in prison.

The toilet was in the room, and this was wonderful; if I felt sick, or whatever, I could use it without having to beg behind the locked door for it to be opened. I could drink as much water as I liked, and turn the light on and off, and breathe fresh air. I would not be shut in all day all alone. I would no longer have to suffer Theophyloyannakos's shouts. What did it matter if I was with the common-law convicts; who knows how and why this unfortunate woman had killed her lover? The guard had told me that she had been there for sixteen months already and had behaved very well, and it was just my bad luck that she had her outburst today. All would be well. Only after nine months and twenty days the kittens would be grown-up cats, and I would not have seen them grow. I slept.

19. *Prison and Release*

I woke at eleven at night. It was about the time when the boys at EAT ESA used to start banging about and cause a general uproar, and I had got used to being woken and then reading, since the light was always on and I had little hope of sleep for one or two hours, when peace might return. This time I got up and turned the light on; being able to turn it on and off gave me a wonderful feeling of freedom. I could not read, as my books had been kept for a second inspection, so instead I went to the window to breathe the cool clean country air, and I looked out. I saw the yard again, and the memory of another yard came back to me, a yard I had never seen but knew and feared: the yard of the men's Averof Prison, which was next to ours. It was the first year of the Nazi occupation, when my husband and I were arrested. Throughout the first and I believe the second year as well, executions took place in the men's yard. Often at about six o'clock in the morning I would hear the hard steps of the squads, the orders of the officers, the clanging of the arms, the shooting. And then for about two hours, while I waited for the German guard to come and tell me, because he was just a soldier and had some compassion, I would stay motionless, holding my throbbing head in my hands, praying the abject prayer, 'Oh Lord, Lord, make it be *others*.' Not mine, not my own, not my husband. I was a second-year student at the medical school when we fell in love, and he was doing his military service, a soldier with cropped hair. The German guard knew my anguish, and whenever he could he would come earlier to tell me the horrible, the wonderful news: it *was* others.

There were lights in some of the cells of the building opposite ours. I could see some men sitting by their window; I could not see their features, but most of them looked young. They were common-law convicts. What had they done? Stolen, killed out of jealousy or in anger, taken or sold hashish or such drugs? Perhaps some were genuinely wicked by nature and beyond human redemption, but probably most of them had committed a crime either because they had been led astray, or in a minute which in Greek we call 'the bad hour', that fate which brings about the circumstances that make one act out of character. Most were surely strong, healthy young men, their dignity crushed, deprived of freedom, of normal life, of women. They were looking longingly at our building full of many young women who were deprived of the same things, of all the things that matter in life.

On the second floor, just opposite my window, but one floor below, there were two rooms with much stronger lights. Men in uniform were in there. They turned and looked at my cell as I put the light on, and one got up, and approached to see what I was doing. I moved back a couple of steps so that he could not see me, and stayed there for a while looking at the sky that I could now see. From the little window of my cell in EAT ESA I could hardly see it; I could only see the top floor of the big building behind the barracks. On the right of the opposite building there was open space and I could see a hill far away, Aigaleo, I suppose.

I heard the key softly opening the iron-barred entrance to our wing, and then soft felty steps. I quickly turned out the light and went back to bed. I noticed that the spyhole in my door, which had been closed when I went to bed, was open now, because I could see the light in the corridor through it. It must have been opened when I was asleep. I also noticed that between the door and the floor there was a two-inch space through which the light could also be seen. The felty steps approached and stopped outside my door. The light from the spyhole was blocked, surely by an eye watching me. I remained motionless. The felty feet moved away, the hole was free again. I remained quiet for a while, and again, about a quarter of an hour later, I was watched through the hole, and I could understand by the continuous soft dragging of the feet that the guard did not stop to look at the others, the privilege was all mine.

After a while I got up again and looked out. The guard on the terrace adjoining the opposite building got out of his watchroom, walked some way on the terrace roof and urinated. It amused me to think that I had caught him at that, that they were not the only ones to watch on the sly. At six o'clock in the morning I was awakened by loud steps and a heavy clatter of keys opening the iron-barred gate first and then all the cells. Free! We were free to communicate with the others. I jumped out of bed, out of the cell and ran to Athena's. She was still asleep, but I could not wait to let her enjoy the fact that we were no longer in isolation, that we could talk, move, walk, meet the new people. First came Ranya. She was a wonderful character: a habitual thief who was in prison for I cannot remember which time, the seventh or tenth perhaps. She had one weakness: she could not resist a locked lock, she had to open it, and she was a master of that art. She offered her services: she would bring a bucket of hot water for me to have a shower every morning, she would bring me coffee, and clean my cell, and wash the corridor for me when it was my day as a common-law convict to do it. This sounded wonderful, and of course I accepted it. She had a number of children, grown up, but also two boys of fourteen and sixteen, and she needed money and food for them, and would work like a slave to get it. I asked her to teach me how to open locks, all knowledge being useful in this world of ours. It took me some time to persuade her to do that, she would not believe that I really meant it, but eventually she yielded and I learned. I do hope that I can still do it.

Coffee bought on credit from the canteen arrived, and I invited Athena to my cell, and this became the routine of every day. Then one after the other we met the rest of the residents of our wing. The lady opposite my cell, who had made all the terrible fuss the day before, shared a cell with Gabriella, a young German girl of nineteen. She and her husband had been arrested at the frontier with something like seventy kilograms of hashish in their car. Her husband, aged twenty-two, was serving a twelve-year sentence in the prison at Corfu, one of the worst prisons in Greece.

In another cell there was a woman who had already been in prison for, I think, fourteen years; at the age of sixteen she had been made by her grandfather, who was her lover, to poison her whole family: in this way the enamoured beast hoped to enjoy the possession of the young girl in ease and comfort.

There were also three women who had killed their husbands, and two others accused of embezzling. One of them was in the cell next to mine, sharing it with an oldish woman, one of the three who had killed their husbands. These two quarrelled continuously, and I often wondered whether one of them would not kill the other in her sleep. I was afraid of these two women, something in both repelled me. In another cell, all alone, was a young woman who had been in prison for some years already. Sometimes she got hysterical and either tried to set fire to her cell, or to break the glass of the window and attack the others. When this happened, she was taken to a mental home until she was quiet again and then she was brought back. She was just back now.

Then Katia got up. Katia was the girl who had rushed to me and embraced me when I had walked into this wing to be taken to my cell. At the moment I did not know who she was; a murderess, perhaps? Katia was a lovely girl. Her fiancé, a student, had been arrested with a group of other students because they had explosives. They meant to use them but had no time to do so. The explosives were not powerful enough to kill. In Greece great care is still taken about this; people do not want to kill.

Katia was arrested because she used to visit the house of these boys to see her fiancé, and she had known of the explosives but had not betrayed her fiancé and his friends, as a good citizen should have done. For this she had been sentenced to four years' imprisonment. She was not allowed to write to her fiancé or to receive letters from him; she had to be married to him to have this permission; but she was not allowed to marry him, either. She was now twenty-five, pale and in a state of complete breakdown, and was taking very strong drugs against depression. Her joy to have Athena and myself, people of her own sort, was very great. All the hours that we were allowed to be free we were together, either in Katia's room or in mine, and we were not only three, we were five, because there were another two girls whom I immediately loved. Mona, twenty, a beautiful Lebanese girl arrested because she had some hashish, and Jo, perhaps twenty-one, a young American also arrested in possession of hashish. Usually the five of us, Mona, Jo, Katia, Athena and myself, were together, the others being occasional visitors. In Katia's room Athena and I saw newspapers for the first time for thirty-two days, and I was told of the three versions that the official spokesman for the government had given of my arrest. When my room was ready, we moved in there.

Almost as soon as we were in my cell, Katia told me to look out to the window opposite, but not to gesture or go too near my window. I looked and saw two men, arms lifted high above their heads, shaking their clasped hands; and this gesture, among Greeks, means 'congratulations'. Then they pointed behind them, and repeated the same shaking of the clasped hands above their heads. I understood it to mean 'Congratulations from the men who are at the back building, the political prisoners.' I was happy to have their approval.

Trying to cheer up Katia, who looked depressed, I told her how

lucky we were to be there, to be among the people who *cared* for
what was happening to our country, to the other people; and that
when our country was going through this calamitous time, when
people suffered as they suffered now, we should either fight our
insolent and barbarous rulers, or, if we were defeated in this unequal
fight, accept prison cheerfully. 'Would you rather be attending a
cocktail party,' I said, 'with all those ridiculous ladies all in glamorous
dresses, all in jewellery, chatting like parrots, living like cabbages their
stupid life, not caring a damn for the misery of all these prisoners and
their families, for the people who were tortured?' Katia agreed that
we were just where nice people like us should be, and I made her throw
away all the tranquillizers and all the other drugs she was taking. She
was no longer distressed to be in prison, she was proud.

My new friends were young; they had not lived the years of the
Nazi occupation, and I could tell endless stories about those days, all
funny, especially when one was looking back at them over such a
distance. And this is the wonderful thing, that one remembers funny
stories—perhaps because one cannot speak of the grim ones and one
keeps them locked deep inside oneself, or pushes them away. I told my
new friends of the dreams we had then, of the beautiful free Greece
which would emerge after such misery and bloodshed. The only
thing that I did not tell them was that I had no more illusions left. I
felt that Greece was betrayed on all sides: by the Western countries
we had fought with, making so many sacrifices, and by America,
which one considered at that time the quintessence of liberty and of
respect for human rights and dignity. Greece was betrayed now by
the majority of countries for the sake of money, advantageous
contracts, and business. This I did not tell them. They were young
and they had to have illusions and dreams.

But once again, because I cannot let myself sink into despair, I
thought of something to comfort myself: that the real human people
would always struggle for a better life and justice and full freedom for
everyone, for those ideals that distinguish genuine human beings from
creatures who are human only in appearance; this struggle might take
us nowhere, its aim might be the struggle itself, but it was worth
fighting. After long years of such a struggle, this thought appeased
and satisfied me. But then, the girls sang beautiful songs about peace
and freedom and love the world over, the Lebanese girl sang Israeli
songs, and Jo the American girl songs against all wars, and it seemed

to me that from all over the world people were getting up, marching
to conquer and give real Freedom and Peace and respect of human
dignity to everyone. And my disillusion wavered: two inches forward,
one inch back—no matter how slowly, humanity *was*, is, going
forward.

We had dinner together in my cell, the five of us. My maid knew
that there would be prisoners who would not be sent food, and sent a
lot. Katia also had food from her parents.

In Averof Prison, during the Second World War, three of our
group received food from home. It was haricot beans, or something
as poor as that, and not much, but it was food. Then again we made
five portions out of the three. There was a Polish woman, pale and
famished and frightened. She had no one to send her anything. Her
husband was at the men's prison next door. So the fifth portion we
managed to send to him through the kind German guard. One day
the couple was taken away and we never heard of them again. We
knew that they were Jews. I cannot remember their names.

On Sunday, the third day of my imprisonment in Korydallos, the
director said that my English doctor Sir Francis Avery Jones was to
come at midday from London to see me. So in the afternoon I was
called to the pharmacy, which was the only place where the doctor
could examine patients, because there was no prison hospital. I entered
and saw the director, with an interpreter I had seen at the military
court; some other people were there who did not speak or smile or
move. They all looked as if they had been changed into marble
statues. They were Sir Francis, my friend Dr Chris Hodges, my own
Greek doctor, and the doctor of the men's prison.

I went to Sir Francis and took his hand in both mine, and thanked
him for coming to see me, and he looked sadly at me and uttered no
word. I went to Chris my friend and got the same reaction. Then the
director ordered me to sit down on a chair in the middle of them all. I
was not to speak English, the translator would translate for me; so that
was it, they were not allowed to speak to me. Through the interpreter
I told Sir Francis of how I felt, about the haematuria, but I was stopped
when I said that I had been deprived of water and sleep. I was pale and
looked ill, and I learned later that this was what Sir Francis reported.
It was a very strongly worded report which spoke of my various
diseases and operations, and of the danger to my life which might
suddenly emerge.

However, as I was told, the British Ambassador asked that a few words be added which were the only ones released to the press: that the doctors had found me in a very good condition, and that I was adequately treated by the doctors in the prison. The young woman doctor was indeed very sweet, but I had no treatment whatsoever in this prison: there was no hospital, no treatment and no laboratory examinations or test facilities whatsoever. I had only been given the drugs which I had said I needed.

In this prison I was treated in a stricter way than the others. I was supposed to be allowed a visit once a week. I was even asked which day I preferred, and I had chosen Tuesday. But Tuesday came and everyone else had more than one visit, and Athena saw a number of relatives and I was allowed no visit, except that of my lawyer. My happiness at seeing him was all the greater because he and another young woman lawyer were my only contact with the outside world.

Much as I may have tried to express my gratitude to George Mangakis, my principal lawyer, he cannot have fully realized that every time he came to see me he gave me so much, such comfort and greatly needed peace of mind. He knew I could see no one but him, and came to see me as often as he was allowed. Someone had overheard the director saying, no doubt to some high official, at the ministry, 'You need have no worry; besides the usual measures, special security measures have been taken. She sees no one but her lawyer, Mr Mangakis.' This explained a number of things. First of all, of course, the fact that I was allowed no visitors, which was against the regulations of the penal code. But also something else, which often amused me and sometimes annoyed me: that so often in the night, as I mentioned before, the soft felty steps would approach my door without stopping at any other door, and the warder would look through the spyhole to make sure I was still in my cell, and had not vanished through the barred window of my third-floor cell. Also every night, outside my iron door, in addition to the strong metal lock, two large pieces of wood were put one on top of the other—this, also, very softly in the hope that I would not hear them. But from the opposite cells my friends could see them, and so could I, going on my knees and looking under the door which left about a two-inch slit to the floor. I could think of only two ridiculous reasons for these special measures, which were taken only for me, for this continued watch and the absurd pieces of timber outside my door. Apparently I was so great a conspirator that I might, like Panagoulis, cut the bars of my window, make a rope out of my sheets, and jump down three floors; or perhaps a helicopter would come to fetch me as I was supposed to be the head of some tremendous resistance organization. As for these logs behind my door, it was again perhaps a measure against my cutting the iron door or the lock, and opening it. Then the logs would fall down and wake the warder who might have fallen asleep. Of course, after opening my door in this way, I had to cut my way through a number of iron barred gates, managing not to be noticed by the guards on the watchtower before reaching freedom; but this, I suppose, must have seemed to them a mere game for a person like me, who had tried to free Panagoulis, the most safely guarded prisoner in the world.

At last, on the twelfth day, I was allowed to see my maid and talk to her. All prisoners spoke to their visitors by means of an inhuman device. We saw each other through a soundproof glass window, and spoke through some sort of a microphone. Both on my side and on hers, a warder stood watching our lips. It was very clear that no exchange of secrets was to be possible.

The other inhuman thing was the absolute isolation of the communist *common-law convicts* from us, the non-communist *common-law convicts*. We were not allowed to say one word to them, not even good morning, when we saw them crowding behind their locked barred gate every time we went down the stairs to go to the pharmacy or to the yard where we were allowed out for a certain time. For the communists there was even another, separate yard, to which they could go to have some fresh air. We were kept good and safe from their contamination—the murderers, the thieves, the prostitutes were a lesser danger and more suitable company for us.

I was trying not to remember anything of the outside world, anything I loved, in order not to miss it. I had made another world for myself inside the prison, one which was inhabited by people worth all my attention, interest and love.

As I was settling down, counting the months and the days, and the remission of one third of the penalty which I might perhaps get for good behaviour, and trying not to think, and wondering sometimes how long my nerves would stand the strain, my lawyer came with a proposal of troubling hope. He said there was a law according to which if the health of a person deteriorates in prison so that it may endanger his life, and if by having a suspension of the sentence his health can be restored so that he can return to resume his sentence, a civil court may decide to grant a suspension of the sentence for a certain time.

My health had certainly deteriorated very much in the horrid thirty-two days of EAT ESA. Following the visit of Sir Francis Avery Jones and of Dr Chris Hodges, the Minister of Justice had sent two professors of medicine to examine me and certify that the diagnosis of Sir Francis was right. They had come, had examined me, and had agreed. On the basis of these reports my lawyer suggested applying for a suspension of sentence.

The newspapers started up again with the front-page news that I was going to be released. My two fighting neighbours, hearing of this, obtained from the director a promise that if I left one of them would have my cell, and the danger of killing each other would cease. Reading every day that I might be released destroyed all the work I had done to close the outside world out. It besieged and defeated me.

The court appointed and sent three more doctors to see me. Two days later I was at court again, a civil one this time. Sir Francis's diagnosis and prognosis were read; my own doctor, the prison doctor, the two professors sent by the Ministry of Justice and three doctors sent by the court all agreed that I should have a suspension of sentence till I recovered enough to go back to prison. A suspension of eight months was suggested, and the court granted the suspension. When I saw the joy on the faces of the grim gendarmes who had escorted me, of the people who crowded the room, and of the people waiting outside the court, I felt again that their happiness for my sake showed that these people were by no means supporters of the Colonels.

With the papers of my provisional release in their hands, the gendarmes took me back to the prison in the police car, followed by the cars of my lawyer, the various television companies, the foreign correspondents, and the photographers. They waited for me to pack, and say goodbye to my happy friends and my sobbing little Mona; the warders unpacked and searched me and everything once more, and I was out free. Free before I could believe it. Free for eight months.

I arrived home still trailing the television, the correspondents and the photographers behind me. My little place looked like a garden. Since the three doctors sent by the court had agreed that I needed this suspension of sentence, everybody was sure that I was coming out.

Flowers had poured in and kept pouring in for days at about a bunch every minute, while the security police standing on the opposite pavement followed this outburst of popular approval with professional hatred.

I had no eyes for the photographers. I got the cats one after the other in my arms, I saw my lovely new kittens, born when I was in EAT ESA. Paschalis, my most intelligent tom, was very reluctant to believe that I had *had* to leave them. The picture which appeared in the *Guardian*, and which he stole, shows him pushing me very determinedly away with his stretched legs and turning his head away. 'Just you keep those stories for the others,' he seems to say. 'Who is this Theophyloyannakos, or anyone else for that matter, who would have the heart to keep you from *me*?'

In my life I have had moments of great happiness, but I don't believe that I have ever felt so conscious of such an intense and condensed happiness as the one I felt that day. The only thing I wanted to do was to stay at home with my cats, my friends, my flowers. But the correspondents and television people who besieged me did not allow that. For five days I did something which I knew was dangerous, but dangerous only to myself. I spoke to the reporters and the television cameras. I told myself that this was the last service I could offer to my country. I knew that whatever I said at these moments would be published in every detail, and I felt it was my duty to do it, whatever the cost; I would be the only one to pay it. So I spoke, I said what I thought it was my duty to say, and then I stopped and refused to speak.

Still the flowers continued coming in, and whenever I walked out, unknown people would stop me, recognizing me from the many photographs in the papers; they would congratulate and kiss me. I remember an old, very beautiful and smart lady who stopped me and asked if I was Lady Fleming. I said yes. She said, 'Congratulations,' and then she whispered, 'What a pity it failed.' I said, 'Yes, a pity.' She bent nearer and said, 'Never mind, next time.' I said there could not be a next time for me, I would be a danger now. She said, 'Somebody else.'

All this enthusiasm of the people, these flowers, this hugging and kissing and congratulations in the street, were once again a sort of referendum. People being for me were against them, and the police ostentatiously standing there and watching were registering this. I

thought that having the security police and the military police against
one under a military dictatorship was no great fun, but I accepted it
as inevitable. They knew I could no longer do anything against them,
they would soon relax.

For fifty-one days I had braced myself not to feel or show any
weakness. Now I let myself go, and suddenly I felt an immense
nervous fatigue. I had not the strength to do anything. Only I forced
myself to go out. I had been locked in all this time, I *should* go out. On
the third day of my release I experienced an additional joy: I realized
that I just had to turn the handle and the door would open! What
marvels there were in the world, and we did not notice them.

I had been released on the evening of October 21st. My car, which
the military police had confiscated, had been returned to me by order
of the military court which thus admitted that I had not taken active
part in the attempt of Panagoulis's escape, and that the three official
communiqués of the government spokesman, first that I was arrested
in my car waiting outside the camp, then that I was arrested in my
car waiting a couple of streets further away for them to hand over
Panagoulis to me, and finally that I got tired of waiting for them and
had returned outside the camp to the meeting place and was arrested
there, were all wrong. Did not they know where and when they had
arrested me? The car had been restored to my ownership, but she was
still a prisoner in the EAT ESA yard, and I had to go and fetch her.

I did not particularly wish to see Theophyloyannakos, so I rang
Major Zissis, the regular military court investigating judge who had
taken my deposition before the trial, to ask him what was the
procedure to follow. He said that I had to go to EAT ESA to sign certain
papers, and then I could take my car. I asked him if he was the
competent authority to deal with the matter, and he said yes he was.
I said, 'So I can see you, only you, is that right?' And he knew what I
meant, and he laughed and said yes, I could see *him* only, and asked me
to go straight away, which I did. It was Saturday, October 23rd.

I went to EAT ESA and told the soldiers at the gate that I had come to
see Major Zissis who was expecting me. The soldiers did not ask for
my name or for any identification; one of them said simply, 'Come
with me,' and I followed him to the building I knew so well. When
one enters it, the commanding officer's office, Theophyloyannakos's, is
first on the left and Zissis's third on the same side. We entered, and two
soldiers were blocking the corridor just beyond Theophyloyannakos's

office, and they told me to enter this room. I explained that I had come to see Mr Zissis and not Mr Theophyloyannakos, but they answered that the commanding officer wanted to see me. I had no alternative but to obey.

There was one more person in the office, somebody he introduced me to, telling me that he was a biologist, a Greek from America, who had been invited by the Junta to come back to Greece to organize research. I told Theophyloyannakos that I did not want to take up his precious time, that I had come to collect my car and had arranged to see Mr Zissis for that. He said that he was delighted to see me, would I please sit down, and he gave orders for the papers for the car I had to sign to be prepared and brought to him. I sat down; he asked me if I would take a cup of coffee, and I said no, thank you, only a glass of water, please.

'As always?'

'As always.'

He asked me how I would like a trip abroad. I replied that I did not feel like travelling.

'Well, just one little journey?'

'No, thank you.'

He asked me why I did not want to go abroad, and I told him I was afraid they might not allow me to return. 'Athens is nice, isn't it,' he remarked.

'Yes,' I answered, 'Athens is nice, and there is more to it for me.'

Then he asked for my address. I asked, didn't he know it? He repeated, 'Give it to me.' So I did, and he said he would come to visit me on Monday or Tuesday between 6 and 7 p.m. I said 'Mr Theophyloyannakos, only my friends come to my home. If you want to see me to ask me any further questions, please send me a summons and I shall come immediately to answer your questions.' He said, 'I want to come to your home, I want it very much.'

I repeated, 'I told you that only my friends come to my home.'

He said he considered himself my friend; I answered, 'It takes two for that.' 'We have given you thirty-two days' hospitality in here,' he went on; 'cannot you give me a cup of coffee just for an hour one evening?' I said no, only for my friends. So he asked, in a honeyed voice, 'Would you like us to give you some more hospitality here?' I said no, thank you. I kept repeating, 'I don't want to take up your time, let me wait in another office for the car papers to come.' I was afraid I would finish by having some more hospitality in there. He said no, he was not busy, and was only too happy to have me there. 'And I shall come to see you,' he added; 'and you will give me a cup of coffee. What can you do if I come? Throw me out?'

I said, 'You will not come to my house.'

Then he showed his anger and said, 'We are ESA and we can enter any house we like.' I said, 'In that way, certainly. Especially with a warrant in your hands.' 'A warrant?' he said, and rolled with laughter.

The telephone rang and he answered, and while he was speaking, the biologist whose name I have forgotten asked me why I was against the regime, and why I spoke in the way I did to the commanding officer who was so friendly. He said he admitted that some misguided people like me were against the regime, but most people he thought were very pleased with it. I said, 'Look, I have come here today to fetch my car, and not to discuss the regime with you. But anyway, if everybody is so pleased why don't they dare lift the military law, and have elections?' Theophyloyannakos jumped up, the telephone receiver still in hand. 'We shall never have elections,' he said. He put the receiver down and went into his old song and dance routine. 'We are honest officers,' he told me in anger, 'hard working, giving our lives for the country. There has not been one scandal, not one abuse, not one embezzlement since we came in.' My own opinion was different, but I could not say so. Instead I said, 'That may well be so, but who can check it?' He got angry again, but again he controlled himself; he is very good at that.

'We want you to be our friend,' he said, 'to collaborate with us, and you *will* be our friend. What about coming out one evening with my wife and myself, and we shall go to a nice restaurant and have dinner together?' I knew that this meant a nice photographer as well, taking a photograph of Lady Fleming having dinner with Major Theophyloyannakos, showing that she had agreed to collaborate with the regime, so I answered, 'No thank you, Mr Theophyloyannakos, I shall not have dinner with you.' Then I said that a few days after my arrest, which seemed years ago now, though it was only two months earlier, he had given me his word of honour that my friend Takis Touloupas would be released in a fortnight, but instead Touloupas was still in prison, awaiting trial.

He said, 'I never gave you my word of honour.' He had, but I could not insist, so I said, 'All right, you did not give me your word of

honour, but you told me so.' He said, 'Well, he may be freed soon.'
Then suddenly he asked, 'Do you want Touloupas freed?'

I said, 'Yes, of course.'

'Well, if you agree to have dinner at a restaurant one evening, that
is, you, Touloupas and his wife, and me with my wife, I shall have him
released this very minute. Do you accept that?'

I said, 'No, I do not.'

He bent towards me as he did on his bad days, and shouted, and
pointed an accusing finger at me. 'You see what you are? You leave
a man in prison just so that it will not be said that you are a friend of
the Junta.'

'And what about all those others you have kept in prison for over a
year now, without trial, changing the charges from one day to
another?' 'There is no one in prison without a sentence,' he said, with
the absolute disregard for the truth which is his quality. 'Just name
me one.' And he knew whom I would name, and I did. 'Christos
Sartzetakis,' I said. 'Well,' said Theophyloyannakos, 'you may also see
him come up your stairs in some twenty days or so. How would you
receive him?' I said, 'With open arms.'

Sartzetakis was released about a month later. But he did not come up
my stairs; he had no reason to do so, because before he was released I
had been forcibly expelled from my country.

The papers for the car came. I signed them, and Theophyloyannakos
gave orders that my car should be immediately given to me and that
they should see that they helped me with starting it (after almost two
months the battery might not work). 'We have technicians here,
everything,' he told me, 'and they will start your car.' Before going
out to the car I said, 'Won't you give me my passports?' When they
had searched my home they had taken both my passports, the British
one as well as the Greek one. 'Why don't you give them back to me?
You do know that I don't want to leave.' I also complained that they
had lost the two little prayers and the verses I loved so much and
always kept in my wallet. He said he would look for the prayers,
nothing was lost in EAT ESA, and as for the passports he would bring
them himself to my house.

I left him, and a new problem arose. I had thought, quite
naturally, that they had kept the keys of the car. But they had put
them in my handbag, which my maid had taken at my request from
Korydallos Prison, and had not yet given back to me: I had been

free for only two days. So I had to come again two days later on
Monday. But that day I did not see Theophyloyannakos. Some young
boys had been arrested with explosives, and, as I heard afterwards,
they had been horribly tortured at EAT ESA. Perhaps on that Monday
Theophyloyannakos was busy 'interrogating' them. But his orders
were executed. Motor technicians charged the battery, soldiers pushed
the car, and in this way I left the place which I hope I shall never see
again.

One day I was having lunch with a friend at her house. I
returned home to find my maid very annoyed. Somebody had rung
up to say that he was a reporter for a foreign newspaper and that he had
to have an interview with me urgently. The maid said that I was having
lunch out. He said it was very urgent that I should give him the
interview, as it was said that I had been released from prison because
I had been the one to give all the group away, that I was collaborating
with the police and the Junta, and that at that very moment I was
having lunch at the Hilton Hotel with someone high up in the
security police and a foreign correspondent. My maid, who knew
where and with whom I was having lunch, and very appropriately had
not let it out, told the man that if he knew so well that I was having
lunch at the Hilton, the sensible thing to do was to go there and find
me instead of ringing me here.

The day after, somebody else rang and this time spoke with me. He
was a newspaper man, he said, and wanted an interview with me. I
said, 'Thank you, but I do not give interviews.'

He said, 'But you must, you have to, because rumour says that you
have betrayed everyone and are a Junta collaborator.'

'I don't mind,' I said. 'I am sorry, but I don't give interviews,' and
I rang off. The man rang again, said the same things, and I rang off
again. He rang a third time; again it was the same, and again I rang off.
Next day it was the same again: another new voice saying almost the
same things and once again ringing three times after I put the receiver
down.

The day after that, the wording changed. A voice said loudly, 'I am
a friend of Alexandros Panagoulis, and of Kostas Androusopoulos.
You will understand that I cannot give you my name, but look here,'
he went on threateningly, 'we thought you were a friend of ours, now
we learn that you gave them away, and you are a collaborator of the
Junta.'

'Are you a member of the security police?' I asked quietly, and rang off.

He rang again immediately, and started threatening reprisals. I put the receiver down again. A friend of mine was with me, and when the man rang for the third time I asked my friend to answer. He did so, and asked the caller to give his name. He refused, saying that he could not, but wanted to speak to me. My friend shouted at him that I was not going to speak to somebody who would not give his name and told him not to dare ring again. He did not, but that was the routine: three times.

Next day as usual somebody rang. He had a cultured young voice, spoke politely and reluctantly, and I thought I could see him as a young soldier, holding the receiver, ordered to tell me these things while Theophyloyannakos or Mallios was holding a second receiver. He said, 'I am a newspaper reporter, Lady Fleming, may I please have an interview with you?' I said once again, 'No, thank you. I do not give interviews.' He went on, 'You know you must, because rumours have spread that you have betrayed everyone.' I said softly, because I was sorry for the boy, that there were no such rumours, and that he need not worry; then I rang off. He rang again, and in an apologetic voice he said that he was the reporter who had just rung and that really there were such rumours. I said, 'There are not, and if there are, let them alone.' And I added in a voice which was sad but not angry, 'What you are doing is cowardly and evil. If you like being one of these things or both, you can go on.' He did not ring back, nor did anyone else after that, but the cold war went on in a different way.

The bell rang one day when my one-room apartment was upside down, as I had decided to find the energy to put my many books in order. So I walked out, closed the door, and went down the few marble steps to my tiny little hall entrance, I think it is one metre and a half by one metre and a half. There stood a woman, looking like a charwoman, whom I did not know. She told me that she was Mrs K., the mother of K., a young man who was in prison. By a lucky chance I remembered immediately who she was, and what she was supposed to have done during her son's imprisonment in EAT ESA over two years ago. I had been told that, coached by Theophyloyannakos, who had promised to free her son if she made him talk and betray his group, and helped betray those of his friends who were not arrested, this woman had co-operated with her son's torturers and succeeded in breaking the poor boy's resistance; he betrayed whatever he knew. I had also been told that if a friend of her son's sneaked into her house after dark, to ask news of him, the woman would keep him talking and would call the police, who would arrest him. Her son was released, and then re-arrested two days before the trial in order to appear in the dock, where he was expected to repeat all he had said during interrogation: to give evidence against his friends, and to say how sorry he was he had been led astray. But those two days before the trial among his heroic friends effected the young man's recovery. He spoke well in court, said he had been made to write the statements he had written, and got a heavy sentence. Suddenly all these things came back to me. I apologized for not being able to take her up to my flat, as it was upside-down, and asked what I could do for her. She said, nothing at all; she had just called 'to pay me a visit'. She did not know me at all, it had never occurred to her before to come and pay me a visit; and if she had the slightest regard for her son's safety I was the last person she should see, since just then I was not high up in the affections either of the security or of the military police.

She added that she would like me to go to her house and sit in the garden and have a cup of coffee with her under the rosebushes—it was November!—and that she wanted us to become friends. I said, 'Thank you very much, Mrs K. Unfortunately I shall never come to your place, because I am afraid of the police, and I shall ask you also never to come to my place again.' And then, standing in this one-metre-square hall, within three minutes, the wretched woman told me all that, I suppose, the police had asked her to tell me when, in a matter of weeks, we would have become friends. Wasn't I the silly woman who was so sorry for the political prisoners and their mothers? The one who could arrange escapes? So she said pleadingly, 'I want my son to get out of prison. I want it so terribly much!'

'I do understand you, madam,' I said, 'and I do hope your son will be freed soon. You have all my good wishes and sympathy.' She saw that her visit was to come to an end, that it had not been successful. But she had been ordered to ask one more thing, so she did it there and then: 'What do you think of the bombs?' She meant the explosives used by the resistance people. She was twisting her hands in embarrassment. It was obviously not the way she had been told to manage things. 'I don't know,' she added. 'I don't know what to think about it. What is *your* opinion about the bombs?' I said, 'I think you should discuss this matter with your son. Thank you for coming to see me, but believe me, you must not come again.' She left.

On the morning of November 12th, I had something that looked very much like angina. It lasted for a good hour, but again I said it must be nerves. In the evening, for four whole hours and in spite of tranquillizers and all sorts of other things, I was sweating and had a pulse of over 150. Next day my friends alerted the doctors, who came, made me stay in bed, and did not even allow me to go to the clinic to have an electrocardiogram. They brought the apparatus to me. The electrocardiogram was excellent, but the doctors said, 'The damage may not show yet, you stay in bed till Monday when we will have a second one, and if it is good, you can get up. *Not before.*'

It was Saturday evening. A friend slept in the flat to keep me company or to be there if I died. The day after, on Sunday November 14th, at 7.30 in the morning, while we were still both asleep, there was a gentle knock on the door. I called my friend, and asked her to see who it was. She was sleepy and said it must be the cats. I said, 'Please go to the door, it is not the cats.' Before opening the door, she asked who it was, and the wife of the concierge said it was she, Zacharoula. So my friend opened it, and six men in civilian clothes walked in. One man approached my bed and said he was sorry to disturb me, but the chief of the police wanted to have a word with me, and would I go with them. I said that on doctors' orders I could not get up. I showed the electrocardiogram on the table next to my bed, and said that they must realize that I had not been expecting them and therefore had not put this electrocardiogram there for them. He said it would not harm me to get up, and I asked him if he were a doctor; he said no, but he understood such simple things as heart attacks.

I told him to ask the chief of police if he would please wait till Monday evening, or, if it was so urgent, to come and see me at home and ask me whatever he wanted. He said, 'That is impossible.' I insisted that I was not going to get up, and gave the name of my doctor for him to tell his chief. A little later the telephone rang and the police officer told me that the chief had asked my doctor, who had said that I could get up. They would take me very slowly in the car to the police station and bring me back just as quietly, and I was not to suffer any discomfort. I asked where this police station was, and they told me. Friends afterwards asked why I obeyed and got up and went with them and why I did not ask them to show me a warrant. I said that they had something much stronger than a warrant; they were six men and I was in my nightdress and I did not see myself being dragged out of bed.

20. *Expulsion*

More men were waiting down at the front door of the building. They asked me to enter a car and sat on both sides of me, while two men sat in front. We started, and the direction was just the opposite of where they had said they were taking me; it was the direction of the airport. I told them that that was where they were taking me, and asked whether they were going to expel me. At first they gave no answers to my questions, but eventually they said yes. I said, 'But you cannot, I am Greek,' and they, halfway to the airport, said that I had been deprived of my nationality two days before. Again I said, 'You cannot, you cannot deprive a Greek of his nationality when he is in his own country,' and they laughed at the thought that there was anything they could not do, or any such thing as the law. 'Anyway,' they said, 'you have one nationality, the British one.' I offered to give up my British nationality if they liked. This seemed to impress them; I also said, 'Why did you lie to me? Why did you say I was to see the chief of police?' and they said that I *was* to see the chief of police, he just happened to be at the airport and that is why we were going there. I could discuss things with him, and it all depeneded on how persuasive I was to be, and anyway, I had the right to three days before being expelled.

When we arrived at the airport I was not taken to the main building but to a small barracks, which apparently belonged to the police and stood at a good distance from the airport building. They were making sure that no one was to see me. One of them made a telephone call from another room and when he came back the general atmosphere changed. Did he tell his chief that I had offered to give up my British nationality? Did this please the chief, did he think it would make good propaganda? 'Lady Fleming says that she does not like the regime, but she prefers it to going to England.' I don't know, but suddenly everybody was terribly worried about the fact that I had had no breakfast and asked me to tell them what I would like to have and whatever it was they would bring it to me.

I had just to express a desire and it would be granted. So I said, 'I would like to go back home, please.' And they said, 'We said anything, and you can have anything, but not that.' They stood all round me, and they all begged me to tell them what I wanted for breakfast. I could not be without breakfast; this seemed to make them all so terribly unhappy. So I said, 'You cannot bring me the breakfast I want,' and they said that *they* could do anything, so in order to forget my despair I said I wanted a double Turkish coffee with a little sugar, fresh milk – I insisted that it should be fresh, not evaporated, as I knew that there was no fresh milk at the airport – and toast and fresh Dutch butter. Three men disappeared, and some twenty minutes later they came back to say that they could not find it. I said, 'What is it that you cannot find?' I had forgotten all about breakfast. They said, 'The fresh milk.'

We had been there for over two hours already. I asked what we were waiting for, and they said the chief was trying to arrange things, and that I should not worry. It was about eleven o'clock when the telephone rang. The officer near me answered with great respect, and then told me that it was the chief, and the chief wanted to talk to me. I took the receiver and a voice said, 'Lambrou here.' Lambrou had been for a long time an inspector at the headquarters of the security police in Bouboulinas Street, with the infamous torture-room on its terrace. Lambrou was known for his gentle manners, his impeccable clothing (although in excessively bad taste), and his terrible cruelty. He had tortured people with his own hands, although he did not like to get them dirty. Lately he had been transferred to the aliens department, as they had learned that there were foreigners who helped the resistance. It was natural that he should be the one to deal with me since, unknown to myself, I had become an alien two days before.

Lambrou used his honeyed voice first: 'With all the respect that I owe you, Lady Fleming, I assure you that I am trying to trace the Minister of Justice in order to beg him to change his mind about expelling you. I was told that he was at Hagios Andreas' (a seaside resort a few miles from Athens) 'and indeed he was, but he had left before I could reach him. I shall go on trying. But if I fail by 11.30 when our last plane leaves for London, I shall ask you like the decent and great lady that you are please to board the plane quietly; when in London, do contact the Greek Ambassador; he will have the new instructions I am trying to get.'

I said, 'Mr Lambrou, I shall not board the plane of my own free will. I may have had a heart attack two days ago, which means that I may die on the flight. I am a doctor myself, and as a doctor, I consider it a serious potential danger to my life. As far as I know I have not been sentenced to death, or have I?'

'Of course not,' said Lambrou's sweet voice; 'nothing at all will happen to you, it has all been discussed with your doctor.' Actually they had never spoken to my doctor, and they had taken the risk of inflicting on someone who was probably suffering from an embolism the ordeal of brutal expulsion and an air flight. 'I promise you I am doing all I can, but you know how it is, if I don't find the Minister of Justice to reverse his order we shall all be punished from the top to the last officer.' My own opinion was that Mr Tsoukalas, the Minister of Justice, was under Lambrou's orders and not the other way round. Still, I cannot have accurate information about the internal affairs of the Junta, nor could I possibly have discussed them at that moment. I asked instead, 'Why this expulsion *now*, Mr Lambrou?' And he said, 'Well, you *did* something.'

I said, 'Supposing I did, I was court-martialled, sentenced, punished.'

A cruel voice in a horrid staccato said, 'Not *enough*.'

I said conciliatorily, 'Will it satisfy you if I go back to Korydallos Prison? I can declare that now I am well enough to resume my sentence and ask for the suspension to be interrupted. I offer to go back to prison and give up my British nationality. Would that appease you?'

His voice was normal again, and with some astonishment he asked me if I really preferred to go to prison instead of going abroad. I said yes, I did. He went back to repeating that he was going to try and find the Minister of Justice, but if he did not manage to do it in time would I, like the decent person that I was, board the plane at 11.30, and he would let me know through the Greek Ambassador in London the success of his efforts. 'Get in touch with the ambassador immediately,' he said. 'He will have instructions for you.'

I repeated that I was not going to board the plane voluntarily, and added, 'Mr Lambrou, it is in no one's interest to expel me now. If I try to help one of our people *now* I shall only harm him, and you know that I would not harm *our* people. Here I am harmless, outside Greece I am armed.' The hard, cruel voice replaced the honeyed one. 'Use your weapons to get back,' he said.

'You know very well that I am not speaking of weapons, I have no weapons, but I can talk. Abroad I can speak out and people will know that I am telling the truth.' The conversation finished there.

We went on waiting. It was past 11.30. A bulky police officer in civilian clothes – they were all in civilian clothes – approached me and said, 'Please will you follow me.' I said no, I would not. 'You heard what I said to Mr Lambrou. I am not going to the plane.' He said, 'But we are not taking you to the plane. Mr Lambrou is here now, at the building, and he wants us to take you to him.' I knew it was one more lie. I had been refused permission to approach the airport building even to go to the lavatory. I knew they were lying, but there were about ten or twelve of them, what could I do? I knew it was all over now, they were going to expel me.

However, just to complete my collection of their lies, guaranteed with their word of honour as officers, I said, 'Will you give me your word of honour that you are not taking me to the plane?' He said yes. I insisted, 'You do give me your word of honour as an officer that you will not take me to the plane,' and he repeated the whole sentence. I got up, walked out, and was asked to enter a little car. Some of them got in with me, and I was driven straight to the plane. I turned to the man who had spoken before and said, 'Is this your word of honour?' and he said, 'Yes,' and I never saw before so much hatred in the eyes of a man. He said, 'Get out of the car.' I sat quietly. He got in the driver's seat, backed the car so that it was just under the steps of the plane, had a bus brought to hide me from the view of the people watching from the airport building roof, got into the car and with a powerful push threw me out. I stayed there. I was not resisting, I just stood passively. He came to me, twisted my left arm hard behind my back, and in that way pushed me up the steps. We entered the plane, and he changed his grip into just twisting my left hand; he made me sit in the back seat of a completely full plane. Still twisting my hand, he pushed something into my handbag. I saw later that it was my British passport and an air ticket in the name of Mrs Konstantinides.

Somebody else brought me my camel coat and said there was a suitcase for me in the plane that my maid had been made to prepare for me. The man was still twisting my hand, wondering what my next reaction was to be. He was looking at me, and my impression is that he had something to say but did not dare to speak to me. I pushed his hand away, whispering, 'Gangsters.' He let my hand go and left. The plane took off immediately. The steward came to me and said, 'The officer asked me to tell you to contact the Greek Ambassador as soon as you are in London.'

A little while before landing, I asked one of the hostesses when the plane was due to return to Athens. She said in forty minutes, and I decided to stay in and go back. Well, perhaps Lambrou had spoken the truth, perhaps he had been trying to find whoever had ordered my expulsion, perhaps my humble offer to go back to prison and give up my British nationality so that I would be completely at their mercy had satisfied them. Hope is such a mad thing.

From time to time throughout the flight one of the pilots had come down to the back seat where I was to have a look at me. The plane landed, and I did not move. I told the hostess I was going to stay in the plane. The pilot who had been watching me got out and then came back. 'This plane is not leaving,' he said. 'It will leave at 10 p.m. The one that was meant to leave at 10 p.m. is going now.'

They had switched the planes. 'This plane has to be locked now,' he said, 'for security reasons,' and he added, 'They asked me how you behaved during the flight, and of course I said that you behaved well.' I looked blank. I did not understand what he was saying. What had they expected me to do—fight, hijack the plane? I asked for the British airport police to come up. In the meantime somebody had whispered to me that all the press, all the photographers, all the television men were waiting on the ground to see me. I sat distraught. I knew that nothing could any longer help me, since the moment I put my feet on British soil, I *was* expelled. This Olympic Airways plane was still Greece.

A middle-aged police inspector came into the plane. He was very nice; I asked him how the law stood in England, did they accept into the country someone who did not want to come? He told me that I was British for them, and therefore welcome. He asked to see my deportation papers. I said I had none. He explained he meant the papers the Greek authorities must have handed me. I told him that no one had handed any papers to me. 'This is very illegal,' he said, thoughtfully, and I was amused to think that the British still seemed to have very strange ideas about how laws are respected in Greece.

He stepped down, then came back again, this time with a press representative of the Foreign Office and my friend Dr Chris Hodges. They all explained to me that the plane was not to leave till 10 p.m., it really did have to be locked according to the law. So I said that where there really are laws one has to respect them, and I got up to get out. The Foreign Office man told me then about the photographers, the press and the television people. He said that if I wanted to talk to them they would arrange for me to give a press conference, or if not, they would protect me. For a fraction of a second I remembered that both Lambrou and the police had told me to contact the Greek Ambassador who would have instructions for me, perhaps to return? For a fraction of a second, I wished it to be true, I wished I could believe it, but I knew that this was another lie, just to prevent me from talking till I stopped being hot news.

They thought that they had worked it out well. They had got me out of my house very early on a Sunday morning, kept me out of sight at the airport, and put me on board the plane almost as it was taking off. As I learned later, a few police officers had stayed behind at my flat in order to prevent any of my people answering the telephone or allowing anyone to enter the house. They thought in this way they could be certain no one would have heard of my expulsion or my arrival in London; and counting on my desperate wish to return to Greece, they produced this deceptive hope of the contact with the ambassador who might have instructions for me to go home again. I would go to see the Greek Ambassador and I would have to keep quiet while I waited for the 'instructions' which would never arrive, and months would go by, during which I would keep ringing the ambassador for news, until in the end my expulsion would no longer be of interest to anyone.

All this went like a flash through my mind, and I said, 'I shall speak.' The press conference took place with television and photographers, and I spoke, and I still do. Somehow the news had reached England that I was coming: the Greek security police had been characteristically unsuccessful in their deception. Since 10.30 a.m., English time, the radio had been giving news of my expulsion and the number of my flight. When five days after my release from prison I had thought I had spoken for the last time to a foreign correspondent, I was wrong. I did not know that the Colonels themselves, with this unnecessary, ill-timed, and, to me, incomprehensible expulsion, would give me the opportunity to speak, almost non-stop for over six months, and to write innumerable articles and this book.

I believe that this was my duty. The expulsion was indeed unnecessary and ill-timed: as I had told Lambrou in Greece, I could do nothing now. I was too well known to the police. I would have been a danger. Why did they choose to do this very wrong thing? Was it, as I said when I came out of Greece, because they wanted to hold the trial of PAK, of the pro-Andreas Papandreou resistance organization? With threats and torture Theophyloyannakos had managed not only to make people say that I belonged to it when I did not, but also to attribute so much to me that if I were in Greece it would be difficult to hold the trial without me in the dock or the witness stand. They knew they could not afford this because they had no evidence against me and they had no wish to let me speak for Andreas Papandreou as I would have done. They were trying desperately to prevent his name being heard.

When I married Alexander Fleming, I refused for six months to take any steps to acquire British nationality from the fear that if I did so I might lose my precious Greek one. We were travelling a lot, and at that time whenever a Greek citizen left England he needed a visa from the British Consulate to re-enter Great Britain. So although my husband was so frightfully busy on every journey, which was usually a packed lecture tour with all sorts of other engagements squeezed in, he had to go to the British Consulate of each place, queue patiently and pay twenty-five shillings to get my visa; and he would never allow me to do it alone and meantime get some rest.

So for six months we travelled, he on his British passport and me on my Greek one. Finally, after six months of this, Fleming's patience came to an end. We were to board the *Queen Elizabeth* to return to London, and had first to rush to the British Consulate for my visa. As we queued quietly, another lady kept indignantly telling me that her husband was an important businessman and could not queue like this, and that some preferential treatment for important people should be established. I heard her complaint patiently and silently. Eventually we all got out, and it happened that the lady and her businessman husband and Fleming and I were boarding at the same time. Photographers rushed to photograph my inconspicuous husband. Later, on board, the impatient lady approached me. 'Never again', she said apologetically, 'shall I complain if I have to queue.'

However, this time Fleming also had had enough of it. 'Look here,' he told me, 'this is the very last time that I pay twenty-five shillings for *my* wife to get back into England.' When we were back in London, I went to the Greek Consulate and explained things to the Greek Consul. I said I did not want to give up my Greek nationality; on the other hand I wanted to please my husband. What could I do? 'There is no problem,' said the Greek Consul General. 'If you are born a Greek, you always remain a Greek. Just apply for British nationality and you will have a dual one, Greek and British.' That is what I did, and every time I travelled I wrote, whenever asked to do so, that I had a dual nationality, Greek and British.

In 1968, while I was in Greece, I needed a birth certificate and went to Athens Town Hall to get one. 'You have been cancelled,' was the unexpected answer that I got. I asked what the man meant. Had I not been born or what? He said that by acquiring the British nationality, I had lost the Greek one. I explained the whole story to him, and what the Greek Consul General had said, and gave his name and the date, but he told me that it had been a bureaucratic error: just before that time a law had been passed adding a formality in cases like mine; I should have put it in writing that although I was getting the British nationality I wanted to keep the Greek one. As the law requiring this formality was new, the Greek Consul did not know about it. But it was simple: if I brought such and such a certificate proving that I was born a Greek, etc., I would automatically get back my Greek nationality. I did so, and regained the Greek nationality I was so proud of.

Greek law says that whatever other nationality you may have, in Greece you are a Greek and subject to Greek laws only. Also at the back of my British passport, under the heading 'Dual Nationality', it says: ' ... when in the country of their second nationality such persons cannot avail themselves of the protection of Her Majesty's representatives against the authorities of the foreign country ... '

The Junta was in power when, with the full knowledge of the above statement, I got back my Greek nationality automatically as I mentioned above with the mere proof that I was born a Greek. My friends were appalled. They knew that I was openly and in a very outspoken way against the Junta; that if I could I would shelter and help whoever they were after; that I had returned to live in Greece for ever before the Junta came. Why on earth did I put myself at their mercy? My non-friends said, 'She must have some sort of interest.' And almost everyone said, 'One would give anything *not* to be a Greek national these days, to have another nationality to protect one, and this madwoman does whatever she can to be deprived of the protection of British nationality.'

Pattakos, the then Minister of the Interior, boasted that the fact that Lady Fleming wanted to be a Greek showed how wonderful the regime was, or something of the kind. Mr Pattakos always mixes his meanings and sometimes his verbs. On this occasion it was his verbs, because the right one was that Amalia Fleming has always been, is and always will be a Greek, because she was born a Greek. And this is an incurable disease that nothing and no one can treat or change.

21. *The Last Lie*

A few days after my expulsion, a foreign correspondent visited Major Theophyloyannakos at his office at EAT ESA to take an interview. Major Hadjizissis, another well-known torturer, was also present. Among other things the foreign correspondent asked Theophyloyannakos why Amalia Fleming was expelled. 'She asked to be allowed to go,' said Theophyloyannakos, with the innocent expression he has when he lies, and which always amused me, even in hard moments.

'You are joking,' said the foreign correspondent. 'After the trial I heard her with my own ears saying that she would rather serve her sentence than agree to leave Greece if she were offered the choice. It is common knowledge that she was almost abducted and forced into the plane to London. It is common knowledge that she refused to leave the plane. I heard her repeat time and time again on the radio, on television, everywhere, making out that she did not want to leave Greece, and she would return if she were allowed in even if it meant going to prison.'

Theophyloyannakos has one great strength; truth neither bothers nor disturbs him. 'Three times,' he said, 'three times, in this very room, she begged me to let her leave the country. Is that not right, Hadjizissis?'

'Yes,' said Hadjizissis.

The Non-V.I.P. Treatment

DOCUMENTARY MATERIAL

That happened twice. Then I was stripped naked in the rain
ged to run in the courtyard of the headquarters in front of the
attalion. They used the torture of drops of water dripping on
head for an hour, while immobilized by being tied, which gave
re headaches, they hung me by the hands and hit me on the
, my shoulders were dislocated and during the night they
big dogs into the cell and left them there. By order of the
dant Manousakakis two soldiers and a sergeant of ESA
y police) tried to rape me; because I resisted their efforts I was
d of food and water. The commandant hit me with his revolver
ving pretended he was going to kill me. My detention, both in
dquarters of the Security Police and Dionysos, lasted three
. I still feel pains on the soles of my feet and in the stomach.
ily was notified of my arrest twenty-five days later and made
t inquiries about my fate, to which the answer was that I was
ained. The Athens Special Military Tribunal sentenced me on
ber 20th, 1968, to twenty-one years in prison.

Signed: P. KLAVDIANOS

ch 1968
Major Anghelos Pnevmatikos's statement: handwritten
uggled out of Salonika Prison. He was charged with
ting the King's group and sentenced to ten and a half

d on March 22nd, 1968.

24th, 1968: I was transferred from the Security to the dis-
y cell of EAT ESA (Special Interrogation Centre of the Greek
y Police), which was dark and so small that it could hardly
a mattress. The interrogation started with the interrogators
g in shifts.

25th or 26th, 1968: Theophyloyannakos slapped me twice
presence of Captain Papageorghiou and a woman called
…

rd, 1968: At noon I was taken to the disciplinary cell of KESA
g centre of the military police). The cell was a stable now used
oners. It still smelled horribly of urine and it was very cold. Two
on which were three planks of wood—no mattress or blankets—
that was in the cell. Food was brought by a soldier who left it

I. *Treatment that was not 'Flowers'*

For five years I have been trying to help stop both the tortures and the
spreading of sadism.

I have failed.

When I was imprisoned in EAT ESA, the commanding officer,
Theophyloyannakos, told me that what I had been through was
'flowers'. I admit it. I have described what 'flowers' were for me.
Here are some descriptions of cases that have not been flowers. There
are some new cases and some old ones. Most speak of the same tortures
and of the same torturers and places I encountered. In these five years,
in spite of everything that has been done to stop them, nothing seems
to have changed.

A few cases follow, chosen at random from 1967–72. Most of these
are the handwritten statements of the tortured. Some are statements
made in courtrooms and reported in the press. All have been checked
and found accurate in every detail reported. A great deal that I know
these people suffered they did not bother to report.

1. August 1967
From Costas Frantzeskakis's statement: handwritten and
smuggled out of prison. He is an accountant.

From the very first day of my arrest (August 25th, 1967) until I was
deported to Leros I was held in solitary confinement in the cells of
Security Headquarters at Piraeus. Any communication with my relatives was strictly forbidden. In the beginning I had no food, no clothes,
no blankets, I remained unshaven for a month and a half. I received
my clothes in Leros and I was allowed to have blankets forty days later
(on October 3rd, 1967). From August 25th, 1967, till October 16th,
1967, I had to suffer a lot. I was allowed to eat properly for the first
time on the seventeenth day after my arrest. The first twelve days I had
to rely on a little yoghourt … and the days after I could eat nothing
because my stomach would not tolerate the yoghourt diet any more.

They beat me with thick twisted cables on the naked soles of my feet (the torture known as falanga) and then they beat my whole body until I lost consciousness. This was done by a team of torturers (Foteinos, Iliopoulos, Kanatas and others) under the guidance of Police Officer Yannoutsos following orders of the head of the department, Sotiris Houvas. These tortures were done in conjunction with the interrogation. Before starting every torture session they first made sure that I was able to walk once more and the sessions lasted from half an hour to three hours, with intervals of about ten minutes. Because of these tortures I started to urinate blood and pus. My stomach—after the beating I got—would not accept any food at all. For ten days I vomited, together with blood, whatever I was trying to swallow. (I had previously undergone a stomach operation.) Before and after the beating I was called to the office (in all I was called about twenty times) and was interrogated. They followed closely my physical and mental condition to see whether I was showing signs of weakening. The interrogation always followed the same lines. There were insults, threats and various 'arguments' drawn from so-called evidence from the archives of EDA. I was repeatedly threatened with court martial. Many times while I was being interrogated the telephone rang and my name was mentioned. I was pressed to inform on people, to change my beliefs because, as I was told, 'Your party will never lift its head again;' 'Now we have a revolutionary right and that is why we treat you in this way;' 'We will not send you to the Royal Commissioner, we will interrogate you as long as we please. But even if this government goes, you will continue to suffer like this as long as there is a NATO.' They also finished the sessions regularly by making the same proposal (or threat): 'You will not come alive out of this unless you agree to become one of our agents.' It seems that all these conversations were recorded by a hidden microphone in the room.

Finally they took a written statement from me for the Royal Commissioner (Public Prosecutor). As I was unable to move and continued to urinate blood and pus, they sent me—in order to recover—to Kallipolis Police Station (Commanding Police Officer Athanasios Hadjis). It was there that the Police Doctor, named Kappos, visited me for the first time after Police Officer Kouvas finally gave his consent. I had repeatedly asked for the police doctor, previously to no avail, however. This police station had been converted into a secret nursing home for tortured people. There were three daily visits by the doctor while the officer on duty and the policeman acted as male nurses,

putting hot towels on the beaten feet, giving a
tion as well as other pain-relieving drugs a
opinion of a high-ranking doctor that I sho
ment in a hospital was not followed. As soon
Leros I was hospitalized on the very same day in
my condition was very serious; I had lost twe
state of complete exhaustion. As, however, the si
still quite apparent, half an hour before the
national Red Cross visited the ward of the exile
under the pretext that I had to undergo a neuro
the Leros Hospital for mental diseases, so that
see me. This was done without the knowl
authorities of the Asclepion under whose care

Signed:

2. February 1968
From Pavlos Klavdianos's statement:
smuggled out of prison. Klavdianos, a stud
Economics and Commercial Studies in A
three, was arrested on February 29th, 19
twenty-one years in prison, charged wit
student resistance organization Rigas Fera

I was arrested by police officer Karathanassis,
Security Headquarters of Athens, and beaten
office of police officer Kalyvas I was beaten up
and Karapanayotis with sticks, rubber straps an
then pulled my genitals with a string. Then I
where there is a shed. They tied me on a bench
my feet with a stick, then ordered me to walk
fifteen policemen hit me in turns, then the
tinued the whole night. I was put in solitary
days. After more torture I was transferred to th
camp at Dionysos and immediately tortured by
hand was burnt by a lit cigarette; transferred t
remained for thirty-eight days there and was s
by Major Boufas, Major A2 (Army Intellige
and other cadets and petty officers. Lieutenant
wires on my forehead and neck and conn

on the floor, without fork or spoon; he also left on the dirty floor some bread. Both food and bread were left next to a large can already full, which I was to use for my bodily needs. A motor-cycle was revved up all day outside the little window. In the night, food was brought in the same way and of course I did not eat either lunch or dinner. All night the soldiers banged on the metal doors or clanged the metal bar and put the light on and off ...

April 6th, 1968: Transferred to Dionysos camp. Cell 1 m. by 2·3 m., ceiling low, covered with a sheet of tin, wooden door, no window. One bed with a mattress—no blankets ... Then another [officer] ordered me to take off all my clothes ... They banged on the door continuously ... They brought dogs, and after beating and enraging them pushed them in my cell so that they would bite me. They abused me [calling me] 'traitor', 'Bulgarian', 'communist', 'Sodomite' ... This lasted till the morning as I refused to 'confess' ... and again till April 8th, 1968. From April 3rd, 1968, I had had neither food nor water.

Major Manousakakis, the commanding officer of the camp, called me into his office, apologized, saying that it had all been done without his knowledge, and gave me fried potatoes to eat ... The same night it all started again.

April 9th, 1968: ... Before I underwent falanga, Major Ioannides used the torture of 'burial' on me. 'Anghelos,' he said, 'you'd better confess, because you will regret it if you don't.' Behind the cell is a pit in which they put the prisoner and cover him with sand, leaving only the head unburied. The time of the burial depends on the resistance of the victim. I don't know how long I was in there. The continual interrogation of alternating interrogators, the anguish, gave me hallucinations.

In the night ... a trainee came who started punching me in the neck and the stomach—I hit back, so more came and beat me and broke my thumb. This lasted till the morning ... Major Ioannides called me to his office, threatened me again with burial and other tortures ... Returned to the cell. The banging of the door continued. I was called again to the office; there were many officers, who beat and punched me. They put me on a bed, and three young trainees started hitting the soles of my feet with an iron tube $\frac{3}{4}$ in. in diameter and with a piece of wood, first with my shoes on, then without them. They took me to the office. I refused to confess. This was repeated three or four times and each time falanga was administered till I fainted ... They told me that they were torturing my brother because of me. Theophyloyannakos ... threatened to bring my nephews and nieces and tell them that their father was in prison because of me ...

Signed: A. PNEVMATIKOS

4. August 1968
From Yannis Klonizakis's statement: handwritten and smuggled out of Aegina Prison. He is a civil engineer and a member of the Greek resistance movement.

... I was arrested on August 19th, 1968 ... I was taken [back to my house] by Babalis, Mallios and Major Theophyloyannakos. They began to question me and beat me ... During the interrogation, Major Theophyloyannakos, who was conducting it, made me lick a very dirty pair of pants ...

From my house I was taken back to the Security Police Headquarters. Mallios, Babalis and Theophyloyannakos became even more methodical in their work. Mallios pulled my moustache and stepped on my toes. Babalis made me undress completely under the threat of the club. After he had had me undress, he started beating me very efficiently with the club. At the Military Police offices (EAT ESA) where I was taken later, Major Theophyloyannakos assumed responsibility ... Shortly after my arrival at EAT ESA, I was taken to the inner office of the interrogators ... In that office I saw Nikolaos Lekanides. It is obvious that they arranged the meeting to demoralize me, for his condition, at least as it appeared to me, was desperate. He was lying down and was barefoot; he later told me that he had been beaten and subjected to falanga. As a result his feet were swollen. Naturally we didn't speak to each other.

They took me back to the office of the duty officer, where the interrogation continued until 1.20 a.m. of August 20th. The screams of those who were being beaten were a torture in itself ...

... A great effort was made by the interrogating officers to slander Alexandros Panagoulis, whom they were trying to represent as a drunkard, an adventurer, a drop-out, a paid murderer, an anarchist and, generally speaking, an anti-social character. On August 29th, at about 9 to 9.30 p.m., the military police Judge Pavlos Panagiotides, an ex-heavyweight wrestler, opened the cell and took me to the office of the interrogating officers ... Panagiotides handcuffed my hands behind my back and threw me on the floor. He tied up my feet very tightly with a rope, leaving enough rope on both ends so that it could be grasped. In other words, we were starting all over again. He took off my shoes and socks. He left me waiting in that state until his assistants came. They were Majors Missailides and Papageorghiou, and they asked me whether I had anything to add to what I had been made to say. I said I had not. The signal for the beating to begin was given ...

... Panagiotides's assistants took the two ends of the rope with which my feet were tied and raised my feet from the ground. My hands were still handcuffed (the marks can still be seen on my wrists). In that upside-down position it was easier for them to beat me. Now the falanga began. For the beating Panagiotides used a thin white cable and sticks from an acacia tree. In the meantime, of course, his assistants were also active, they kicked me all the time with their boots in the stomach, in the ribs, and in general wherever their boots happened to land.

... From time to time Missailides and Papageorghiou would come in to see if I had any intention of speaking. As I refused, the order to go on was given. When Papageorghiou got tired, he stopped the falanga, he undid my hands and my feet, he took my head between his knees and then he started punching me about my waist, my back and my bottom, while his assistants were kicking wherever it was possible. After that they carried me in their arms to the corner next to the door and made me jump on water, while they slapped my face and punched me in the kidneys and from time to time tried to dislocate my thumbs by twisting them. The same torture, falanga, etc., in all its various phases, continued until 1 a.m. Many times they poured water on my feet. From time to time Missailides and Papageorghiou came in to make sure that the torture was applied efficiently. At about 1 a.m. Major Theophyloyannakos came in, ordered the beating to stop and started interrogating me ...

... Later I was taken to the prosecutor's office, where they gave me a mattress to sleep on. Needless to say, whichever position I tried, the pains all over my body were insufferable. They had crippled me. My feet were covered with blood, my hands were covered with wounds from the handcuffs. Many months had to pass before I was able to sleep without pain. Even now I still suffer pain in the kidney area.

Next day I gave supplementary evidence in connection with the things I had said on the previous night ... From that day on, physical torture ceased but psychological torture naturally continued in a more persistent way. Of course I was not the only member of the Greek

Resistance who has been arrested and tortured. Every single one of us was tortured to a greater or lesser degree. Many of us bear clear marks of torture. Later in Korydallos Prison I was told about the nervous shock which my brother, Dr Artemios Klonizakis, had suffered. He was not only left without any kind of medical care, but also, at a moment of hysterical crisis, he was beaten up, as many eyewitnesses testified, by a petty police officer named Phocas ...

Aegina Prison, October, 1969

Signed: YANNIS M. KLONIZAKIS

5. July 1969

From Dionysios Karageorgas's statement: handwritten and presented to the court by his lawyers.* Translated and published in the resistance journal 'The Greek Observer', April–May 1970. He was charged with handling explosives, and sentenced to life imprisonment. He is now in prison in Crete. Karageorgas should have an ear operation. Because he was not allowed treatment, the infection spread to the facial nerves. He should also have an expert operation on his hand.

I was arrested in the afternoon of July 14th, 1969, at the Aretaiion Hospital [Athens] where I was transferred to be operated on, having been gravely wounded. At about 10 p.m., just out of the operating theatre and still semi-conscious, I became aware that two persons in civilian clothes, each one standing on either side of my bed, were pulling the flesh of my chest with great ferocity. At the same time they were shouting at me to confess to them who had given me the explosives which they had found in my house. Obviously these two persons were policemen. As I was not replying to their questions the two policemen continued for a long time to pull my chest with ever growing harshness, until exhausted by the operation and by such ill-treatment, I lost consciousness ... they began threatening me that they were going to arrest my wife, as well as my mother who is eighty-four years old, my brothers and other relatives. Tzavaras started to insult me in vulgar terms.

For about two hours these two officers insulted me, and this process went on for about a week ...

At the beginning of August ... they said that their patience was exhausted, and as I was not telling them the truth they had arrested my

---

* Reported in its entirety in *Bima*, March 29th, 1970.

wife, my mother, my brothers and my parents-in-law. 'They are rotting in the detention houses and curse you for that.' 'They will remain in detention to die a slow death, if you don't speak.' They said also that my children – a six-year-old boy and a five-month-old girl – were left to their fate and that no one was taking care of them any more. The threats I had heard for the past week and the convincing manner of these last statements made me believe that the police had indeed decided to exterminate my whole family. So, when the policemen left me I was overtaken by fear and had a stroke. It was about 6 p.m. that I felt that my jaw twisted to the right while the right side of my head was getting numb, and when I tried to speak I realized I was stammering ... Later I knew I had had a stroke.

At the beginning of September ... I was transferred from the hospital to the detention house at Neon Irakleion police station ...

On September 13th, Mavroidis again began the threats and the rest were all at the same time shouting in a deafening way over my head. One hour later Favatas came in in a frantically wild mood and began hitting me on the face, shouting, 'You dirty beast, I will break you. You are offending the prestige of the gendarmerie and its hundred years' old tradition by making us learn from the ESA things you should have told us by now.' That moment Mavroidis stood up to go and said: 'Take him to the little room.' They took me to a small room next to the office. They ordered me to stand up with my back to the wall. There, in that position, Favatas, but mainly Moroyannis, began to hit me in an inhuman way. Favatas standing on my right was hitting my face. Moroyannis in front of me, with his hands linked, hit my head; with his knee he hit my belly and my genitals, and he kicked my legs. The beating lasted for a long while. Weakened by the operation I had had a fortnight ago I couldn't stand the beating any more and fell unconscious on the floor.

When I recovered I realized that they had put me on a writing table. Favatas was taking my pulse and someone else was wetting my head. The beating was repeated next day in exactly the same way. Upon leaving the office Moroyannis kicked me many times from behind on the waist and on my bandaged amputated right hand. This made me sink on the floor, my face was bruised while my bandages became red with blood.

Two days later I was taken again to Nea Ionia subdivision for questioning ... I was submitted to new beating. But this time being so exhausted I couldn't stand it for long. With the first blows from Moroyannis I began losing consciousness. That moment I felt they were putting something on my head, but I was not in a position to know what. Next day in my cell I realized to my utter disgust that sputum, mixed with cigarette ends and other dirt was stuck on my head. It seems that the moment I was losing consciousness they put on my head the paper basket full of rubbish and sputum.

During the last ten days of September and for the first time something strange happened to me. Although I was fully conscious of my daily transfers from Neon Irakleion to Nea Ionia for questioning, this was not so while on my way back after the end of the questioning. Although the questioning had ended and I was being taken back to Neon Irakleion I was under the illusion that the questioning was still going on. That they continued to ask questions, to threaten, to insult and to beat me. When I regained my senses I was surprised to find myself in my cell. Often these hallucinations went on until the next day. I had nightmares that my wife was maltreated by policemen and calling for help to me, my boy in rags, a beggar wandering in the streets, my daughter dead in her cot. I could not explain to myself these hallucinations which caused a nervous shock to me to such an extent that I had completely lost my willpower ...*

To the above I should add that the strict solitude I was confined to for five whole months was for me one of the most terrible ordeals. During this time I knew nothing of the fate of my family, as any sort of communication with them was forbidden. Conditions in the Neon Irakleion police station were horrible. The cell was a filthy place, 2 m. by 3 m., damp walls, a cement floor and an opening a few centimetres wide to let in light and air so to speak. For three months I was locked in that horrible place from which I was not allowed to go out except to get to the nearby W.C. I slept on the cement floor on a very thin and filthy mattress which because of the dampness was unbearably wet. I ate my food on the floor of my cell. In spite of my repeated requests I was not allowed books or periodicals or any sort of print. By the end of November the natural resources of my resistance were finally exhausted and I was often in a terrible anguish.

They let me then have books and transferred me to Nea Philadelphia police station where I was detained with another person. A few days later, when visits to political prisoners by representatives of the Inter-

* Many of this group were given hallucinogenic drugs.

national Red Cross were due to start, they took me to the General State Hospital to treat my ear. It should be noted that since mid-October I had asked for treatment as my ear was continuously secreting pus, but no one paid any attention then. This delay caused a chronic otitis which I could have been spared had I been treated in time ...

Averof Prison, January 12th, 1970
                                            Signed: D. KARAGEORGAS
                                            Professor of Panteios High School
                                                    for Political Sciences

6. September 1969
From Nikolaos Konstantopoulos's statement: handwritten and presented to the court by his lawyers.* Translated and published in 'The Greek Observer', April–May 1970. Konstantopoulos, aged twenty-eight, a student, was sentenced to eight years of prison. He is in the worst prison of Greece—in Corfu. This handsome and brilliant young man, absolutely innocent, is now after so much suffering a human wreck. It was Konstantopoulos, as was mentioned before, about whom the defence counsel asked after the trial, 'Now tell me, why eight years for Konstantopoulos? On what evidence?' and the military judges answered, 'He is a potential leader!'

I was arrested on September 3rd, 1969 ... I was not shown any warrant of arrest nor given any explanation for my arrest ... I was immediately transferred to the Special Interrogation Centre of the military police (EATESA) where Major Hadjizissis ... threatened that if I did not confess he would submit me to a 'special process of torture' ... He then locked me up in a cell so small that only an iron bed could fit in it, and full of dirty mouldy bread and other disgusting things.

At 05.30 next morning (September 4th, 1969) ... they threatened to arrest my fiancée and torture her in front of me. They did in fact arrest her after an hour, and detained her in the same building until September 15th, 1969.

I remained in my cell until 9.30 p.m. on September 4th, 1969. At that time, I was taken to Majors Hadjizissis and Theophyloyannakos for a first interrogation. As I refused to fall in with their suggestions, special interrogator Theophyloyannakos started hitting me. He gave me a series of slaps, blows and kicks while Major Hadjizissis had

* Reported in its entirety in *Bima*, March 29th, 1970,

removed my glasses and was hitting me with a wooden rule on the ears, the head and the shoulders ... They threatened to 'make me impotent', to 'cut me', to 'make a useless invalid of me', to 'hang me', to 'hand me over to the falanga', to 'rape me', to 'torture my fiancée' and so on ... 'they do not fear any pressure and are not accountable to anyone'; and they do not hesitate to use any means for achieving their purpose'. Major Theophyloyannakos, his face altered with fanatic rage, hit me ruthlessly ... In the 'prosecution office', in which I was locked up, a sentry was put with instructions not to allow me to sleep, to drink water, to sit or to rest, but to oblige me to walk around the office day and night. I was to remain sleepless, hungry and thirsty till exhaustion broke down my physical resistance, undermined my mental lucidity and made me 'mature' enough to confess what my torturers wanted. Every time I stopped walking or slowed down, every time I attempted to lean on the wall or to close my eyes, my guards hit me savagely in order to remind me of instructions. Every now and then Major Georgacopoulos or Captain Economou came round to watch my condition ... Whenever I asked for water, they replied cynically that I could drink my urine, as others had done before me. At the same time they called other soldiers to enjoy sadistically, in my presence, various refreshments. They pretended to offer me some too, but when I came near they beat me. In order to escape the torture of thirst I was forced to drink water from the flush in the toilet. They realized this and after September 7th they allowed me to use the toilet only once every twenty-four hours. In the afternoon of September 7th I fainted. I was brought back to my senses by savage beating. I kept asking for a doctor, mostly with inarticulate cries, while a whole group of military policemen were beating me. They called a doctor only when they saw I was no longer able to stand on my feet, and told him I was a soldier of their unit who was being punished for a disciplinary offence. The examination showed I had tachycardia and temperature of 39° but the duty officer did not permit the doctor's prescriptions to be applied. I shouted to him that I was a political prisoner and described to him the inhuman treatment I was being subjected to. The result was that after the doctor's departure I was again beaten with the same ruthlessness until I fainted once more. They revived me and started beating me again. I vomited in my hands, and was not allowed to wash them.

During the following night (September 7th, 1969) I suffered from intolerable pain in the stomach. It was impossible to go on walking.

They gave me aspirin in a spoonful of water. I again vomited in my hands and fainted. When I came to my senses they once more started to beat me up. They knocked my head on the wall and held their cigarettes close to my eyelids. One of my tormentors held a photograph of Papadopoulos and shouted to me that 'if I licked it he would let me sit down for half an hour'. My fiancée, who had been deliberately put in the adjoining cell, heard my cries and began to protest. They forced her to shut up and came back to me. An entire group started beating me up once more pitilessly. Owing to my high temperature I found myself in a nightmarish world. Every now and then a fresh soldier walked in and hit me with true savagery, shouting that because of me they were missing their leave and sleep. That same night I heard two other prisoners being tortured ...

Next day, September 8th, I was brought once more to Majors Hadjizissis and Theophyloyannakos. In order to increase my torment they had placed on their desk refreshments and ice-cold water. My reflexes worked automatically. Before asking me any questions they began to discuss if they should offer me water or not. Theophyloyannakos appeared willing, while Hadjizissis would have it depend on whether I confessed or not. Upon my refusal to confess to the concoction of imaginary evidence which they quoted, I was subjected to the same threats and insults which ended up in an attempt to blackmail me by declaring that they would treat my fiancée like myself and that they would subject me in her presence to sexual torture. They used the dirtiest imaginable language, spat on me or punched me, insulted everything I loved, talking with vulgar contempt about my parents. The more I refused to co-operate, the more they lost their self-control. Major Theophyloyannakos kicked me with genuine rage. They handed me back to my guards with clear instructions to break me down. And indeed, till September 10th I continued to walk day and night, without a moment's rest, without sleep, food or water, with beatings and hallucinations ...

During the night following that same day, at about 4 a.m., they allowed me to sit on a chair. My belief that I would find some relief, however, was wrong, because they forced me to stare at an electric bulb without closing my eyes and without sleeping. My exhaustion was unimaginable; I suffered from hallucinations which made the objects in the office take on fantastic shapes, I had nightmarish sensations and had the impression of living in an unreal place. Naturally I was overcome by an invincible need for sleep, but the sentry woke me up by loud banging on the wooden table. Till 7 a.m. I fell asleep every minute and was instantaneously woken by the nightmarish banging. I felt a hammering in my brain; pain from the beating was intolerable; I had high fever; hunger, thirst and lack of sleep caused an unbearable physical and mental condition ...

Signed: NIKOS ANDR. KONSTANTOPOULOS

7. October 1970

Andreas Frangias's statement at his trial, March 17th–22nd, 1972. Frangias, aged fifty-two, a civil engineer and hero of the resistance against the Nazis in the Second World War, belonged to the PAK resistance organization. (See the photographs of Frangias before and six months after his arrest.)

MANGAKIS (*defence lawyer*). I declare, on the authorization of my client, that his first confession of January 29th, 1971, was extracted from him involuntarily and is not true. This confession was extracted from him when he was almost unconscious as a result of the tortures he suffered at the hands of the security police. He was beaten twice by a team of torturers and after the first beating he was sent to the Polykliniki Hospital where he stayed from October 31st, 1970, to November 30th, 1970, where the doctors testified that he was covered with wounds and had suffered internal and brain injuries. I give you now the hospital certificate. On November 30th he was transferred from this clinic to Military Hospital 401. I present you with Mr Frangias's photograph to show you his condition ...

FRANGIAS. I would like to beg you, because of my general health, if I may make my defence sitting and not to ask me dates, because I cannot remember dates ... I was not in my right senses under interrogation. I had continuous transfusions and injections. For four and a half months I was in the psychiatric ward in Military Hospital 401 although I was sane. The methods used in Soviet Russia are used in Greece, I am beside myself with indignation, Mr President, because of all this ... I was transferred twice to the hospital unconscious. The first time was the night of my arrest.

PRESIDENT. You must have been ill.

FRANGIAS. They ill treated me. The next morning they took me back to my cell as soon as I recovered my senses, and while I was in that condition, the policeman Tzaferis took down my first statement. After that, I was locked in under terrible conditions, and Sunday night or Monday morning they attacked me for the second time. This attack was maniacal; they asked me to tell them about the explosions. I lost consciousness and I was transferred to Hippocratiou Hospital. When I recovered, I saw that I was covered in blood, and for a period of twenty days after that I could not see or hear well. I had lost my eyesight and my hearing. I was dizzy and I had spasms and I vomited blood continuously. Because of the beatings, terrible damage had been done to my stomach, and I could not eat. The smallest portion of food made me vomit. For twenty days I lived on serum. As the damage to my brain was very serious, and as at the Hippocratiou they did not have the proper medical equipment, I was transferred to Polykliniki. There I was treated with cortisone and had continuous serum and transfusions for one month. On November 30th I was transferred to Military Hospital 401 where they locked me into the psychiatric ward with other madmen. I spent four and a half months there ...

(*After this, Mangakis presents to the court a signed statement enumerating the tortures Frangias underwent, in detail. The following are extracts.*)

FRANGIAS. ... A group of seven or eight men was around me and they howled insults I am too ashamed to repeat. They started to beat me unmercifully on my head, my chest, my stomach and my abdomen. They asked me continuously, 'Tell us why we have brought you here,' and they threatened me, saying that I had to answer this question if I wanted to leave alive and see my wife and daughter again ... During the second attack, they removed my shoes and some of my clothes, and they began to beat me again, while someone was giving instructions as to method: 'Beat him on the head and stomach. Be careful not to leave marks.'*

8. January 1971

From George Spiliotis's statement: handwritten and smuggled out of Korydallos Prison. Spiliotis, aged thirty, was sentenced on August 6th, 1971, to two years in prison. He has recently been in Korydallos Prison.

My name is George Spiliotis (the son of Theodoros Spiliotis). I am a graduate of Pantios University.

* *Bima*, March 19th, 1972.

I was arrested by members of the General Security Police of Athens on January 3rd, 1971 ...

They entered my apartment at about 8 p.m., pointing a revolver at me. As soon as they arrested me they started to hit me and to make threats such as, 'We are going to kill you,' and, 'We are going to throw you from the top of Mount Parnis.'

At the headquarters of the security police, they tortured me, first in an office. They punched me on the face and in the stomach, gave me electric shocks and poked my eyes with their fingers. My nose started bleeding as a result of the blows.

They then took me up to the terrace. I was tied on to a bench, half naked, and they started to hit the soles of my feet with an iron bar. Some of the policemen sat on my chest while one of them, whom I recognized as Gravaritis, hit my genitals and other parts of my body with a stick. He also punched me on the head with both hands or sometimes stuffed a wet cloth on a stick into my mouth in order to smother my cries. Another policeman was squeezing my testicles with his hand. The pain made me writhe, and the ropes cut into my ankles. I was then untied and two policemen held me and forced me to walk around while they swore at me. They then released me and started to throw me one to the other, and then two policemen would pull at my arms in opposite directions. They tied me on to the bench and the whole process of falanga and beating started again, and was repeated about four times.

Then I was taken into an office, and they started to hit me again. They made me stand with one arm in the air, like the Statue of Liberty, and I kept falling down. A policeman was hitting my genitals. They put me on a chair and started to hit me again.

They then threw me into a cell and left me lying on the cement floor. During the next days Gravaritis would take me out into an office and hit me. His favourite tortures were to poke my eyes with his fingers, grab me by the hair and bang my head against the wall, and punch me on the head and inflict tortures on my genitals with his hands.

While this was going on, I could hear the screams of people being tortured, which grew louder all the time. I could hear names being called for questioning. In my cell I heard continuously my name being called for interrogation. I heard the cries of the others who had been accused with me being tortured; I heard them being murdered by being thrown through a trapdoor into the basement. I was delirious all the time.

Because I was in this state a doctor was sent to look at me. I was even shown one of those accused with me to prove that they had not been killed.

There were about seven policemen present at my tortures, of whom I can give the names of only three: Gravaritis, Kalivas and Smailis.

Signed: GEORGE SPILIOTIS

9. October 1971
From George Sayas's statement: handwritten and smuggled out of Korydallos Prison. Sayas is a physics and mathematics student.

On October 20th, 1971, I was arrested at the house of a friend. There were six or seven men of the security police, and they took both of us to the Athens security station at Messogion Street.* They took me to the office of an officer called Karapanagiotis. There they asked me to tell them what I knew about the organization called '20th of October'. When I refused to answer, Karapanagiotis started beating me with his hands, and after that someone else continued beating me with a thick, double cable. There were a number of them in Karapanagiotis's office; they started abusing and beating me all at once. One was kicking, another was treading on my toes with his heels. Another, pulling me by the hair, was knocking my head on the wall. Afterwards they threw me on the floor and kicked me, and one stamped with all his strength with his heel on my hands and shoulders.

When I stood up, Karapanagiotis came again holding in his hand something like a club with a wire all around. When he touched me with it, I felt electric shocks shaking me. As I continued to refuse to answer their questions, they handcuffed me and took me down to the basement.† They were about six or seven men, with Officer Gravaritis as their chief. They obliged me to undress completely, they made me lie down on a bench, they tied me so that I could not move, they covered my eyes and they started beating me with a metal rod on the

* The headquarters of the General Security have recently been transferred from Bouboulinas Street to Messogion Street.

† At Bouboulinas Street the tortures took place in the room on the terrace of the building; in Messogion Street, in the basement of the new building.

soles of my feet and on my genitals. At the same time the one who was covering my eyes was pressing them with his thumbs so that I felt them sinking in their sockets. When they took me to the upper floor again, I could not stand by myself, and they had to support me all the time. They put me into a cell. For about three or four days they took me again and again to Karapanagiotis's office and the same things were repeated. Fortunately, they did not take me down to the basement again. Among my torturers was also Police Officer Smailis. I don't know the name of the others. Finally, they detained me at the Security for about one month, and afterwards I was transferred to Korydallos Prison.

Signed: GEORGE SAYAS

10. October 1971
Nikos Manios's statement: handwritten and smuggled out of prison. Manios is a fifth-year student in the faculty of Medicine at the University of Athens.

I am a member of the '20th of October' resistance organization and was arrested, without a warrant, by the security police of Athens on October 20th, 1971. I was driven directly to the Athens Security Police Station, Messogion Street.

The interrogation started the same day, accompanied by continual threats of torture.

The same night I was removed from the cell where I had originally been put, my eyes covered so that I could not see, and was taken down to the basement while at the same time being kicked and slapped.

There I had to undress. I was tied on to a bench and someone started to hit the soles of my feet with a piece of piping. In the meantime, someone else had tied a nylon string around my penis and pulled it tight. The one who was doing the falanga hit me every so often on the testicles with the pipe and they all kept telling me that they would make me impotent for life. A third man hit me on the stomach and on the face. Then they stopped for a while and threatened me with even worse methods of torture. This respite didn't last long; the falanga started again until someone grabbed me around the neck and tried to suffocate me by pressing on my nose and throat—then once again they started to hit me on the soles of my feet and my testicles.

I don't know how long this torture lasted. After that they got me up and made me run around the room with my eyes bandaged while they banged my head against the wall. After I had dressed, they took me up into my cell again and on the way they pulled my hair so hard that whole tufts of hair came out.

I was given a yoghourt and dry toast for supper and advised not to take off my shoes or walk around the room. My feet had swollen up and more than ten days passed before I could walk properly again. I was kept in solitary confinement for eleven days, under the continual threat of torture. Among my torturers were Police Captain A. Gravaritis and Police Captain A. Smailis.

I didn't learn the names of the rest.

Signed: NIKOS MANIOS

II. *The Suppression of* Anti

Athens, May 25th, 1972

Christos Papoutsakis, an architect, who published a weekly magazine *Anti (Against)*, called reporters, among them Reuter's,[*] Agence France Press,[†] U.P.I.,[‡] the London *Times*,[§] and told them that under military police pressure he was obliged to interrupt the publication of his magazine, which had been launched only the previous week and was immediately sold out. All contents of the magazine were absolutely within the press law.

Since the publication, Christos Papoutsakis was summoned almost every day to the EAT ESA (the Special Interrogation Centre of the Greek military police which is next to the American Embassy) and was each time interrogated for many hours. The last time the interrogation lasted thirty hours. Mr Papoutsakis did not say what he went through during these thirty hours, but the reporters saw him in bed, haggard, with arms and hands badly bruised, and with badly swollen and bruised feet. He could not stand on his feet or walk. He said that he had been told to go again the day after to EAT ESA, but he could not do so because he could not walk. 'If they want me they must come and take me,' he said. Besides, his doctor had ordered him to go immediately to a hospital.

Not seeing her son return home, his aged mother had a 'cerebral incident'. At the same time, according to *The Times*, 'a tax investigating squad raided the magazine's premises, then searched Mr Papoutsakis's offices and a shoe shop run by the managing editor's wife. Two other members of the staff were invited to hear some "friendly advice" from the police. Mr Papoutsakis said tonight that the military police interrogators wanted to know "who was behind me in publishing *Anti*. I explained that the magazine was in accordance with the law, the law of the revolution. I explained that I had the idea, possibly false, that there existed in Greece limits within which one could express ideas. I explained that no one was behind me." '

[*] Reuter's, May 25th, 1972.
[‡] U.P.I., May 24th, 1972.
[†] Agence France Press, May 25th, 1972.
[§] *The Times*, May 24th, 1972.

III. *Postscript to the Panagoulis Case*

July 5th, 1972

After his arrest in August 1969, Alexandros Panagoulis was kept in solitary confinement for about a year. Then followed a period when his mother was allowed to visit him once a fortnight and bring him food once a week, but after an escape attempt he was again held in strict isolation. Since June 1971 Panagoulis's mother has been allowed to see him only four times, and this through the meshed spyhole of his metal door while she has to stay outside in the open. It must be noted that since he was sentenced, almost four years ago, no other person has seen Panagoulis except the Representative of the International Red Cross who, I think, saw him once. His lawyer was never allowed to see him. On February 29th Alexandros through the spyhole, in the presence of the officers listening to their conversation, told his mother that he had been asked to write and sign a statement denying that he had ever been so much as beaten, and saying that he was receiving very humane treatment (presumably this demand followed my description of his tortures at the military court in the presence of foreign correspondents). He added that because he refused, he was so savagely beaten while tied in a straitjacket that he remained semi-conscious for three days and he was still in great pain; he thought that he had broken ribs, he could hardly stand, and he asked his mother to go. The mother then lodged a complaint with the Public Prosecutor against the people who were torturing her son. The next visit was allowed on April 27th, 1972, under the same conditions described above. She had begged in vain to be allowed to see him on April 9th, the Greek Easter, which is the greatest Christian festival in Greece. Again, on April 27th, she was not allowed to leave any food, not even one orange. On this visit Alexandros told her that he had been given foul-smelling meat and that he was not eating for fear that they might poison him. When he said this the officers shut the spyhole, which, according to Mrs Panagoulis, is as large as an envelope, and brusquely ended the visit. When she begged the officers to allow her to leave some fruit for him she was thrown out.

Athena Panagoulis had been told that she could see her son on May 15th, but she was not allowed to do so; instead she was given a new date, May 30th. On May 30th, running a high temperature herself, she waited in the rain for half an hour to be told that she could not see him as he was being punished. The truth, as she learned later, was that he was in a very bad condition because he had been on hunger-strike since April 27th—that is, for thirty-three days. On May 30th an officer told her in secret that if she could see her son she would not recognize him because of the terrible state of health to which he was reduced, and that they had orders to exterminate him before the end of the year. Utterly distressed, Mrs Panagoulis tried to start a hunger-strike outside the American Embassy on May 31st, but twenty minutes later she was dragged away by the police, who threatened to beat her, kept her for two hours at the Security Police Headquarters and then took her to her house under guard. She was kept under house arrest for two or three days with three policemen outside, who the 3rd day had to take her to a doctor because she had suffered a haemorrhage. The house arrest stopped then, but she is still followed wherever she goes and the police car is always near the house.

On June 20th she was at last allowed to see her son, of course only through the spyhole. He was in a terrible state of debility. He told her of his hunger-strike, and that on May 31st two doctors had come to feed him. He also said that he was again beaten on May 3rd, 5th and 9th. His main torturers were Nikolaos Zacharakis, Major Anastasso-poulos, commander and vice-commander of the Military Prison Boyati, and Lieutenant Zoulas of the Military Judicial Body. On May 3rd, besides the beating, officers came into his cell, had his head forcibly shaved, and laughed at him in an effort to break still further his shattered nerves. They also removed his shoes and left him barefoot for twenty days. On June 9th Major Theophyloyannakos, the sadistic torturer commanding officer of EAT ESA, went into his cell and ordered him with shouts and threats to write a letter asking Papado-poulos to forgive him: otherwise they would exterminate him. He was also told that no intervention by anyone would save him. As usual, Panagoulis refused. On July 4th his mother was allowed to see him again through the spyhole, and this time she was allowed to leave him oranges and other fruit, but no other food. He told her that X-ray machines had been brought into his cell to X-ray his ribs about six months after they were broken; he also said that he had not been beaten again. Perhaps the intervention of the Pope, President Nixon, Senators and Congressmen which I tried to secure brought some results: after a concentrated effort to break him they seem now to have stopped torturing him, at least for a little while. Foreign public opinion and pressure always bring results. But it has to continue.

What are they trying to do? Lead Panagoulis to a slow death? Make him insane so that they can shut him in an asylum and finish with him? Panagoulis was sentenced in June 1968. Greek law says that if a death sentence has not been carried out after three years have elapsed, the sentence is automatically commuted to life imprisonment. Also according to the law a military who has been deprived of his military status purges his sentence in a normal prison and not a military one. The sentence had deprived Panagoulis of his status as a soldier, and in November 1971 the three years were over, and Alexandros has now a life sentence. His lawyer tried in February 1972 to raise this matter: why was Panagoulis still in a military prison? In March 1972 an addition to the law was enacted: the life sentence of a prisoner who is no longer a soldier should be spent in a normal civil prison. *But under emergency law (like the martial law we are under now) the military authorities can decide where the sentence will be served.* In this way the dictators tried to make legal the illegal keeping of Panagoulis in a military prison. However, as the lawyer had lodged his appeal to the court before this addition was enacted, it cannot apply to Panagoulis, and his lawyer has now appealed to the Council of State about this case; it will be heard in February 1973.

Mrs Athena Panagoulis received a summons to appear on the morning of July 5th before an investigating judge on the charge that she had harboured a 'criminal'. She was accused of having hidden Nicholas Zambelis, the young man who escaped from Aegina Prison in June 1971.

Are they trying to put her in prison as well? Or to intimidate this mother? Stifle the only voice which speaks up for Panagoulis, sever his only connection with the outside world?

COMPLAINT

of Athena, wife of B. Panagoulis, Asklipiou Street 57, Glyfada,

against

1. Major Anastassopoulos, Vice-commander of the Military Prison of Boyati;

2. Nicholas Zacharakis, Commander of the Military Prison of Boyati;

3. Any other responsible party, either civilian or military, whose name and position are unknown to me.

To the Public Prosecutor of Athens:

On February 29th, 1972, which was the day on which I was permitted to visit, I went to the Military Prison of Boyati, to a small building which stands apart from the main area of the prison camp and resembles a tomb (2 metres by 2 metres), to visit my son, Alexandros Panagoulis, who is there serving his sentence.

My son told me — and I was able to see it for myself — that he was in a lamentable condition, that he had extreme difficulty in standing in order to talk to me through the very thick, coloured, wire screen which covers the tiny ten-centimetre-square aperture of his cell. This was due to ill-treatment about which he told me in front of Adjutant Andreas Vezyris, a sub-lieutenant and six soldiers, all of whom followed the entire conversation with my son and showed no reaction nor tried to deny what my son said about the unprecedented inhuman treatment to which he was being submitted, which was:

On February 17th, 1972, following an order given by the vice-commander of the prison, who is cited first in this complaint, seven men in civilian clothes grabbed him and forceably put him into a straitjacket of the type used to restrain psychotics during violent seizures. Having thus immobilized him, they threw him on the floor and began to beat him, prompted by the leader of the group who was giving orders with terrible rage, saying, 'Beat him, kick him, make him black and blue.' They hit him with their fists and feet indiscriminately all over his body.

All during this savage beating, which continued until my son completely lost consciousness, the sub-lieutenant from the section of Military Justice who was present was urging the soldiers like a maniac, encouraging them to beat their victim even more, and when they stopped for a rest, he threatened them, biting his thumb with rage. Many times during the beating in addition to hitting and kicking him they grabbed my son by his hair and with indescribable fury banged his head against the wall.

The result of this barbaric, inhumane and cowardly treatment of my son, held absolutely powerless and defenceless because of the solitary confinement in which he is kept incommunicado and the immobility to which he was reduced, was that his body became bruised all over, and, as my son told me—and I have no reason to doubt the truth of what he described—the fracture of several ribs and the wounds on his head reduced him to a state of semi-consciousness that lasted for three days. After that a military doctor visited him and saw these dangerous and grave injuries, and a fortnight later my son told me that he still suffers terrible pain and fears for his life.

Mr Prosecutor: Although some time has passed, the traces of the appalling mistreatment endured by my son are still quite visible and it is essential that he be examined by a specialist in forensic medicine, thus making possible the necessary treatment and enabling you to act against all those responsible;

Because the above-mentioned acts constitute the commission of the crime of inflicting serious and dangerous bodily injury, which is within the scope of the provisions of the Criminal Code and subject to punishment under the Code, and against which the public prosecutor is obliged to act whether or not a private complaint is lodged;

For all these reasons I bring this complaint against the individuals cited above and all those responsible for the actions described herein.

And I demand that they be prosecuted under the provisions of the Criminal Code and severely punished.

I propose as witnesses:

1. Commander Christos Kaggelaris (Ret.), Korthiou Street 2, Athens;
2. Anastassia Mela, Asklipiou Street 57, Glyfada, Attica.

The complainant, A. PANAGOULIS